Linguistic Variation and Change

Edinburgh Sociolinguistics

Series Editors:
Paul Kerswill (Lancaster University)
Joan Swann (Open University)

Volumes available in the series:
Paul Baker, *Sociolinguistics and Corpus Linguistics*
Scott F. Kiesling, *Linguistic Variation and Change*

Forthcoming titles include:
Kevin Watson, *English Sociophonetics*
Theresa Lillis, *The Sociolinguistics of Writing*

Visit the Edinburgh Sociolinguistics website at www.euppublishing.com/series/edss

Linguistic Variation and Change

Scott F. Kiesling

Edinburgh University Press

© Scott F. Kiesling, 2011

Edinburgh University Press Ltd
22 George Square, Edinburgh

www.euppublishing.com

Typeset in 10/12pt Adobe Garamond
by Servis Filmsetting Ltd, Stockport, Cheshire, and
printed and bound in Great Britain by
CPI Antony Rowe, Chippenham and Eastbourne

A CIP record for this book is available from the British Library

ISBN 978 0 7486 3761 4 (hardback)
ISBN 978 0 7486 3762 1 (paperback)

The right of Scott F. Kiesling
to be identified as author of this work
has been asserted in accordance with
the Copyright, Designs and Patents Act 1988.

Contents

Figures	ix
Tables	xii
Preface and acknowledgements	xiii
Terminology and notation conventions	xiv
Phonetic notation	xv

Part I: Questions and method

1	Questions about language and variation, and where we got them	3
	Questions about language	3
	Where we got the questions: from comparative philology to variationist theories	4
	Orderly heterogeneity and constraints on its form	8
2	The linguistic variable	13
	Definitions and types	13
	Linguistic variables at different linguistic levels	14
	Variable rules and their 'quiet demise'	17
	Criticisms of the notion of linguistic variable	20
3	Discovering and describing patterns of variation and change	26
	Ethical linguistics	30
	Finding language to measure	31
	Speech communities and sampling	32
	Getting speech: interviews and other talk	36
	Recording and managing recordings	38
	Coding variables	39
	Describing patterns	41
	Finding structure in variability	45
	Testing statistical significance and modelling variation	45

Part II: Variation and social relationships

Introduction to Part II 51

4 Social patterns I: interspeaker variation 53
   Stratification 54
   Canonical patterns: accommodation 64
   Canonical patterns: differentiation 70
   Challenges to canonical patterns 79

5 Social patterns II: intraspeaker variation 90
   Intraspeaker patterns, community patterns, and style 90
   Register, speech activity, speech event, genre, frame 94
   Stance and identity 98

6 Meaning and social patterns 104
   Indexicality: meaning in the sociolinguistic variable 104
   Experimental evidence for meaning 107
   Indexical webs, cycles, and fields 114
   Dimensions of social meaning in language 117

7 Acquisition of variation 119
   How is variation learned? 119
   Early childhood 119
   Older children and adolescents 123
   Adulthood 124
   Transmission and incrementation of changes 124

Part III: Variation, change, and linguistic structure

Introduction to Part III 129

8 Structural patterns I: phonology and morphology 131
   Phonological variation: patterns of change, structural effects, and
   explanation 131
   Change in progress 131
   Shifts and chain shifts 135
   Mergers 141
   Regularity vs. lexical diffusion 143
   Phonological patterns of variety contact 144
   Morphological variation 145

9 Structural patterns II: syntax, lexical variables, and suprasegmentals . . . 153
   Description: the problem of 'saying the same thing' 153

Syntactic variables	154
Pragmatic and discourse variables	161
Lexicon	164
Suprasegmentals: intonation and rhythm	166

Part IV: Conclusions

10 The life and times of linguistic changes 171
    Sources and actuation of change 171
    Early development and spread of change 172
    Propagation, diffusion, transmission, and completion 174

References 177
Index 189

Figures

0.1	The International Phonetic Alphabet	xvi
2.1	Cross-product display for /d/ in Detroit (Fasold 1991: 5)	19
3.1	Sample coding spreadsheet	40
3.2	Percentage of (aʊ) variants by age category	43
3.3	Percentage of (aʊ) variants by age and gender	43
3.4	Monophthongisation percentage by age and gender (better version)	44
3.5	Monophthongisation percentage by age and gender (best version)	44
4.1	Social stratification of (r) in New York interview data (adapted from Labov 1966: 240)	57
4.2	Percentage r-fulness by age and class for reading style (adapted from Labov 1966: 345)	58
4.3	Stratification of (ing) in Norwich (adapted from Trudgill 1974: 92)	58
4.4	Negative concord by age and social class in Philadelphia (adapted from Labov 2001a: 107)	61
4.5	Negative concord by gender and social class in Detroit (adapted from Labov 2001a: 82; Wolfram 1969)	61
4.6	Low-density (left) and high-density (right) networks	65
4.7	(ae) variation in Belfast neighbourhoods by gender and age (adapted from Milroy 1980: 124)	66
4.8	(th) variation in Belfast neighbourhoods by gender and age (adapted from Milroy 1980: 128)	66
4.9	Major dialect areas of North America (based on Labov et al. 2006; http://commons.wikimedia.org/wiki/File:StatesU.svg)	71
4.10	AAVE features in five communities (adapted from Wolfram 2000: 342)	73
4.11	[ɪn] use in Norwich by gender and class (adapted from Trudgill 1974: 94)	76
4.12	Negative concord in Detroit by gender and school category (adapted from Eckert 2000: 113)	76
4.13	/aʊ/-monophthongisation in Pittsburgh by age and gender, 2005	77
4.14	/oʊ/-fronting in Philadelphia by gender and occupation (adapted from Labov 2001a: 298)	77

4.15	Amount of English *ai* used by individuals in Cane Walk, ordered by class (adapted from Rickford 1986: 218)	81
4.16	(ae)-raising in Philadelphia by gender and occupation (adapted from Labov 2001a: 298)	84
4.17	/aʊ/-monophthongisation in Pittsburgh by gender and education	84
4.18	Cajun English variants by age (adapted from Dubois and Horvath 1999: 293)	86
4.19	Nasalisation in Cajun English by gender and age (adapted from Dubois and Horvath 1999: 294)	87
4.20	(dh) and (th) stopping by Louisiana women, by age group and network type (adapted from Dubois and Horvath 1999: 295)	87
5.1	Labov's decision tree for coding attention to speech (adapted from Labov 2001b: 94)	91
5.2	[ɪn] use probability by speaker and speech event (adapted from Kiesling 1998: 81)	97
5.3	Sue's mean rate of /t/-vocalisation when speaking to clients of varying classes (adapted from Bell 1984: 165)	101
5.4	Use of *eh* by ethnicity and gender (adapted from Meyerhoff 1994: 373)	102
6.1	Sample Likert scale response sheet for a matched-guide experiment	109
6.2	Perceptual boundaries between /s/ and /ʃ/ by gender stereotypicality (adapted from Strand 1999: 92)	112
6.3	Perception of intelligence by perceived region (adapted from Campbell-Kibler 2009: 148)	113
6.4	Indexical field of (ing) (adapted from Eckert 2008a: 466)	116
7.1	Coronal stop deletion (CSD) by age and following environment (adapted from Labov 1989: 93)	120
7.2	Percentage of monophthongisation by speaker and speech activity (adapted from Smith et al. 2007: 75)	122
7.3	Percentage verbal (-s) by speaker and speech activity (adapted from Smith et al. 2007: 84)	122
8.1	/r/ use in New York City by department stores at two different times (adapted from Labov 1994: 88)	132
8.2	Change in /r/ use by department store and age (adapted from Labov 1994: 93)	133
8.3	Vowel space core and periphery (adapted from Labov 1994: 177)	135
8.4	The Philadelphia Vowel Shift	136
8.5	The Northern Cities Vowel Shift (adapted from Labov 1994, in press).	136
8.6	A more complex view of the Northern Cities Vowel Shift (adapted from Gordon 2001)	137
8.7	Southern Shift peripheral vowel raising (adapted from Labov 1994, in press)	138
8.8	Southern Shift in Sydney, Australia	138

9.1	S-curve as defined by the logit function	156
9.2	Definite article use before possessive in Portuguese (adapted from Kroch 1989: 209)	157
9.3	Probability of definite article before possessive in Portuguese by constraint type and century (adapted from Kroch 1989: 210)	157
9.4	*Do*-support in Modern English (adapted from Kroch 1989: 219)	158
9.5	*Do*-support in English by constraint type and century (adapted from Kroch 1989: 223)	159
9.6	Compliments by gender in New Zealand (adapted from Holmes 1995: 123)	163
9.7	Intensifier use in Toronto by age (adapted from Tagliamonte 2008: 372)	165
9.8	Use of *dude* by gender of speaker and addressee (adapted from Kiesling 2004: 285)	167

Tables

3.1	Possible design for a sociolinguistic study	36
3.2	Percentage of (aʊ) variants by age category (number of tokens in parentheses)	41
3.3	(aʊ) variants by age category (poorly constructed table!)	42
3.4	Percentage of (aʊ) variants by age and gender	42
3.5	Observed monophthongisation in Pittsburgh by age group	47
3.6	Expected monophthongisation in Pittsburgh by age group	47
4.1	Class scores in Labov (1966)	56
4.2	Class division in Labov (1966)	56
4.3	Summary of canonical variation patterns	78
4.4	Percentage of negative concord among Detroit high school students	83
6.1	Orders of indexicality and Labovian variable types for (aʊ) in Pittsburgh	108
8.1	Factors in coronal stop deletion (CSD)	140
8.2	Types of sound change (Labov 1994: 543)	144
8.3	Grammatical category effect on (ing) variation	147
8.4	(ing) assimilation	148
8.5	(sSpan)-deletion in Philadelphia by grammatical category, following segment, and stress	149
8.6	Weights for s-deletion by preceding environment	149
8.7	*were* probability by polarity and grammatical subject (Tagliamonte 2008: 176)	151

Preface and acknowledgements

The book you have here attempts to survey and organise all of the various interdisciplinary work that falls under the rubric 'linguistic variation and change'. Students (and teachers) are encouraged to follow the literature cited for topics that they want to pursue further. A short look at the references indicates that some journals are central to the field: *Language Variation and Change, Language in Society, Journal of Sociolinguistics*, and *Language*; others such as *English World Wide, Diachronica, Language and Communication*, and the *Journal of Phonetics* are also ones to review. The *Linguistics and Language Behaviour Abstracts* (LLBA) from Cambridge Scientific Abstracts is my favourite bibliography.

I imagine the student using this book as a beginning (post)graduate student or an advanced undergraduate. I expect that in addition to an introductory linguistics course, the student will have taken a course in phonetics and phonology, and a very basic syntax course. The level needed lies between a general introductory course and completion of these other courses.

Finally, some thanks are in order. First is Esmé Watson, who was been instrumental in prodding me to finish and patient as well, and to Vicki Donald for getting things over the finishing line. Also patient are Paul Kerswill (who is responsible for getting me into this project) and Joan Swann. Peter Patrick provided some important feedback and guidance. I cannot express the debt I owe to my distinguished list of variationist teachers, whom I consider it an amazing privilege to have known and learned from: William Labov, who taught me my first linguistics course and is responsible for my being a linguist (in addition to pretty much being responsible for the field this book surveys), Gillian Sankoff, Ralph Fasold, Roger Shuy, Walt Wolfram (a generous mentor even though I was not his student), and Peter Patrick. Barbara Johnstone has been an invaluable colleague and mentor as well as an exemplary scholar. Christina Schoux Casey stepped in near the end to clean up my mess. The various students who have taken my variation courses have taught me much about the topic. The most patient and encouraging of all are my family, especially my spouse Julie, for enduring frustrations, distraction, and more than a few late nights and insanely early mornings.

Terminology and notation conventions

I will use the term *variety* most of the time as a cover term for language, dialect (or lect of any sort), etc. When it is important for me to differentiate two languages, I will do that as best I can, but there is an unsolvable issue when it comes to more specific terms. Where such entities begin and end, and how to define them, is problematic, so I ask the reader's patience with my vagueness when I judge the issue to be irrelevant to whatever the current point is. I will generally use names for varieties that other authors use, although this can be contentiousas well; again I ask for patience in this matter. Most abbreviations are introduced in the text, and refer to variables, varieties, or key pieces of literature; below are some important notations used throughout.

- [x] phonetically represented segment (see the International Phonetic Alphabet chart in Figure 0.1); this notation also represents *variants* of a variable
- /x/ phonemically represented segment
- {x} morpheme; {-x} represents a suffix and {x-} a prefix
- (x) sociolinguistic variable

Phonetic notation

Phonetic notation will follow the International Phonetic Alphabet (IPA), as shown in Figure 0.1. Readers are assumed to be familiar with phonetic terms (a good introduction is Johnson 2003).

ENGLISH VOWEL NOTATION

Because English vowels are disproportionately important in the field of linguistic variation, it is worth mentioning the notation adopted for them in this book. In general, I use the IPA vowel that most closely approximates the vowel class. I generally gloss each with an example word. However, because of differences in the pronunciation of vowels in different varieties of English, it is inevitable that a speaker's native pronunciation (or the primary variety learned, if English is a second language) will differ in some details. This variety of vowel classes is also the reason for not using the keywords of Wells (1982). Here are the general representations.

/ɑ/ lot
/ɔ/ thought
/ə/ <u>a</u>bove
/ɛ/ bet
/e/ bait
/ɪ/ bit
/i/ beet
/æ/ bat
/u/ boot
/ʊ/ foot
/ʊ/ boat
/ʌ/ but
/aʊ/ house
/aɪ/ bite
/oʊ/ boat
/oɪ/ boy

THE INTERNATIONAL PHONETIC ALPHABET (revised to 2005)

CONSONANTS (PULMONIC)

	Bilabial	Labiodental	Dental	Alveolar	Postalveolar	Retroflex	Palatal	Velar	Uvular	Pharyngeal	Glottal
Plosive	p b			t d		ʈ ɖ	c ɟ	k ɡ	q ɢ		ʔ
Nasal	m	ɱ		n		ɳ	ɲ	ŋ	ɴ		
Trill	ʙ			r					ʀ		
Tap or Flap		ⱱ		ɾ		ɽ					
Fricative	ɸ β	f v	θ ð	s z	ʃ ʒ	ʂ ʐ	ç ʝ	x ɣ	χ ʁ	ħ ʕ	h ɦ
Lateral fricative				ɬ ɮ							
Approximant		ʋ		ɹ		ɻ	j	ɰ			
Lateral approximant				l		ɭ	ʎ	ʟ			

Where symbols appear in pairs, the one to the right represents a voiced consonant. Shaded areas denote articulations judged impossible.

CONSONANTS (NON-PULMONIC)

Clicks		Voiced implosives		Ejectives	
ʘ	Bilabial	ɓ	Bilabial	ʼ	Examples:
ǀ	Dental	ɗ	Dental/alveolar	pʼ	Bilabial
ǃ	(Post)alveolar	ʄ	Palatal	tʼ	Dental/alveolar
ǂ	Palatoalveolar	ɠ	Velar	kʼ	Velar
ǁ	Alveolar lateral	ʛ	Uvular	sʼ	Alveolar fricative

VOWELS

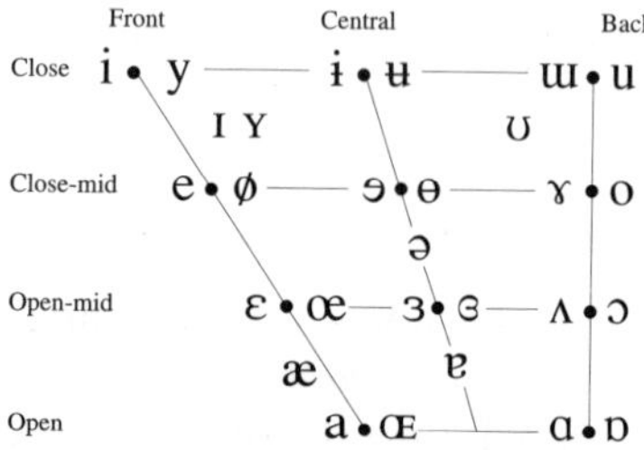

Where symbols appear in pairs, the one to the right represents a rounded vowel.

OTHER SYMBOLS

ʍ Voiceless labial-velar fricative

w Voiced labial-velar approximant

ɥ Voiced labial-palatal approximant

ʜ Voiceless epiglottal fricative

ʢ Voiced epiglottal fricative

ʡ Epiglottal plosive

ɕ ʑ Alveolo-palatal fricatives

ɺ Voiced alveolar lateral flap

ɧ Simultaneous ʃ and x

Affricates and double articulations can be represented by two symbols joined by a tie bar if necessary. k͡p t͡s

SUPRASEGMENTALS

ˈ Primary stress

ˌ Secondary stress

ˌfoʊnəˈtɪʃən

ː Long eː

ˑ Half-long eˑ

˘ Extra-short ĕ

| Minor (foot) group

‖ Major (intonation) group

. Syllable break ɹi.ækt

‿ Linking (absence of a break)

DIACRITICS Diacritics may be placed above a symbol with a descender, e.g. ŋ̊

̥	Voiceless	n̥ d̥	̤	Breathy voiced	b̤ a̤	̪	Dental	t̪ d̪
̬	Voiced	s̬ t̬	̰	Creaky voiced	b̰ a̰	̺	Apical	t̺ d̺
ʰ	Aspirated	tʰ dʰ	̼	Linguolabial	t̼ d̼	̻	Laminal	t̻ d̻
̹	More rounded	ɔ̹	ʷ	Labialized	tʷ dʷ	̃	Nasalized	ẽ
̜	Less rounded	ɔ̜	ʲ	Palatalized	tʲ dʲ	ⁿ	Nasal release	dⁿ
̟	Advanced	u̟	ˠ	Velarized	tˠ dˠ	ˡ	Lateral release	dˡ
̠	Retracted	e̠	ˤ	Pharyngealized	tˤ dˤ	̚	No audible release	d̚
̈	Centralized	ë	̴	Velarized or pharyngealized	ɫ			
̽	Mid-centralized	e̽	̝	Raised	e̝ (ɹ̝ = voiced alveolar fricative)			
̩	Syllabic	n̩	̞	Lowered	e̞ (β̞ = voiced bilabial approximant)			
̯	Non-syllabic	e̯	̘	Advanced Tongue Root	e̘			
˞	Rhoticity	ɚ a˞	̙	Retracted Tongue Root	e̙			

TONES AND WORD ACCENTS

LEVEL			CONTOUR		
e̋ or	˥	Extra high	ě or	˩˥	Rising
é	˦	High	ê	˥˩	Falling
ē	˧	Mid	e᷄	˧˥	High rising
è	˨	Low	e᷅	˩˧	Low rising
ȅ	˩	Extra low	e᷈	˧˦˧	Rising-falling
ꜜ		Downstep	↗		Global rise
ꜛ		Upstep	↘		Global fall

Figure 0.1 International Phonetic Alphabet (copyright International Phonetic Association)

Part I: Questions and method

Chapter 1
Questions about language and variation, and where we got them

QUESTIONS ABOUT LANGUAGE

This book is about the study of language and the search for explanations of why languages are spoken the way they are. This is a search that is shared by all types of linguistic theory, but in the perspective taken in this book (which I will variously refer to as variationist or Labovian linguistics), the goal is not the search for a 'universal grammar' (although there will be discussion of universals). Rather, the goal of variationist linguistics is to understand why language varieties *become different* from one another (or, in some cases, become more similar). The Chomskyan question 'What underlies all human languages?' is thus not replaced, but other questions, at least as important, are added:

- If all human languages share a common universal grammar, why aren't they all the same?
- Why don't all speakers of a language speak the same way all the time?
- What forces produce this variation across languages? Are the forces universal?
- How do languages get from one 'state' to another?
- What does the 'state' of a language look like if it is changing? Is it different from a 'stable' one?
- Does variation have a function? Given that in some case it impedes understanding, does variation serve a meaning function?

The goal of this book is to enable its readers to explain what our current best answers to these questions are, and to be prepared to begin adding to our knowledge of these questions. The book is mostly focused on theory, but since the methods of variationist linguistics are closely tied to the theory, a discussion of methods is essential. However, for students and instructors who wish to have a full methodological training, I would suggest supplementing this text with a methods book (such as Milroy and Gordon 2003) and a statistics text (such as Tagliamonte 2006, solely focused on the Varbrul statistical method, or Baayen 2008 and Johnson 2008, which are good general statistical introductions for linguists).

In this first chapter, we will be concerned with understanding the full scope of the questions asked above. We will take a historical perspective, because the theories, questions, and ideas about language discussed in the variationist field are not the result of an ahistorical process, but, even though by most accounts it is a 'new' field, are owed to the questions formulated decades and centuries ago. From the historical roots of the variationist programme come questions and assumptions that reverberate (even if they are not subscribed to) to this day in variationist studies.

WHERE WE GOT THE QUESTIONS: FROM COMPARATIVE PHILOLOGY TO VARIATIONIST THEORIES

The roots of the variationist programme reach far back, to the beginning of modern Western linguistics. This beginning may be traced to observations made by Sir William Jones, who is often credited as the first European to remark, in 1786 (Seuren 1998: 79), that the similarities among Sanskrit, Greek, and Latin suggest that they somehow derived from a common source (although most linguistic historians believe that these ideas were floating around before Jones made his famous speech; see Weinreich et al. 1968). This insight led to the development of the comparative method in historical linguistics (see Seuren 1998), and the nineteenth century showed a rapid development in the understanding of relationships among languages. In addition to the 'discovery' of the Indo-European language family, one of the intellectual currents in European society about this time was a move towards rationalism and the discovery of 'natural' laws based on direct observations. This current led to a rapid leap in an understanding of the natural world; linguists of the era were therefore inspired to approach language in a similar way. Comparative historical linguistics, then, arose out of the same trends in science that produced physics, chemistry, and evolutionary biology.

The most important innovation in linguistics of this time was the development of a method for the comparison of languages. One of the first lessons learned in historical linguistics is that it is easy to find false cognates: words that look similar in two languages but are not related, due to a systematic change that has taken place in the phonology of one or both of the languages. The comparative method provided a way in which comparisons could be made between languages in a more systematic and less error-prone manner. This research agenda, based on comparison across languages, also suggested the need for systems of transcribing sound that were not language-specific, so that such comparisons could be made; this need gave rise to phonetic alphabets culminating in the International Phonetic Alphabet (IPA), which was derived from the work of phonetician Henry Sweet (Sweet 1911). Another intellectual current arising especially in the eighteenth century was the development of prescriptive grammars. Grammar until this time had mainly been seen as something that was a property of Latin and Greek, and one learned grammar by learning to translate ancient texts in these languages. As shown by Mugglestone (2003), it was in the eighteenth century that European scholars began to write grammars and dictionaries for 'vulgar' languages such as German, French, and even English.

All of these developments changed the way people, and especially the developing scientific community (or 'natural philosophers' as they called themselves), thought about language. For example, language needed to become an object that could be studied, and it needed to acquire regularities that one could write laws about. Biology, physics, and mathematics were dominant fields in the burgeoning scientific world, so it is not surprising that their study gave rise to two ways of looking at language. An early way of thinking about language was through a biological metaphor, in which languages were seen as organisms. Another view held that language was the 'personal property' of an individual. This argument was debated vigorously, with the opposing view being that language is a community object. This argument continues to this day, with generative linguistics in some ways taking the former view, and variationists the latter.

In the late nineteenth century a group of young, mostly German men had the audacity to argue against their teachers, and radically rethink the relationship of language and the individual. These *Junggrammatikers* or *Neogrammarians*, as they have become known, postulated that it is not individual words that change in a language, and at the same time rejected the biological metaphor. Rather, they argued, linguists should be searching for regular and predictable laws of sound change, just as physicists search for laws of nature. That is, languages change through individual sounds (or categories of sound) rather than word by word. Although it may seem obvious to modern linguists that change should affect classes of sounds, the Neogrammarians were working without the benefit of the theoretical notion of the abstract phoneme, and in fact their work may have helped to spread the term more widely. The Neogrammarians were (and still are) central to variationist work because they began to look for 'laws' of sound change. They began to describe changes in ways that look similar to phonetic and phonological changes as they are described in modern historical linguistics.

The first revolution in linguistic thinking in the twentieth century (Seuren 1998: 157) was started by Saussure's *Cours de la linguistique generale* (1983 [1916]) and especially by the notion of the phoneme. Phonemes are defined by their structural relationship to other phonemes in the linguistic system, and not by their phonetic character. In this view, the significance of /p/ in 'pin' is not its phonetic character combined with the other phonetic characters of the word, but its difference from other phonemes such as /b/ or /d/, and this can easily be seen by the fact that replacing /p/ with these other two consonants produces words with completely different meanings. A structural relationship is one of difference that produces meaning, crucially only within a particular linguistic system (language or variety). Although the way we now discuss the phoneme is not identical to that described in the *Cours*, the notion of a category of sounds has its beginning there.

While Saussure worked in Geneva, in America the field of anthropology was beginning to develop. Franz Boas (Boas 1911) saw the project of linguistics as part of anthropology and as revealing the folly of racism, challenging the view that American Indians were somehow inferior to Anglo-Americans. One of his tools in this endeavour was to describe American Indian languages in a rigorous way. This concern with method can be traced in the present-day variationist focus on method as a central part of the research programme. In addition, Boas stressed the 'unconscious' nature of language, and aligned this character with 'culture'. Indeed, it is central to Boas's argument that language should be aligned with culture, since both have categories that develop organically rather than through conscious thought and discussion. Boas's student Edward Sapir elaborated this notion. He developed Boas's ideas and expanded the anthropological linguistics tradition of description in his influential 1921 book, *Language*. This current became an important one that in the later twentieth century influenced sociolinguistics considerably (see Shuy 1990), both because of its focus on descriptive methods and because in this tradition language was always seen as a cultural rather than individual property.

The tension between language as an abstract object and as the property of an individual, however, is still present. In a central early programmatic article on variationist linguistics which we will discuss extensively, Weinreich et al. (1968; henceforth WLH) spend a considerable amount of time engaging with the theories of change outlined by Hermann Paul (Paul 1970, originally published in 1880, with the fifth edition published in 1920). Paul was an extremely influential linguist of the late nineteenth and early twentieth centuries, whose view of linguistic change rested on a concept of language as something that belonged to an individual: he argued that the 'idiolect' is the proper object of linguistic study. For him, individuals are fairly consistent in their language knowledge (or language 'image', a translation of Paul's *Vorstellungen*); however, pronunciation randomly varies around a target. A dialect (or language) for Paul is a collection – an average – of idiolects. Language changes when idiolects change in parallel, and dialects split from one another when groups of idiolects diverge. These changes are explained by contact with other dialects and accommodation by speakers to that new dialect. WLH spend considerable space refuting this view in favour of a view of a dialect as a community object. They argue that Paul's view cannot account for the reality of language change, and indeed can account only for phonetic change and not for change in the case of lexical replacement. There are other unanswerable questions, as well: why do speakers move their idiolects in the same direction (in parallel)? If everyone is varying randomly, why do they end up moving in the same direction? In addition, if change tends to come from idiolects in contact, why are those idiolects different in the first place?

WLH delve deeply into many other approaches to change, and we will not go into all of them here. But their critique of other theories constitutes the real innovation in the study of language considered in this book. The best-known passage from the article states their central claim most eloquently; it is worth quoting in full and spending some pages on this passage to understand the innovations in the study of language change established by WLH (pp. 100–1):

> The generative model for the description of language as a homogeneous object ... is itself needlessly unrealistic and represents a backward step from structural theories capable of accommodating the facts of orderly heterogeneity. It seems to us quite pointless to construct a theory of change which accepts as its input needlessly idealized and counterfactual descriptions of language states. Long before

predictive theories of language change can be attempted, it will be necessary to learn to see language – whether from a diachronic *or* a synchronic vantage – as an object possessing orderly heterogeneity.

The facts of heterogeneity have not so far jibed well with the structural approach to language . . . For the more linguists became impressed with the existence of structure of language and the more they bolstered this observation with deductive arguments about the functional advantages of structure, the more mysterious became the transition of a language from state to state. After all, if a language has to be structured in order to function efficiently, how do people continue to talk while the language changes, that is, while it passes though periods of lessened systematicity? Alternatively, if overriding pressures do force a language to change, and if communication is less efficient in the interim (as would deductively follow from the theory), why have such inefficiencies not been observed in practice?

This, it seems to us, is the fundamental question with which a theory of language change must cope. The solution, we will argue, lies in the direction of breaking down the identification of structuredness with homogeneity. The key to a rational conception of language change – indeed of language itself – is the possibility of describing orderly differentiation in a language serving a community. We will argue that nativelike command of heterogeneous structures is not a matter of multidialectalism or 'mere' performance but is part of unilingual linguistic competence. One of the corollaries of our approach is that in a language serving a complex (i.e., real) community, it is *absence* of structured heterogeneity that would be dysfunctional. [emphasis added]

The focus of this passage is on the heterogeneous nature of language, as opposed to the homogeneous states that most other theories of language up to this point assume. Underlying this focus is an understanding of language as existing in a community of individuals, rather than completely and perfectly in one of those individuals. This view is embedded in the key statement from the second paragraph above: 'The key to a rational conception of language change – indeed of language itself – is the possibility of describing orderly differentiation in *a language serving a community*.' The main difference between WLH's view and that of previous (and many current) theories is that a language or language variety (dialect, etc.) is not the averaging of individuals, or even something locatable in a *single* individual's mind, but rather an external, community 'object'. In this view, individual variation is not to be averaged, but rather seen as the pattern or texture of the variety: variation is part of the very description of a language.

WLH argue that 'the identification of structuredness with homogeneity' is one of the main conceptual problems preventing linguistic theories from developing an adequate account of linguistic change (and as we will see, it also fails to account for many so-called synchronic linguistic facts). Really, there is no observational or scientific reason to assume that language is homogeneous (whether in a community or in someone's mind). This view is rather an ideology about language that has persisted throughout the history of Western linguistics, and it is related to the ways that language is assumed to work more widely. In fact, as Anderson (2006) shows, the idea of a homogeneous, national language was one of the notions that helped create the modern nation-state and the very idea of 'a nation' and 'a language' (see also Agha 2007).

One of the most obvious examples of this ideology of homogeneity is the focus of structuralist (and to some extent generative) phonology on exceptionless (what I will also call categorical), predictable rules or constraints. That is, in describing a language, the focus is on predicting categorically the phonetic character of phonemes. If they cannot be categorically predicted, then any phonetic alternation is thrown into the 'free variation' dustbin, and often attributed to issues of 'performance'. In this view then, if something is not categorically predictable – i.e., if the rule does not apply always – then it is 'free' or without order.

So WLH introduced the term 'orderly heterogeneity' as the key for unlocking the problem. Orderly heterogeneity is essentially the pattern or texture discussed above. This term addresses the fact that earlier theories had viewed any type of heterogeneity as disorderly. Of course, we see heterogeneous order all the time in almost all human practices. For example, when do you get out of bed every morning? At dawn? In fact, it would silly to suggest that everyone gets up exactly at dawn, and if we were to construct a theory of circadian rhythm, we wouldn't argue that everyone has this as the necessary ideal. But this doesn't mean that there isn't a predictable, generalisable structure to the way a community, a culture, or an individual wakes up each day: In fact, researchers have found that there is an approximately four-hour window in which most people wake, and the waking times of those outside those patterns can be accounted for in other ways (Horne and Ostberg 1976). The point of this non-linguistic example is to show that it is not hard to think of human knowledge and behaviour as being heterogeneous, or variable, but still possessing predictable structure.

ORDERLY HETEROGENEITY AND CONSTRAINTS ON ITS FORM

So what then is 'orderly heterogeneity' in language? It refers to the fact that speakers of a language have many choices in how to assemble any utterance (that's the heterogeneity part), but that these choices form predictable patterns in terms of the linguistic system and social factors (that's the orderliness part). This is the basic insight from which all the research discussed in this book flows. Let's look at this difference with an example. One of the earliest and best-known variation studies is Labov's (1966) investigation into linguistic change in New York City, which we will discuss in detail later on. As an example here we can focus on his study of postvocalic /r/ (the pronunciation of /r/ after vowels in words such as *floor* or *fourth*). In New York the /r/ is not always pronounced, unlike in most other varieties of North American English. Labov studied whether there was a pattern in who pronounced the /r/ and when. Part of his method consisted of going to three different department stores and asking where some item was located in the store, knowing full well that the answer was the fourth floor. He pretended not to hear the response, causing the clerk to repeat 'fourth floor', and thus got four productions of /r/. Both the pronunciations of individual speakers and pronunciations across speakers were variable: sometimes people had a 'constricted' approximant [ɹ] pronunciation (or 'r-ful'), and sometimes a vocalic pronunciation ('r-less'; in the case of *fourth* it would be [fo: θ]). By looking at the historical record and by comparing older and younger speakers, Labov determined that the r-ful pronunciation was increasing in New York.

We can use this example to see that there are two dimensions of orderly heterogeneity. First, speakers behave differently (heterogeneity), but *which* speakers and *which* utterances are more r-ful will be statistically predictable (orderliness). In the department store study, for example, Labov found that salespeople in all stores had variable pronunciations, but that those who worked in the high-end store used the r-ful pronunciation more than those in the other two stores. Second, pronunciation will be affected by linguistic factors: in this case, the pronunciation of /r/ will be *statistically predictable* on the basis of some other linguistic fact, such as whether the /r/ is followed by a consonant in the syllable (this is orderliness). Labov investigated two phonetic environments, and while there was variation in both *fourth* and *floor*, the *fourth* pronunciations were more often vocalic than the *floor* examples. Not all such effects were phonetic. When Labov had the salespeople repeat their response, so that they were more 'emphatic' the second time, the utterances that were more emphatic were more likely to have r-ful pronunciations. So Labov found heterogeneity, or *variation*, both across individuals and within individuals, and this variation was not random, but patterned in statistically predictable ways. Orderly heterogeneity allows us to see a change such as in /r/ not as an abrupt change in which one generation is all r-less and the next generation suddenly r-ful, but as a more gradual and organised affair, and this removes much of its mystery. This reconceptualisation also sets up new questions, such as whether there are universal patterns of variability. WLH articulate a set of problems that a theory of linguistic change must answer, and one riddle that may be unanswerable:

1. The **constraints** problem, or that of 'the set of possible changes and possible conditions for changes which can take place in a structure of a given type' (p. 101): In what linguistic and social conditions are certain changes likely or unlikely? For the New York example, what linguistic structural factors might have led to the 'strengthening' of /r/? Were there vowel changes that supported the shift?
2. The **transition** problem: What intervening stages 'can be observed, or must be posited, between any two forms of a language defined for a language community at different times'? The New York example tells us that there needs to be some kind of variability in the transition. We might also observe phonetic gradients such that some speakers exhibit very definite [ɹ], some sound a little less so, and some completely r-less. Theoretically, we will want to try to predict what these stages will look like for all changes, or perhaps

for different kinds of changes (or changes in phonetics, phonology, morphology, or syntax). Finally, the transition problem encompasses the regularity question (also known as the Neogrammarian controversy): do changes move regularly as changes to phonemes (and, relatedly, by syntactic category), or do they move at different rates from word to word (and for syntax, by individual constructions)?

3. The **embedding** problem: 'How are changes embedded in the matrix of linguistic and extralinguistic concomitants of the forms in question (what other changes are associated with the given changes in a manner that cannot be attributed to chance?)?' (p. 101). This is the problem on which the vast majority of variation studies have focused. The New York city study provides several examples of embedding. First, the observation that speakers in the high-end department store were more r-ful is an embedding of the change to r-fulfulness in the social fabric of the city. In addition, the change is embedded in the linguistic system in that /r/ is more likely to be r-less when followed by a consonant. The theoretical goal in this area is thus to find regularities such that we can predict the ways that changes are likely to expand through a community and through a language.

4. The **evaluation** problem: 'How can the observed changes be evaluated – in terms of their effects upon linguistic structure, upon communicative efficiency, and on the wide range of nonrepresentational factors involved in speaking?' (p. 101). This problem is almost as much studied as the embedding problem and they are almost by necessity studied together. In New York, we want to know what a shift to /r/-fulness does to the structure of the language (for example, in the way that vowels before /r/ are pronounced), and whether or not the shift leads to misunderstandings. More common is a focus on the social evaluation: is the newer pronunciation valued in some way or viewed with disdain? Theoretically, we want to look for predictable, repeated patterns of how such changes are usually evaluated in the community, and whether there is agreement or disagreement on how and even whether to evaluate the new and old ways of speaking.

5. The **actuation** riddle: How and why do changes begin? This is a riddle because changes probably begin unobserved, making it difficult to identify their start.

Once we take variability to be a basic design feature of language, we then need a way of theoretically, or at least *heuristically*, representing it. In variationist approaches, this representation has been accomplished through the notion of the linguistic *variable*. The traditional way of defining a linguistic variable is to see it as more than one way of saying 'the same thing'. As we will see in the next chapter, the notion of 'the same thing' is slippery. But the essential idea is that there is one, isolable linguistic feature that carries meaning, such as the pronunciation of a phoneme like /r/, and the community has more than one way of representing it in language. The 'variable' notion is discussed in detail in the next chapter.

Note that a view of language that takes ordered heterogeneity as a given does not rule out categoricity; in fact the field assumes that there are some parts of the grammar that may be categorical. In describing a grammar with probabilities, it is trivial to describe a part of that grammar that is categorical: it simply has a probability of one (acting 100 per cent of the time). For example, at some point in the future, New Yorkers may use a consonantal pronunciation for all of their /r/s.

WLH end their essay with some general principles for the study of language change, which summarise the variationist perspective and suggest issues important in variationist linguistics:

1. '[Language change] is not random drift proceeding from inherent variation' (p. 187). This is a reaction to an idea that Saussure suggested, and is still the view of some linguists (who argue that more radical change is always the product of language or dialect contact). However, there seems to be more directionality in language change than would be predicted if change were random and unstructured.
2. 'The association between structure and homogeneity is an illusion' (pp. 187–8). As discussed above, we can find structure, or orderliness, in variability, if we know how to look and how to describe it.
3. 'Not all variability and heterogeneity in language structure involves change; but all change involves heterogeneity and variability' (p. 188). In other words, variability is a 'natural', even stable state for language, but if language does undergo change, we are logically going to see some variability.
4. 'The generalization of a change is neither uniform nor instantaneous' (p. 188). This is a corollary to (3); changes happen faster in some parts of the language and for some speakers, and there will be many speakers who show variability in the transition.
5. 'Grammars of change are grammars of speech communities' (p. 188). This seems simple, but it is important and one of the most difficult principles for students to understand, because it requires thinking about our object of study very differently. We cannot understand language change by assuming a single, ideal individual who represents the only grammar during the change. Rather, the grammars we represent are those of a speech community. Labov described /r/ in New York City, not in a particular New Yorker. Given the variability across individuals such a task would be problematic. Of course, speakers do have linguistic knowledge, and the problem of how to represent variable knowledge is an important one.
6. 'Linguistic change is transmitted within the community as a whole; it is not confined to discrete steps in the family' (p. 188). The word 'discrete' is important here, because there are patterns by generation. But there are no big jumps from mother to son, for example, and the change is not restricted to families but affects – and is moved forwards by – the entire community.
7. 'Linguistic and social factors closely interrelate' (p. 188). Linguistic change does not happen in every speaker in the same way, but rather certain types

of speakers will adopt the change before others. The linguistic and the social constraints (or factors) affecting a change are to some extent independent (at least theoretically), but they will interact. Thus, almost everyone in New York will show the effect of a following consonant (everyone's rate of /r/-lessness before consonants will be greater), but their overall rate of /r/-fulness will vary as well.

In addition, I will include a third type of factor. These are cognitive factors, and they constrain what speakers cognitively perceive and produce. That is, how are such perception and production cognitively organized in the individual? I include this factor in order to bring research on individual 'abilities' into our discussion. One of the central problems in variationist linguistics is to determine exactly how different factors relate to one another. For example, does the following environment for /r/ in New York work the same for everyone? Why does the following environment have that effect and how might it be 'overridden' (for example, if you point the pattern out to someone, can they consistently use one variant or another)?

All three of the major constraints (structural, social, and cognitive) act on language simultaneously, and it is the tension among them that ends up driving and determining the direction of changes. The problems and principles outlined by WLH and explained above focus the questions we ask, and the three main constraints will help to structure the answers. We will begin with a more in-depth look at the concept of the variable.

Chapter 2
The linguistic variable

In this chapter we will investigate the 'variable' construct in detail, and consider some criticisms of the notion and responses to that criticism. We begin with an investigation into exactly what is meant by 'the linguistic variable' beyond the straightforward definition, and explore how this definition has changed since it was first used by Labov in 1963. We then consider some of the important objections to the concept.

DEFINITIONS AND TYPES

The usual definition of a linguistic variable is that it is two or more ways of saying the same thing, where 'the same thing' refers to what is denoted by an utterance. So, for example, the alternation between *walking* with [ɪŋ] and *walkin'* [ɪn] in most spoken English shows that there are (at least) two ways of uttering the {ing} morpheme without changing the central meaning of the word as referring to the act of walking. This notion was introduced by Labov (1963) in his groundbreaking article on variation on the island of Martha's Vineyard, off the northeast coast of the United States. From preliminary investigations on the island, Labov noted that some islanders had a distinctive way of pronouncing /aʊ/ and /aɪ/ as in *down* and *bite:* 'one frequently hears on Martha's Vineyard [ɐɪ] and [ɐʊ] or even [əɪ] and [əʊ]' (1972b: 9). He showed, on the basis of historical evidence and other evidence we will review in the next section, that these phonemes were undergoing a change towards centralisation of the first element of the diphthong. Labov also introduced the notation convention of using parentheses for variables, so when discussing the Martha's vineyard variables he used (aʊ) and (aɪ). This notation distinguishes them from the phonemes /aʊ/ and /aɪ/, and also still allows a discussion of their phonetic characteristics with square brackets, so that the *variable* (aʊ) might have the phonetic *variants* [əʊ], [aʊ], or [æʊ]. It is important to get this terminology correct: when discussing, for example, the increase use of centralisation of (aʊ) in younger speakers, we are discussing the change taking place in the *variable* generally. However, when we want to be more specific, we might say that 75 per cent of the individual *tokens* of (aʊ) are of the [əʊ] variant. For the morpheme {ing}, the variable is (ing), with variants of [ɪŋ] and [ɪn].

LINGUISTIC VARIABLES AT DIFFERENT LINGUISTIC LEVELS

Linguistic variables can occur at any linguistic level: phonological, morphological, lexical, syntactic, pragmatic, discoursal, and suprasegmental. The trick is to define carefully the part of the variable that 'stays the same'. This is not always easy. The most important issue is to be able to identify the *variable context*. That is, we need to be able to find every place that a speaker must make the choice we are interested in. Let's look at some examples of variables and variable contexts in each.

Phonological

The two examples given so far – (ing) and centralisation in Martha's Vineyard – are examples of *phonological* variables. For the Martha's Vineyard (aʊ) variable, the variable context is every instance in which English phonology requires this phoneme, no matter how it is said. For (ing), the variable context is a little more complex. It is tempting simply to identify any *-ing* spelled cluster as the variable context. But this definition would be too broad, because there are certain instances in which there is no option of using the [ɪn] variant, such as in words like *king*. The variable context thus excludes these instances, because they are not variable. If the variable context is not completely clear, it is best to define it broadly and then exclude contexts that do not show any variability.

Morphological

The variable context of morphological variables is usually identified by the morpheme's grammatical function, such as tense or aspect marking on verbs, or plural marking on eleents of a noun phrase. So for example we might say that plural agreement on nouns in Spanish is a variable. But note that in this case we need to look beyond the plural morphology on the verb and also take into account the form of the determiner and any modifying adjective, each of which can show plurality.

Lexical

Lexical variables are fairly straightforward, as long as we can show that the two variants – such as the choice between *soda* and *pop* for a carbonated beverage in American English – refer to the same entity. Thus, in the case of *soda* and *pop,* we need to take into account that for many US southerners, *Coke* (when used to refer to a beverage and not the steel-making fuel or the illicit narcotic) has the same referent as *soda*, whereas in other parts of the US, *Coke* refers to a single brand/flavour of the beverage (see the excellent maps at http: //popvssoda.com).

Syntactic

Variables at the level of syntax are some of the most difficult to define, because it is not always clear whether or not two variants are equivalent at some abstract level. We will return to this problem when we discuss variable rules below. Nevertheless, speakers generally have some choice in what clause structure to use in their utterances. For example, there is the alternation in English between passive and active constructions (as discussed by Weiner and Labov 1983). Pronoun use has also been well studied from a variable perspective. In these studies, speakers might have a choice of using more than one pronoun (for example, the choice in Montreal French between *on* and *tu/vous* studied by Blondeau 2001). In 'pro-drop' languages such as Spanish the use of an overt pronoun is optional, so *Yo hablo Espanol* 'I speak Spanish' is equivalent grammatically to *Hablo Espanol* '(I) speak-1sg Spanish' (see Cameron 1992 for a study of this variable). Another example of a choice of pronoun in a situation of language change is Zilles's (2005) analysis of the rise of a new first person plural pronoun in Brazilian Portuguese, in which *a gente* (lit. 'the people') replaces *nós*.

Pragmatics/Discourse

The most difficult type of variable to determine is at the pragmatic level, in which an abstract pragmatic function is taken as the variable. One successful research paradigm is the analysis of information status in texts (either written or spoken: Prince 1981, 1992; Ward and Birner 1995; Birner and Ward 2009). However, more often this work finds a syntactic difference, such as a choice of word order, and assumes that there are functional reasons for the choice. In this sense, the choice is assumed *not* to be equivalent in terms of meaning, but the choice is nevertheless important. For example, Ward and Birner (1996) show that in syntactic constructions in which there is 'rightward movement' in English (that is, the subject is moved to a later position in the sentence), the noun phrase referred to has the status of 'unfamiliar information'. An example of this type of construction is inversion, as in the second sentence in (1), from an aircraft announcement, in which the 'canonical' order *Red and white wine are also complimentary* has been inverted (Ward and Birner 1996: 2).

(1) We have complimentary soft drinks, coffee, Sanka, tea and milk. *Also complimentary is red and white wine.*

In this case, the noun phrase *red and white wine* involves entities unfamiliar to the hearer. The variable is thus subject to realisation before or after the copula, and both the inverted and the canonical types of sentence communicate an identity relationship between the adjective and the noun phrase.

Suprasegmental

These variables are most often pitch contours or intonation, and very little work has been done on them. One example is the investigation of so-called 'high rising tone' (HRT) or *question intonation* on declarative sentences. Like variables above the morphological level, these present challenges in defining the context. For example, when studying HRT, do we count syntactic clauses, so-called intonation phrases, or some other unit as the variable context? We may want to include declarative sentences as well.

There are therefore choices in how to say something at every level of language, and every possible choice can be considered to be a variable. The difficulty is in determining exactly what possible choices exist. For example, note that there are other possibilities for communicating (1), such as 'Complimentary red and white wine are also available', or 'We also have complimentary red and white wine.' This observation points out other difficulties with syntactic and pragmatic variables, namely the possibility of defining the variable context. We will return to this definition in the section on criticisms of the linguistic variable below and when we consider methodology in more detail in Chapter 3, but here it is important to note that the way in which variable contexts are defined is one of the main differences among variables at different levels of language.

Most of the variables outlined above constitute *discrete* variants, enabling a clear choice between one form or another: [ɪŋ] or [ɪn], *soda* or *pop*, passive or active. Indeed, this discrete organisation of variants is the most common way of conceiving of linguistic variables, and many research practices reflect this assumption, as we will see in the next chapter. However, it is possible in the phonetic realm to have *continuous* variables, with an unlimited number of choices on a continuous scale. It is possible to measure vowels instrumentally and produce a continuous variable (called acoustic measurement or coding), or alternatively, a trained phonetician can do an *auditory* analysis in which each vowel uttered is placed into a particular category. In the Martha's Vineyard study, Labov had four levels of centralisation for each vowel, which he coded auditorily. (However, he also measured some vowels acoustically to make sure his auditory codes were reliable.) Whether we have a discrete or continuous variable is important in choosing a statistical method for analysis.

It is also important to realise the extent to which the variants are imposed on the data (as in creating categories out of continuous data). In other words, any category is created by the analyst, and may or not be 'salient' for the user of the variety being analysed. We will investigate this point further in Chapter 3.

A further important distinction is between those discrete variables that have only two variants and those that have many. Here again the imposition of analytical choices makes a difference in how the data are understood, and we will return to these points in Chapter 3. The manner in which variables are understood today is related to their earlier conceptions, to which I turn in the next section.

In sum, we have two different ways to characterise linguistic variables: based on the level of language (phonology, morphology, etc.), and on the discreteness of the variants. Given the variability of what counts as a variable, we must define what counts as a *variable* more broadly than 'two or more ways of saying the same thing'. We will simply say that a *linguistic variable is a choice or option about speaking in a speech community*. Choice in this sense is not necessarily (although it could be) a volitional choice, but simply an option. Note that this definition does not in any way require us to state that the meaning be the same, although there should be some kind of equivalence noted. Notice that this broad definition is based on the speech community, which is important because something that is a variable in one speech community may not exist in another. For example, the deletion of word-final /s/ is variable in some Spanish speech communities, but in others it may not be so at all. Our definition thus keeps the focus of the variable on the speech community.

VARIABLE RULES AND THEIR 'QUIET DEMISE'

The *variable rule* is an important concept in the development of variation theory. Although the concept is no longer generally used, it must be grasped in order to understand what objections to the notion of variable have already been addressed (or not), and also in order to appreciate more fully what the concept of the variable is.

The first variable rule

We have seen that the first discussion of a linguistic variable was by Labov in 1963, but it wasn't until a 1969 article that he devised the first formal *variable rule*. This article was on the realisation (or deletion) of the English copula in African American Vernacular English (AAVE) and mainstream American English (for want of a better term). Labov's concern in this article is to show the regularity with which the copula is deleted in AAVE in sentences, as illustrated in (2).

(2) He ØØ the first one started us off. (Labov 1969: 716)

The ' Ø' in (2) indicates that the copula *is* (or the contraction *-s*) has been deleted in this utterance. Labov formulates generative morphophonological rules in the fashion of the time. These rules are ordered (so that there is a rule that applies for contraction of [ɪz] to [z] before [z] is deleted), and apply at different rates. Labov's rule for contraction is shown in (3).

(3) Contraction

$$\begin{bmatrix} +\text{voc} \\ -\text{str} \\ +\text{cen} \end{bmatrix} \rightarrow (\emptyset) / \begin{bmatrix} *\text{pro} \\ \alpha V \end{bmatrix} \#\# \begin{bmatrix} - \\ +T \end{bmatrix} \begin{matrix} C_0^1 \\ [*\text{nas}] \end{matrix} \begin{bmatrix} \alpha Vb \\ \beta gn \\ -\gamma NP \end{bmatrix}$$

This rule states that a schwa is deleted variably (the part before the slash; parentheses around Ø indicate variability). The rule applies variably in certain contexts (the part after the slash). For example, the deletion occurs on a tense-bearing item (that is, a verb), as indicated by the '+T' underneath the dash, which symbolises where the segment is. The '##' symbol is a word boundary, so whether or not the preceding word is a pronoun and ends in a vowel is important. The 'C' with numbers means that the segment is followed by one consonant, and the '*nas' means that the consonant is not a nasal one. Finally, the last bracket gives the effects for the following words, which tell us there are effects on whether the following word is a verb, a noun phrase, or the future *gonna* or *gon*.

The lower-case Greek letters (α, β, γ, etc.) are Labov's innovation, representing the strength of each constraint. So 'αV' tells us that whether or not the preceding segment is a vowel has the strongest effect on whether or not contraction takes place. The important point here is that ordered heterogeneity was being inserted into formal linguistic theory: The fact that the rule is variable is a representation of heterogeneity: the rule applies sometimes, and sometimes not. But it does not apply randomly, and this is indicated by the ordering of the different constraints. With the variable rule concept, Labov thus provides a proposal for how to implement the claims made by WLH in formal linguistic theory.

A short detour is in order here to discuss terminology. The things (like 'following consonant' or 'speaker's socioeconomic class') that affect the rate at which a variant appears I have been referring to in a non-technical way as *constraints* (as in phonological constraints); the same terminology is used by Labov in this original formulation. So he noted that whether or not the noun before the copula is a pronoun strongly affects the contraction of the copula. However, later variationist terminology, which I will use from now on, discusses constraints as *factors* or *factor groups*. Students may see either terminology, and while there may be slight differences in how they are related to statistics in variation research, they should be treated as essentially the same thing.

Now, back to the ordering of constraints or factors: the way this ordering was represented in early variationist work was through a *cross-product display*, which shows all the possible combinations of factors and the rates of variation for each combination. Fasold (1991) provides a particularly good example of such a representation in his discussion of variable rules. The variable in question is /t/ or /d/ deletion in English, or coronal stop deletion (CSD) as I will refer to it, which is the variable deletion of a word-final /t/ or /d/ in English words such as *test, missed, caught,* and *raised*. CSD is extremely well studied in many English varieties (see Guy 1980; Santa Ana 1991, 1996), and the relevant constraints are well known. In fact, it has been a crucial variable in the development of variationist theory and methods. Fasold provides a cross-product display based on data from Wolfram (1974), a study that focused only on the deletion of /d/. Fasold includes three constraints: whether or not the following word begins with a vowel, whether the syllable with the coronal segment is stressed or not, and whether the final segment is part of a suffix. It is reproduced here as Figure 2.1.

This figure shows that /d/ is present 17.1 per cent of the time if there is a following vowel, the word is stressed, and the /d/ is part of a separate morpheme on the main lexical item (for example, it is a past tense marker). Each of the eight possible contexts from three factors is thus represented. This representation is fairly straightforward for three factors with two options each, but there are often more factors, and they are not always so readily organised.

There are two problems with this kind of schematisation. The first is that some combinations of constraints may not be possible. For example, as Fasold points out,

The linguistic variable   19

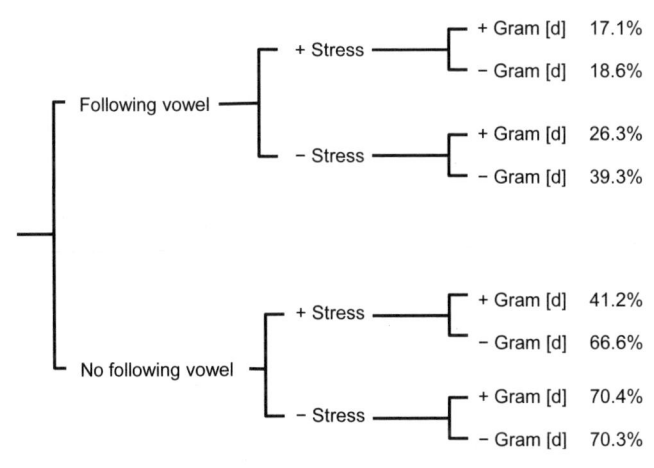

```
                                        ┌─ + Gram [d]   17.1%
                    ┌─ + Stress ────────┤
                    │                   └─ − Gram [d]   18.6%
   Following vowel ─┤
                    │                   ┌─ + Gram [d]   26.3%
                    └─ − Stress ────────┤
                                        └─ − Gram [d]   39.3%

                                        ┌─ + Gram [d]   41.2%
                    ┌─ + Stress ────────┤
                    │                   └─ − Gram [d]   66.6%
No following vowel ─┤
                    │                   ┌─ + Gram [d]   70.4%
                    └─ − Stress ────────┤
                                        └─ − Gram [d]   70.3%
```

Figure 2.1   Cross-product display for /d/ in Detroit (Fasold 1991: 5)

we may find a constraint for CSD that depends on whether a segment is a consonant or a vowel, and whether the following segment is nasal or oral. In a language that has no nasal vowels (like English), the logical cross-product combination of vowel–nasal will not exist. A further complication arises if there is a three-way option rather than a binary one. For example, we could note that in CSD the morphological status of the /t/ or /d/ is actually three-way rather than two-way. Guy (1980, 1991) used this division, such that each word ending in /t/ or /d/ was monomorphemic (*mist*), a regular past tense morpheme (*missed*), or a 'semiweak' past tense (*felt*), in which the /t/ is part of an irregular past tense suppletive morpheme. Such a three-way branch makes it difficult to decide which constraint produces the strongest effect.

Elaboration and development of variable rules

A more sophisticated statistical method and representation was developed by Cedergren and Sankoff (1974). They tweaked the variable rule notation, and more importantly provided a statistical method for determining the probabilities which should be assigned to constraints (the program which would later become Varbrul and GoldVarb, discussed in Chapter 3). In this formulation, angled brackets – '< >' – were used to show both the variability of the resulting form of the rule and the variability of constraints. They rewrite Labov's rule for contraction as shown in (4).

(4) $\begin{bmatrix} +\text{voc} \\ -\text{str} \\ +\text{cen} \end{bmatrix} \longrightarrow \langle \emptyset \rangle / \begin{array}{c} \langle \text{Pro} \rangle \\ \langle [-\text{cns}] \rangle \end{array} \ \#\# \ \begin{bmatrix} \overline{} \\ +\text{T} \end{bmatrix} \ \begin{array}{c} C_0^1 \\ [*+\text{nas}] \end{array} \ \#\# \ \left\langle \begin{array}{c} \text{Vb} \\ \text{gn} \\ \text{NP} \\ \text{PA-Loc} \end{array} \right\rangle$

The method they use, called *logistic regression*, produces the probability that a rule will apply for a particular factor independent of the other factors. Recall that Labov had argued that factors in variable rules should be ordered, and that the final frequency of the rule application was obtained by adding up the frequency for each factor, as seen in the cross-product display. Cedergren and Sankoff (1974) argued that we should calculate the *probability* that a rule will apply given a particular constraint. Moreover, these probabilities should be *multiplied* to determine the final rate. One important consequence of operating in this manner is that that the strength of the constraint would be represented by the magnitude of the probability. To understand this, remember that probabilities range from 1 to 0; 1 means that a rule will always be successful, while 0 means that it will always fail. A probability of 0.5 (for a binary variable) means that a factor has no effect – the rule applies randomly. So stronger constraints will have a value closer to 0 or 1, weak constraints closer to 0.5. These probabilities are then shown in probability tables associated with the variable rule.

Once we get the probabilities from the statistical program, they can be multiplied together to arrive at the predicted frequency of the variable. Moreover, each factor is assumed to be *independent*. For example, in CSD, we assume that the following segment factor group and morphological status factor group do not *interact* in some way. An interaction would occur if the following segment factor group had different probabilities of rule application when the coronal segment was a suffix and when it wasn't. In this case, we would need to make rules that incorporate probabilities for all the permutations of the variable (as in a cross-product display).

Rather, we assume that the following segment always contributes the same probability no matter what is happening in the other factor groups, and each operates independently of the overall tendency if no factors are taken into account. For example, for the variable rule for /d/-deletion for the study by Wolfram discussed above, the rule and the weights are as in (5).

(5) Overall tendency: .410

Following vowel?	**Stress**	**Grammatical /d/**
Present .275	Stressed 0.45	Suffix .451
Absent .725	Unstressed 0.55	Monomorphemic .549

We can tell that the following vowel factor group has the biggest effect by the fact that the range between the two factors for following vowel factor group is 0.45 (.725 minus .275), while the ranges for the other two factor groups are 0.10 and 0.098.

It is the weightings from these tables that we see in most variation studies performed in the 1990s and 2000s. For the most part in these studies, variable rules have been abandoned in favour of simply noting the probability that one variant will surface. Although the integration of ideas of ordered heterogeneity and probabilities into linguistic theory has only intermittently been attempted, there has been some renewed interest in how variation can be formally modelled in dominant forms of linguistic theory.

CRITICISMS OF THE NOTION OF LINGUISTIC VARIABLE

Recall that an early definition of the linguistic variable is 'two or more ways of saying the same thing.' This definition, at least on the surface, is unproblematic for allophone-like situations such as the vowels on Martha's Vineyard. However, we noted above that this sort of meaning is more problematic when it comes to syntactic, discourse, and to some extent morphological variables. For example, in many varieties of English, the marking of past tense on a verb is variable, as shown in the CSD studies above – if we delete the /t/ from *passed,* it is indistinguishable from the present tense form. This variable assumes, first, that past marking is identifiable in all contexts. However, it is also possible that this variable actually encodes a meaning difference. For example, the verb that otherwise have past tense marking but in which the -t/d is deleted might have a 'less remote' past tense (that is, something that just happened rather than something that happened a long time ago). This possibility of previously unknown meaning marking is one criticism aimed at the original definition of the variable. On the other hand, it is possible to define the variable on the basis of *function* rather than form. In this English past tense case, we could ask what choices are presented for the marking of simple past tense in a variety, holding aspect constant. We will return to this issue in the next chapter on methodology, but for now it is important to understand that while the objection that two forms may not have the 'same' meaning is important, it can be addressed through careful attention to the methods of defining the variable.

Along the same lines, another criticism that has been levelled at the original definition of variable is that it privileges a particular ideology of language with a limited view of what counts as meaning: a way of thinking and talking about language that sees the only function of language as a system of referring unproblematically to ideas and things. This is the most common Western ideology of meaning, but it is not the only kind of meaning that language exhibits, and some approaches privilege this *symbolic meaning* less than dominant generative approaches (see, for example, Halliday's Systemic Functional Grammar: Halliday and Mathiesson 2004). Symbolic meaning holds when a linguistic form unproblematically 'means' or stands for an abstract idea or thing. Thus, *three* in English refers to a number, and in another language it will be arbitrarily represented differently (*drei, san, troi,* etc.). There is nothing about the number that ties it to the word, and no matter what circumstance it is used in, it still means three. So if someone in an English-speaking speech community sometimes says [tri] for *three*, we can argue that the /θ/-/t/ alternation is a variable, because the symbolic meaning is the same.

However, there is another kind of meaning, very important for sociolinguistics, which is called *indexical* meaning. An *index* is a sign which takes its meaning from contextual associations. For example, a word that is always used by a particular person may take on a 'meaning' that indicates this person is speaking. So if someone other than that person says it, that person can be seen as 'voicing' the person who usually does. For example, if Uncle Eric always says 'by jingo', and I start an utterance with that phrase when speaking to someone who knows him, then I am indexing that I am speaking as if I were Uncle Eric. So we might argue that the use of 'by jingo' versus another interjection like 'holy cow' has a different meaning.

Haas (1944) reports that there are different words used in Koasati for at least some items depending on the gender of the speaker. For example, the paired words *lakawwíl — lakawwís* mean, respectively, 'Woman saying I am lifting it' and 'Man saying I am lifting it.' The gender of the speaker is part of the meaning in this case. Of course, these are categorical examples, but one could argue that any choice or option in language is likely to have some kind of indexical meaning. If we consider meaning in this way, then the classic definition of 'variable' is again problematic. However, we can respond to this criticism by using our expanded definition of 'variable' (*any* choice made by a speaker), and then argue that one of our interests is in discovering what meaning differences hold for the various choices.

The criticisms discussed so far resulted from the way that the variable was defined, and have been met by making our definition and methods more careful. Other criticism focuses not on the variable itself, but on the more fundamental claim that variables and the frequencies of their variants represent a consistent *community* pattern or grammar, rather than an *average of individuals* or individual uses. This claim is at the heart of Bickerton's (1971) criticism of the variable rule notion. He points out that it is at least theoretically possible that a variable pattern in a community could arise because there are individuals categorically using one variant or the other. For example, in the case of CSD discussed above, it is possible that a large group of the speakers had individual frequencies of deletion of zero, and another group had a 100 per cent deletion rate. When the group is averaged overall, it may look as though the entire community is variable, but it is actually the case that there are two groups of categorical speakers.

This criticism is easy to test by investigating the rates of individuals. The most careful and complete refutation of the criticism was produced by Guy (1980), using again the CSD variable among White Philadelphians and New Yorkers. He showed first that for his data, there was ordering for three factor groups, just as Wolfram found. For our example, let us just consider the morphemic status of the coronal segment: it is monomorphemic if it is part of the word, as in *mist*, ambiguous if it is part of an irregular past, as in *sent*, and a past tense marker if part of the regular *-ed* past tensesuffix, as in *missed*. Guy shows that for all of his data, there is an ordering such that the monomorphemic words have the highest probability of deletion, while the past tense morphemes have the lowest probability of deletion (and in fact he cites data from other studies with similar rates of effect). Guy used the Varbrul program developed by Cedergren and Sankoff to calculate probabilities for each individual in his study, and then compared the relative ranking of factors in factor groups for each individual to that of the overall community (none of the speakers always deleted or never deleted). The ordering of rankings for each individual mirrored the rankings in the overall data set; the only speakers who did not mirror the community pattern were those who could be shown to have the fewest measured instances (or *tokens*) of CSD. In other words, the only people who did not mirror the community rates were those speakers for whom there weren't enough data to determine the ranking of probabilities reliably. This result showed that the variation, and the ordering of constraints on that variation, were not an artefact of grouping speakers together.

We could take another methodological tack and decide that these three grammatical categories should be separate variables (so, for example, we considered only monomorphemic words in our analysis), but in this case we would then look to another factor group to test our orderings. This is exactly what Guy did, and the method worked for other factor groups as well. He found that the following phonetic environment also had the same effect for individuals as it did for the community as a whole. Interestingly, in this case there was some difference among speakers with respect to the ordering of the following pause, in which the pause environment had a higher probability of deletion for New Yorkers than for Philadelphians. This difference provided even more evidence that speakers' patterns of variation reflect those of their speech communities, because the differences were directly related to speech community membership (Philadelphia or New York), and not random individual differences.

The introduction of the idea of the variable rule had a profound effect on the way variables are conceived of. It made it possible to formulate the variable and its variants by simply outlining alternative realisations of the variable. For phonological variables, this conception would have the possible effect of increasing the number of variants to infinity. For morphosyntactic variables, there is a similar expansion of alternatives, but in ways that are more likely to change the denotation of the utterance. The variable rule introduced ideas from generative linguistics into the mix, most importantly by suggesting that variation was the outcome of a process or rule rather than of choices among alternatives. This imposes a more restricted set of alternatives on the variable, because (at least as originally outlined) they need to represent 'underlying forms' and the output of a rule. Thus, (r) in New York is seen as having an underlying /r/ which is then vocalised. This view has meant that the majority of work in variation has had variables that are limited to two variants. Even when three or more possibilities are recorded in the coding, two or more variants are usually combined in order to produce a binary variable. The early development of the variable rule thus led to a statistical procedure – Varbrul – which is expressly designed to handle binary variables, and in fact forces one to create a binary variable. As this statistical procedure became the dominant one in use for variationists, studies were in a sense forced to create binary variables, and forced to assume a rule-like organisation.

This organisation is appropriate for some variables, but is certainly not for all. Milroy et al. (1994) provide a case study of just such a 'problematic' variable. They analyse voiceless stops in Tyneside in northern England. These consonants have many different possible articulations in English: flap, /r/, aspirated, fricated, glottalised, and glottal stop, among others. Most importantly for Milroy et al.'s argument, there is a difference between a glottalised variant, in which there is some glottal closure with the consonant articulation, and the full glottal stop. We might assume that the glottalised variant is just a 'weaker' version of the glottal stop, and thus collapse them together. But Milroy et al. show that the two variants do not pattern in this way, are distributed differently geographically, and most importantly are not evaluated in similar ways by the speech community. In other words, if we were to collapse these variants, we would be glossing over important patterns of structured heterogeneity that we wish to describe and explain.

These criticisms of the notion of the variable have not stopped linguists from using the idea, but rather have led to a more flexible and nuanced understanding of optionality and choice in language and linguistic change. The requirement for identical meanings has been relaxed, and new statistical methods, discussed in Chapter 3, have been developed to handle situations in which one speaker may have undue influence on an overall data set, and situations in which there are more than two variants available to speakers. The variable thus continues to evolve as a concept, but at the same time maintains its central location in variationist theory and method.

I will conclude by mentioning two criticisms that are aimed not necessarily at the variable concept itself, or at the variationist project, but at the dangers in taking the means of variationist analysis to be the ends. These issues are normally set aside in most variation studies, but they are important to consider. Both have to do with the relationship between the methods of variationist analysis – which are based on the notion of the linguistic variable – and conclusions that can be reached from those methods.

Variationist linguistics is a deliberately data-driven and empirical method, but there are issues of interpretation at many points, and we must be careful not to lose sight of the fact that interpretation and qualitative analysis also inform methods from the very start – our methods are not 'objective' in the sense of 'mechanical'. Two dangers to watch out for are the tyranny of correlation and the atomisation of category. The former arises from the fact that the method of variationist linguistics is based on correlating a linguistic variable with other factors. What comes next, however, is interpretation. The *tyranny of correlation* comes about when this interpretation attributes too much to the correlation, in terms of either meaning or significance. For example, in Pittsburgh we might assume that the correlation between being a Pittsburgher and using /aʊ/-monphthongisation suggests that (aʊ) has a 'Pittsburgher' meaning. But Johnstone and Kiesling (2008) have shown that this understanding of the variable is simplistic at best, because when asked about this way of speaking, and about specific tokens of the 'Pittsburgh' variant, speakers diverged considerably on their identification of the variant and the Pittsburgh way of speaking. Similarly, we might assume that patterns of morphological deletion, such as /s/-deletion in Spanish, would reflect when the plural /s/ marking is most important. But Labov (1994) shows that careful investigation into such patterns often reveals other reasons for a correlation, such as the tendency to repeat /s/ or to continue to delete in adjacent tokens (for example in *las manos grandes*, with three successive tokens of /s/). This problem is only solvable by being linguistically and socially thoughtful in our analyses, and by always being sceptical of our results. The temptation is just to 'read off' our answers in correlations; even (or especially) in statistical patterns, it is important to read *critically*.

The *atomisation of category* is similarly a potential problem with the correlational methods, but at the other end of the process of performing a variationist analysis. That is, in variationist work we atomise different aspects of language, identity, and community into small, component parts, the better to correlate with the linguistic variable. There is an almost infinite number of possible factors potentially influencing a linguistic variable, and we choose among them. Thus we have already delimited the possibilities of describing the behaviour of a linguistic variable in a speech community by creating these categories for analysis. Moreover, we assume that there is independence among all of the linguistic variables in a community, and independence among the different factors in a community. That is, we assume the factors don't influence one another separately from the linguistic variable. However, this assumption of independence is simply that: an assumption. It is entirely likely that some linguistic variables and factor groups may interact. These problems, as with most discussed above, can be met with thoughtful methods and careful, evidence-based interpretations. In the next chapter, we will approach the central issue of methodology.

Chapter 3
Discovering and describing patterns of variation and change

Methodology is an integral part of variationist linguistics. Variationists take the view that methodology is inherent to theory and to the understanding of language. We will therefore discuss methods in this chapter, before we address the findings of variationists from the past forty or so years. However, the details of variationist methods can, and do, fill multiple book-length works. The discussion here is to get students started, and can be supplemented by methods books such as Milroy and Gordon (2003), and for statistics Tagliamonte (2006), Johnson (2008) and Baayen (2008). We will begin with some general points about variationist methods, and then move on to some more specific issues, roughly following the methodological steps involved in performing a variationist project.

Ultimately, methods are in the service of the questions we are asking about language, so these questions shape the methodology. The main question we want to answer in any variationist study is this: *'How does speech pattern in a speech community – what is the order in its orderly heterogeneity?'* Since we are searching for answers about speech communities and not individuals, we must analyse language that is representative of the community and not just an individual (and we want to find out how representative each individual is of the community). We will discuss the status of the speech community below; the general point now is that the perspective that we are studying the speech community and not individuals requires us to study more than one individual, and those speakers whose speech we do sample must be in some way representative of the speech community of interest. We will also study speakers' reactions to different kinds of speech, but treat these reactions not as representative of the individual's grammar, but as community-mediated attitudes that can help in understanding and explaining patterns of variation an change. In sum, by focusing on the speech community, we will want to record speech from many members of the community in order to understand the language of that community.

The problems outlined by WLH, introduced in Chapter 1, also provide us with questions that our methods must serve. First, of course, we must identify a variable or variables to focus on. This might be done on the basis of known variation in the community, but it also might be the focus of a preliminary study. We also want to determine whether we think the variable is undergoing change or whether it is stable. (Labov 1994, in analysing the entire Philadelphia vowel system, identified a variable undergoing the early stages of change, which would not have been identified if the variation in all vowels had not been analysed.) Recall that there were five main problems outlined by WLH, which can be turned into the questions that might drive a research project:

1. The **constraints** problem: What are the linguistic, or internal, constraints on the variable? What linguistic conditions have led to the change?
2. The **transition** problem: If the variable is changing, how is it spreading through the linguistic system and through the speech community? At what stage is the change (e.g., incipient, accelerating, slowing, almost completed), and why? Who adopts the change first and who adopts it last? How does one generation move the change forward?
3. The **embedding** problem: How is the variable patterning in the community and the language?
4. The **evaluation** problem: Does the change affect the communicative efficacy of the variety? How do speakers evaluate other speakers who use one variant more than another? Why do they evaluate speakers this way? What effect do these evaluations have on the change, if the variable is undergoing change?
5. The **actuation** riddle: How and why did the change begin?

For the most part, the *actuation* riddle has been set aside because the methodology required to study it does not exist, since we do not know ahead of time what parts of a variety are about to start changing. However, there two likely mechanisms: one is that there is always some variation in a language, especially in phonology, and so one generation could easily begin to shift that variation to the point that it starts a change. Alternatively, and more importantly, speakers use language creatively, using linguistic forms in new ways, and this expressive creativity may lead to many changes. Most probably the answer is a mix of these two mechanisms, and we can investigate the actuation riddle indirectly by understanding variation in language that doesn't change, and also how speakers use language creatively in interaction. The actuation riddle is of course related to every other problem since actuation precedes everything else. For example, a change perhaps only really 'takes off' when it gets evaluated in certain ways by some in a speech community, or once a certain number of speakers have adopted it (the evaluation and embedding problems). In addition, we don't really have a change until it moves from one generation to the next, which is related to the transition problem. Finally, the constraints problem suggests that there might be some changes that are more likely to get actuated.

Given those issues with the actuation riddle, let's turn our attention to the other four problems and their relationship to methods. The first two problems – constraints and transition – clearly demand that we observe language in the speech community, and record many other factors along with the status of any one token of a variable we find.

The *constraints* problem suggests that we need to know a lot about the entire variety we are concerned with. That is, we need to record many aspects of language that *might* affect the variable. We have seen examples of this already in the CSD example, in which following environment and morphological status are constraints on whether or not a coronal segment is deleted. How we decide on what constraints to record depends on our knowledge of linguistic theory and on likely effects that have been previously documented for the variable or for similar variables. For example, until recently most variationist studies with phonological variables did not record a measure of the frequency of the word the segment appears in. However, work by Bybee (2000) and Pierrehumbert (2001) has suggested that at least sometimes word frequency has an effect on some variables (but Labov in press and Dinkin 2008 find otherwise). The constraints we find are therefore intimately tied up with our methods: what kinds of recordings we have made, and what kinds of measurements we have made of the possible constraints. Real-world limits on resources (especially time) usually require that we select only those possible constraints that our models of language tell us are most likely to have a significant effect on the variation.

The *transition* problem suggests that we want to try to find linguistic changes in progress, and be able to identify which linguistic variables are involved in change and which are variable but not really changing. Of course the most obvious way to do this is to record speakers from the speech community at different times. However, most studies do not have the luxury of the several years or decades needed to detect changes that take place in generational time. The few studies of this type which have been performed have been very important in variationist work, but they are rare. When this kind of study is impractical, it is sometimes possible to find records of earlier studies of the speech community, even if performed using different methods. Labov (1963) used records from the Linguistic Atlas of New England (LANE) study to compare, in a fairly rough way, the amount of centralisation present in Martha's Vineyard in the early 1960s with that in the 1940s. The possibility of such work has increased as the variationist research programme has expanded. Indeed, there have been re-studies of both Martha's Vineyard (Blake and Josey 2003) and New York City Department stores (Fowler 1986, cited by Labov 1994; Becker 2009). In addition, linguists occasionally uncover early recordings of speech several generations removed (see, for example, Gordon et al. 2004 on early New Zealand English, based on recordings made in the 1940s). For studies of syntax, real-time historical studies of texts have yielded important results. Syntactic changes seem to happen over a much longer time span than phonological changes, but they have the advantage that texts of many languages exist over hundreds of years. There are other issues in this kind of study, such as whether texts are comparable in terms of genre, but the point is that there is much available material for syntactic studies.

The studies that compare speech recorded at different times are called *real-time* studies, and give us the most information about changes in a speech community. However, the vast majority of variationist work is done with *apparent-time* studies, which are apparent because they compare speakers of different ages or age groups recorded at a single time. If there are significant differences in the use of a variable from the older to the younger generation, then it is hypothesised that we are seeing a change in progress in the direction of the younger generation's usage. Of course, it is entirely possible that as speakers age they change the way they talk, a pattern known as *age grading*. However, in general these changes reflect generational changes, or changes in the speech community, rather than age grading, especially for phonological systems. Different kinds of variables seem to be more or less susceptible to age grading. Labov (1994) presents evidence from a number of real-time studies to suggest that phonological variables are fairly resistant to age grading. Sankoff (2006: 111) reviews thirteen real-time studies and concludes that

> in none of the follow-up studies do we find age grading alone. The most important implication of this conclusion is that apparent time is a truly powerful concept in locating the presence of change. In other words, a researcher who locates a gradient age distribution in a new community under study is virtually assured of having identified change, whether or not age grading is also involved.

In addition, all of the changes that Sankoff surveys which find some age grading show that older speakers change in the direction of overall change in the community. For example, Sankoff and Blondeau (2007) investigated the (r) variable in Montreal French, finding an age pattern in which younger speakers used more of the dorsal [R] variant than the coronal [r]. They re-interviewed theirty-two speakers thirteen years after previously interviewing them (a *panel* study), and in addition recorded thirty-two new, younger speakers (a *trend* study). The researchers found that for the most part, the speakers from the panel study did not change their rate of [R] use, but of the minority who did, all used more [R] than they had thirteen years before. This finding, along with the other studies surveyed by Sankoff (2006), suggest that, if anything, apparent-time studies *underestimate* the rate of change, because if there is any age grading going on, it is happening in the direction of the change.

These results taken together show that, in addressing the transition problem, ideally we triangulate how a transition is happening by using both apparent-time and real-time evidence. However, we can also be fairly confident that if we find differences in variable usage by age, we are finding a change in progress and the study can inform our understanding of the transition problem.

The *embedding* problem points to other issues in methodology. Recall that the embedding problem focuses on how the change is embedded in, or moves through, the speech community. The central issue in addressing this problem is making sure that our data are representative of the speech community such that we aren't missing important parts. This means that we have to be careful about which speakers we record, and that we keep track of the identities and practices of those we record and their positions in the community. For example, we need to have speakers of different ages in order to make claims about change in apparent time. More important for the embedding problem is that some speakers of the same generation adopt linguistic changes before others. Our goal is to discover these patterns and then try to find a reason why they exist. So we need to know also whether, for example, women adopt changes before men, or upper-class speakers adopt them before lower-class speakers, etc. This problem, then, is one of sampling a particular speech community in a way that represents the important types of person in it. It may be that ethnicity is more important in one community, while class is more important in another. Strategies to address this problem are discussed below.

The final problem is the *evaluation* problem. Rather than focusing on how different people *produce* language, this problem focuses on how people *evaluate* other speakers who use the different variants we are interested in. This problem is thus one that points to more experimental methods of presenting language to members of the speech community and measuring their reaction to it (including whether or not there are misunderstandings) by various means.

All of these problems therefore lead us to methods of performing a research project. The main issue in the process is to move from these general questions to specific ones about a particular speech community, a process we will explore after a short detour to discuss research ethics.

ETHICAL LINGUISTICS

From very early on, sociolinguists have been concerned with helping the people who agree to provide data. This concern begins, of course, with permission to record someone's speech. We always obtain informed consent for recordings before those recordings are made, usually in written form. Ethics panels and internal review boards (IRBs) will need to provide approval as well, and will insist on informed consent. (If you are studying a speech community with low rates of literacy, you may be able to obtain consent verbally.) Informed consent means that speakers need to know more than the simple fact that they are being recorded. They should also have some idea of what we will do with that speech. 'Informed' does not mean that we need to explain to them how we will measure the formants of their vowels, for example, but we should at least provide a statement something like this: 'We will use the recordings to describe how people use language in this community, and how and why some people sound different from and similar to other people in the community.' It is usually best to not be too specific, for two reasons. First, speakers are probably not interested in the intricate details of the project, and one does not want to sound too academic in most cases, since we want them to do the talking. Second, if we tell them very specific things like what variable we are interested in, then we have called attention to it and speakers may adjust their use of the variable whether they mean to or not.

Sociolinguists, however, have long argued that our ethics can go further. The question ethics panels ask is 'Do the benefits of this research outweigh the potential costs?' Some sociolinguists argue that in fact we should have a net positive effect on the communities we study. There are three principles that Wolfram (1993, 1998) outlines, the first two of which originate with Labov (1982):

1. **Principle of error correction**: 'A scientist who becomes aware of a widespread idea or social practice with important consequences that is invalidated by his [sic] own data is obligated to bring this error to the attention of the widest possible audience' (Labov 1982: 172).
2. **Principle of debt incurred**: 'An investigator who has obtained linguistic data

from members of a speech community has the obligation to use the knowledge based on that data for the benefit of that community, when it has need of it' (Labov 1982: 173).
3. **Principle of linguistic gratuity**: 'Investigators who have obtained linguistic data from members of a speech community should actively pursue ways in which they can return linguistic favours to the community' (Wolfram 1993: 227).

It should be evident that many variationist sociolinguists argue for the importance of going beyond research reports in order to explain findings to the public. Both Labov and Wolfram (among others) have provided examples of how to go about this. Both have written popular books or in popular magazines in order to educate the public about the systematicity of vernacular dialects (especially AAVE). Wolfram has been very successful in creating popular materials (print and film) that show the importance to the community of ways of speaking (Hutcheson 2001, 2004, 2005). These linguists and others have also helped to create reading materials to aid in removing barriers to reading faced by speakers of 'non-standard' varieties. When designing a research project, therefore, we should keep in mind ways of benefiting and involving the members of the community in our research.

FINDING LANGUAGE TO MEASURE

The basic outline of a variationist study is the following:

1. A speech community or communities (see below) to study is or are identified, and at least one linguistic variable, if this can be identified in advance (perhaps from previous studies).
2. If the researcher is not already familiar with the community, preliminary ethnography and study should be performed, focusing on understanding how members of the community understand its boundaries and what identities and social practices are likely to correlate with variation in the linguistic variable(s). Exploratory interviews may be performed.
3. The parameters of the speech community are defined, and a strategy for recording speech samples, attitudes, and social practices of members of the community is designed.
4. The data, as outlined in stage 2, are collected.
5. Linguistic variables and factors are coded.
6. Significant factors affecting the linguistic variables are discovered using statistical tests.
7. Other data are brought to bear to explain the correlational patterns that are found. Follow-up studies might include further interviews asking about speech, or experimental procedures to test attitudes towards language in the community.

On the face of it, this process is pretty straightforward, but the outline above hides many potential complications and problems that require further consideration. We will begin with the first three steps in this section, which focus on getting the speech and experimental data in a speech community.

SPEECH COMMUNITIES AND SAMPLING

Because the speech community is the basis for our 'grammar' in variationist studies, the first problem is to decide what counts as a speech community, and specifically what counts as the speech community for a particular study. There are many definitions of speech community, and researchers have debated both the theoretical and the practical definition of the concept (see Patrick 2004 for a thorough review of these issues; a useful list of definitions is Patrick 2002). In addition, some have argued that the term *speech community* can be replaced or supplemented by other concepts such as *network* or *community of practice* (Milroy 1980; Eckert and McConnell-Ginet 1992; Eckert 2000; Meyerhoff 2001). Why has this central variationist concept been so difficult and contentious? The problem stems from the fact that it is one of those ideas that is intuitively obvious and appealing, while at the same time the production of a definition that matches these intuitions is almost impossible. If the definition is too precise, speakers who we intuitively think ought to be included in the community are not included, while if it is too vague, then we don't really know whom to include. Let us approach this problem by focusing on the concepts that recur in the definitions and discussions of speech community.

There are two central ideas that recur in many definitions. First is the notion of some kind of *shared linguistic norm*. These shared norms can refer to similar ways of producing speech, but also often refer to language more generally (e.g., Labov 1972b). The shared norms thus do not entail everyone speaking alike, but could mean that speakers produce language differently and at the same time evaluate speech in a similar manner (for example, speakers of 'non-standard' varieties sometimes apparently agree with speakers of standard varieties that non-standard speech is not as good as standard). The second central idea that often appears in definitions is that there are some kinds of communication lines that link the members of the community. In other words, a speech community is a group of people who talk to each other more than other possible interactants, whether for social or physical reasons (such as living in relative proximity). There are many problems with both of these central recurring ideas: what of someone who has only recently moved to a city, and has regular and frequent interactions with others in the city – is this person a member of the speech community? In addition, the focus on norms assumes that everyone who is knowledgeable about speech norms agrees with them, whereas it may actually be the case that there is conflict about norms in what we want to call a community, an issue we will address in later chapters.

There are more practical issues that add to the problems with the speech community idea. The first is that, in practice, sociolinguists have tended to use geographical boundaries of varying sizes and precision to define speech communities and their members: Martha's Vineyard, the lower east side of New York City, Philadelphia, Panama City, and all of England are examples of geographical entities that have been used to describe speech communities. However, in none of the definitions of speech community do we find an essential focus on residence or provenance for inclusion or exclusion in a speech community. Moreover, while *space* can be defined by precise coordinates and boundaries, *place* – how people think about their physical surroundings – may not be as precise and in fact different speakers in the same space may think of place differently. For example, in Sydney, Australia, the entire city could be divided into very small areas corresponding to local governing bodies or treated as one speech community. Sydneysiders tend to think of the city in a much more intermediate manner, however, with areas like the 'Northern Beaches' having their own character in the talk about place there. Another convenient way to label a speech community is by identity category such as race, ethnicity, class, or gender. Here again we have the problem that some convenient external label is applied, which may not actually match the speech community. For example, in the USA, there are African Americans (whom we would identify by African ancestry) whom we might not want to count as belonging to an African American speech community, and there are non-African Americans who perhaps should be counted as part of the community.

But this is a chapter on methodology, so the focus is on making an operational definition of our speech community. From the above discussion, it should be clear that any operational definition that outlines criteria for membership will always be imperfect. The important question is: how do we know *before* we perform a study who should be included in the speech community? We want to know this because if we decide what speakers are in or out of the community after we interview them, then we could bias our study (and we might even unconsciously use a person's ways of speaking as a criterion on which to determine their membership). The practice in most studies is to decide in terms of geographical residence, identity category (ethnicity for example), or other non-speech property of individuals, informed by some knowledge of the variety in question ahead of time. There are methods for determining how much speakers consider themselves to be from the same community or region. For example, Zelinsky (1980), a geographer, mapped regions of the United States by recording regional names used by businesses in different cities. In order to find the western limit of New England, for instance, he looked for cities with fewer businesses having 'New England' in the name. While indirect, this type of method could be employed to decide the geographical limits of a speech community. One could also survey speakers as to their ties to a particular community, either by frequency of interaction, by residence, or even by just asking them a question like 'Do you consider yourself to be a Pittsburgher?'

Such methods avoid, for the most part, the problem of circularity. The danger is that one might argue that a speaker is not part of the speech community because he or she has a different pattern of variable use from others originally in the speech community. If the speech community concept is to be useful at all, we need either to avoid this circularity or to build it into the methods. We avoid it by using objective methods such as the regional naming discussed above. We build it in by taking a wide view of the speech community and declaring that one goal of our research is to discover the extent to which a variant is used geographically or socially.

The theoretical issues surrounding the speech community are still unsolved in sociolinguistics. Because it is a concept of analysts and not of speakers themselves, controversies surrounding the concept will no doubt continue. At the same time, it remains a central concept in variationist sociolinguistics, and this status is likely to continue as well. The best advice that can be given in the practical case of designing a research project is to think carefully about how we are going to use the speech community concept, and to be explicit about the assumptions we are making about a speech community in each study. Ideally we would have enough speakers and information in order to discover exactly to what extent norms are shared and how often every member talks to another. But research is an art of compromise between the theoretically desirable and the practically attainable, so some tough decisions need to be made about how to exclude speakers from the speech community.

Here are some questions about speech communities to answer when beginning a variationist project (and to ask about any published study):

- What are the precise characteristics of a person who is in (or out of) this speech community?
- What is the motivation for those criteria? That is, why are these the criteria for membership?
- What are the benefits and drawbacks of defining the speech community in this way? How do the benefits outweigh the drawbacks?
- If we are *discovering* the speech community, what criteria will count for being in or out of it (ways of speaking, self-report of belonging, evaluative norms of language, etc.)?

There are other concepts which, like speech community, serve to group people together for sociolinguistic study. Two of the most common are *social networks* and *communities of practice*. We will discuss the theoretical significance of these terms further in Part III; methodologically, they can complement the speech community concept or replace it to some extent.

The idea of *social networks* is well developed in sociology (Scott 2000; Hanneman and Riddle 2005), and is probably at least somewhat familiar to readers through so-called 'social networking' websites such as Facebook and MySpace. Social networks, put very simply, are groups of people who have some sort of social tie to one another (as family, friends, co-workers, neighbours, etc.). It should be obvious that this way of looking at a group of people is similar to the 'mutual contact' criterion sometimes posited for a speech community, and in that sense a network could be seen as a kind of speech community. One could identify a network, or even a single speaker's network, as the group from which to sample. In fact, one method often used by sociolinguists is essentially a network sampling: We start with a few individuals whom we already have met in the community, or introduce ourselves, and then ask them to introduce us to friends, and keep asking for introductions. This 'snowball' sampling strategy (sometimes called 'friend of a friend') allows us to follow several networks within a particular community.

Community of practice is a relatively recent idea, introduced to sociolinguistics mainly by Penelope Eckert (Eckert and McConnell-Ginet 1992; Eckert 2000). A community of practice is a group of people that is organised around some practice or activity, such as a chess or book club. The practice can be explicitly socially oriented, so that a group of people who dress similarly or have similar musical tastes can form a community of practice. Such a community is similar to a network, with the difference that the community of practice is organised around the common practice, rather than around individual ties to other individuals. Essentially, then, the community of practice is a network in which the network ties are very narrowly construed – that is, people must engage with each other through the practice. Eckert argues that it is at this level of social organisation that social meanings arise and are negotiated. A community of practice is thus again not necessarily a unit from which to sample; however, it might be a way of identifying a sample of a community, by identifying members of several communities of practice in a larger speech community to record. We will review the significance of this concept in Chapter 4.

From a methodological point of view, these concepts – speech community, network, and community of practice – provide us with different ways of identifying speakers whom we would like to record. I will not go into detail about sampling here (see Bernard 2006), but it is important to know a few things about choosing speakers. Ideally, we would record speech from every single individual in our speech community, but of course this is impossible. This group of everyone is called the *population* by statisticians. Since we cannot record everyone, we have to record a small group of the population, called a *sample,* that is as close as possible to the population in every characteristic. The most statistically rigorous is the *random sample*, in which a certain number of people are chosen from a population (speech community) completely at random, perhaps by choosing telephone numbers randomly in a particular city. However, in sociolinguistic studies this type of sampling is almost impossible to achieve, because the methods used to contact speakers are likely to *bias* the sample in one direction (for example, some people might be more likely than others to answer the telephone, or to agree to be recorded). Most studies therefore use a *judgement sample*, which is as random as possible but also determines ahead of time how many people of certain characteristics should be included, often on the basis of the proportion of that characteristic in the population as a whole. For example, the sample might be balanced in terms of age group, gender, class, ethnicity, or any other social aspect that the researcher suspects may affect the use of the linguistic variable under study. One problem with these samples is that they can bias the sample towards one group if the quota is not correct. In addition, they may extend the time it takes to complete the recordings because the last few speakers may take an inordinate amount of time to track down. These problems are not as prevalent for snowball sampling, discussed above.

These are the primary types of sampling used in variation studies, each with its strengths and weaknesses. The key is to make sure that the kinds of research questions one is asking match the methods. For example, are we producing a survey of a speech community never studied? In such a case a random sample might be

Table 3.1 Possible design for a sociolinguistic study

	Men				Women			
	Child	Young adult	Middle-aged adult	Old adult	Child	Young adult	Middle-aged adult	Old adult
Lower class								
Lower middle class								
Upper middle class								
Upper class								

desirable. If on the other hand we are studying the meanings attached to variants in interaction, then a snowball sample or even a small community of practice might be the best choice. For more on sampling and recruiting, see especially Bernard (2006) and Milroy and Gordon (2003).

Finally, we come to the question of sample size. 'How many interviews should I do?' is a common question from students. The answer is: 'It depends.' Note that statistics are generally based on the tokens of the variable and not on, for example, on the average of each speaker. Thirty people are generally assumed to provide a decent sample size, although for really robust statistic reliability one wants more (see Johnson 2008 on measures of determining the power of a sample size). The most important issue for this question, however, is what, and how many, groups of speakers you want. If you want to compare, for example, four age groups, two genders, and four social classes, you have to have a category for each combination of age, gender, and class. Each interaction of all three is called a *cell*, since the design can be represented as in Table 3.1.

The question then becomes how many speakers should be in each cell. Some researchers, such as Horvath (1985), opt for five, which is another somewhat 'magic' number for some statistical tests, but the more the better. The sample does not need to be balanced, but we should try to have a minimum for each cell. Note that our design in Table 3.1 has thirty-two cells, so that if there are five per cell we need to find 160 speakers to record (five multiplied by thirty-two). This is not a small number of speakers (nor would it be a small amount of coding), so the ideal design must as always be balanced against our resources available for performing the study. Recruiting speakers and recording speech is time-consuming work, as will be evident in the next section.

GETTING SPEECH: INTERVIEWS AND OTHER TALK

How to go about getting people to talk so that we have enough data on our variables of interest is another topic that could fill a book. When we record speech, there are several characteristics we might wish for. First, we might be trying to record the speaker's most 'natural' way of speaking (Labov 1982 argues that we are searching for the speaker's 'vernacular'). Second, we might be striving to record with the most fidelity possible. Finally, we want to record enough speech so that we have a large number of tokens of the variable we wish to study. These goals are sometimes at odds, and can also be at odds with our ethical goals. For example, 'natural' speech is more likely to take place when someone doesn't know they are being recorded, but for reasons of fidelity and ethics, the speaker needs to know we are recording.

It is for this reason that most variationist studies rely on the sociolinguistic interview, in which a researcher asks questions of a speaker and records the answers. We use various interactional 'tricks' to attempt to make the interview as close as possible to a 'normal' casual conversation, but the fact remains that the interview is not the type of speech event that speakers engage in during their day-to-day activities. Other methods are possible, but there are always trade-offs. For example, I recorded a conversation among eight women (Kiesling 2009) and was able to increase fidelity by having a microphone on each one. However, because this was a conversation and not an interview, there was an imbalance in the amount of speech each woman produced, and the conversation was still somewhat artificial given all of the wires snaking away from the table. Recording truly 'naturally' occurring speech – for example, when a linguist follows a speaker around – is even more difficult, as there will be long stretches with no speech, and the fidelity will fall. I have also recorded the speech of a meeting in a single room (see Kiesling 1998), but with one microphone only some speakers are unintelligible, and in addition only some speakers can even be identified.

The sociolinguistic interview has therefore been thought to represent the best compromise among 'naturalness', fidelity, and amount of speech. Researchers have developed quite sophisticated techniques that create a much more conversation-like atmosphere for the interview (see Labov 1982; Milroy and Gordon 2003). Nevertheless, our findings based on such interviews should always be viewed with the right amount of caution, because there are always factors that affect variability that we are not controlling for. For example, Rickford and McNair-Knox (1994) show the importance of the identity of the interviewer in how a speaker uses some variables. The researchers analyse two different interviews with the same speaker, with different interviewers in each. The speaker, Foxy, is an African American woman, and Rickford and McNair-Knox's focus is on her use of five variables known to characterise AAVE. The researchers find that although both occasions are framed as sociolinguistic interviews and have the same general format, the fact that in one the interviewers were African American and in the other the interviewer was White made a significant difference in Foxy's rate of use of these variables. There were also three total participants in one interview, and only two in the other. In addition, Rickford and McNair-Knox report that there are wide differences according to topic. The point here is that in designing and listening to interviews, we need to realise that a speaker will always be talking in relation to the person they are talking to. Therefore, even though we hold the interviewer constant, the differences we find in linguistic variable use among interviewees may not be differences in their 'vernaculars', but rather in how they relate to the interviewer.

RECORDING AND MANAGING RECORDINGS

The technical details of recording have changed considerably since Labov made his recordings on Martha's Vineyard. Modern equipment makes it possible to record speech on one's mobile phone, whereas before such recording required bulky reel-to-reel equipment. However, we must not lose sight of the fidelity requirement in the fog of convenience. Even if one does not plan to perform sensitive phonetic analyses of speech, it is important to get the best fidelity possible, if only because one might later on wish to perform that phonetic analysis. Given the pace of technological advance, I will not provide any specific recommendations for equipment. However, in general, the best way to record a speaker is by using a high-quality lavalier microphone, that is, a small microphone which clips on to clothing, usually at the collar or lapel. People often focus more on the recording device quality in their equipment, but in general there is better value in spending more on a high-quality microphone than on a high-quality recorder, although ideally both will be very good.

Most recording is now digital, and good-quality digital recorders can be purchased for a reasonable price. For a few years there were some critics of digital recording, arguing that because digital recorders only *sample* the sound, we don't know what we are losing. But if the sampling rate is high enough (e.g., 44.1 kHz or 48 kHz) there is no noticeable loss of data. Most laptop computers now come with recording capability, but this is not the first choice for field recording (the built-in microphone on the computer will not be of good quality, and the sound card that performs the digitising is usually not of very high quality either). I cannot stress enough that the microphone is at least as important as the recording device; the microphone is the first filter the sound passes through, and even the best recorder cannot make up for a poor microphone. In general, XLR connections (thick connections with three pins) are better than the more common ¼-inch jacks (as long as your recorder has XLR inputs). There are plenty of microphone sources on the internet, and I encourage researchers to learn as much as possible about their equipment.

Always familiarise yourself with your equipment before you begin research; perform several 'mock' interviews with friends in which you set up your equipment. The more you have to fiddle with equipment when doing interviews, the more likely you will be to call attention to the recorded aspect of the interview. You may want to write out a checklist; many good interviews have been lost through simple oversights such as the recorder or the microphone not being turned on!

On a final practical note, be very careful to keep track of all recordings, and to make more than one backup, kept in at least two places. You may wish to pay a service to house your backup recordings securely; these recordings are a big investment, so expenses on backups should be thought of as insurance, and are worth it. Do not think you are immune from loss; while I have never lost recordings due to theft, damage, or computer malfunction, I have known too many others who have lost data for all of these reasons to be complacent. Label the file names logically, and keep a catalogue of what is in each file (including date, place, and participants – using pseudonyms – as well as any field notes that go with the recording). Do this in a way that makes sense to you; that is, in a way that will enable you to find what you are looking for.

CODING VARIABLES

Coding the speech means measuring and recording each token of the linguistic variable and recording any social or linguistic variables that go with that linguistic variable. Let's use as an example a study based on my own work: the monophthongisation of the English diphthong /aʊ/ in Pittsburgh, such that the word *house* is pronounced [haːs]. This vowel varies from a completely monophthongal, open [aː] to a more standard [aʊ].

The first decision in coding is to determine what counts as the variable. For example, in my vowel example, I might decide that I want vowels only from monosyllabic words, or at least only in stressed positions. One important factor is to make sure that one kind of token does not dominate the coding. So in this example, I might want to limit the number of tokens of 'our' that can be used, or not count it at all. This is called *determining or defining the variable context*, and is one of the most important decisions we have to make in performing a variation study. See 'Linguistic variables at different linguistic levels' above for more on the variable context for other types of variables.

Next we need to know the best way to *measure* the linguistic variable. This could be a numeric measurement. For example, I could use a phonetic analysis program (I recommend the free and powerful Praat, used by many linguists; Boersma and Weenick 2009) in order to measure the formants in hertz at two points of each token of (aʊ), and use the difference between the two measurements for each formant as the variable. This type of measurement will provide a fairly fine-grained view of the variation, with theoretically an infinite number of measurements (there are also techniques to measure and represent continuous trajectories: see Nycz and De Decker 2006; Baker 2008).

On the other hand, I could simply listen to each token and auditorily decide whether to categorise the variable as monophthong or diphthong (or possibly use an 'in-between' category), so I would have a categorical or *discrete* variable. There are advantages to each approach: the interval variable can presumably capture more subtle levels of variation, and is more objective and not susceptible to uncontrolled biases of the analyst, as might be the case for the categorical version. On the other hand, it will probably take longer to perform the coding for the continuous measurement. I might also suspect that it is only clearly monophthongal variants that make a difference in the speech community, and not subtle changes in the diphthong, which argues in favour of using a categorical coding.

We are looking for measures that are *reliable* and *valid*. Reliability refers to the extent to which the measures will be the same if repeated at another time or by another rater. Validity refers to whether the measurement is a 'true' or accurate representation of the thing being measured. In my example, there are ways that I could test the potential problems for reliability and validity. I could perform an

40 Linguistic Variation and Change

Value	Speaker	Word	Preceding	Following	Sex	Age	AgeCat	Ethnicity	Birth city	Residence	Occupation	Income	School
D	3	southside	s	th	Female	24	18-34	polish welsh	stubenville, O	Belleview	Child Care S	20K-40K	18
M	3	Cowher	k	r	Female	24	18-34	polish welsh	stubenville, O	Belleview	Child Care S	20K-40K	18
D	3	(down)town	t	n	Female	24	18-34	polish welsh	stubenville, O	Belleview	Child Care S	20K-40K	18
D	3	down(town)	d	n	Female	24	18-34	polish welsh	stubenville, O	Belleview	Child Care S	20K-40K	18
D	3	south hills	s	th	Female	24	18-34	polish welsh	stubenville, O	Belleview	Child Care S	20K-40K	18
D	3	towel	t	l	Female	24	18-34	polish welsh	stubenville, O	Belleview	Child Care S	20K-40K	18
D	3	Browns	r	n	Female	24	18-34	polish welsh	stubenville, O	Belleview	Child Care S	20K-40K	18
D	4	Cowher	k	r	Female	36	35-59	White	Mount Pleas	Mount Pleas	Housewife	40K-60K	16
D	4	towel	t	l	Female	36	35-59	White	Mount Pleas	Mount Pleas	Housewife	40K-60K	16
I	4	down	d	n	Female	36	35-59	White	Mount Pleas	Mount Pleas	Housewife	40K-60K	16
I	4	Johnstown	dg	n	Female	36	35-59	White	Mount Pleas	Mount Pleas	Housewife	40K-60K	16
D	4	Browns	r	n	Female	36	35-59	White	Mount Pleas	Mount Pleas	Housewife	40K-60K	16
M	4	down	d	n	Female	36	35-59	White	Mount Pleas	Mount Pleas	Housewife	40K-60K	16
D	5	(down)town	t	n	Female	53	35-59	Greek and Ir	Pittsburgh	Monroeville	Social Secu	0-20K	12
D	5	southside	s	th	Female	53	35-59	Greek and Ir	Pittsburgh	Monroeville	Social Secu	0-20K	12
D	5	Browns	r	n	Female	53	35-59	Greek and Ir	Pittsburgh	Monroeville	Social Secu	0-20K	12
D	5	towel	t	l	Female	53	35-59	Greek and Ir	Pittsburgh	Monroeville	Social Secu	0-20K	12
D	5	town	t	n	Female	53	35-59	Greek and Ir	Pittsburgh	Monroeville	Social Secu	0-20K	12

Figure 3.1 Sample coding spreadsheet

experiment which asks listeners to tell me whether they hear a difference in the pronunciation of different words, and control exactly how different they are. If I find that listeners only notice extreme differences, then I know a categorical variable might be more faithful to the speech community. In addition, I could measure the formants of a subset of the vowels that I have already coded into categories to determine whether or not those categories are objectively different. I could also have other raters code a subset to determine whether or not they put most vowels in the same category. The goal here is to balance validity and reliability against practicality, and any study should be explicit about how all of these decisions were made and why. This concern will hold for any kind of linguistic variable we have.

One very practical detail that is often asked is exactly how one sets up the record for coding. The easiest way is to use a spreadsheet program such as Microsoft Excel or its open source (free) equivalent OpenOffice.org Calc, a data sheet in a statistics program such as SPSS or SAS, or a database program such as FileMaker Pro. When setting up a spreadsheet, it is best to have each row represent one token. Within that row, the first item should be the variant of the linguistic variable, followed by any factors that you code for, such as linguistic environment or speaker characteristics. Figure 3.1 is an example. Because each row is a different token, tokens from the same speaker will have the same speaker characteristics. The rest of the details are not crucial, but it is useful to see an example of a properly laid-out coding sheet.

Note that the information in this spreadsheet is as independent as possible. For example, not only the word that the vowel appears in is recorded, but also the preceding and following phonological environments. This way, we can explore the effect of the following environment separately from the word, and we can investigate the preceding environment separately from the following. Notice also that age is recorded as a number and as a category. We would not include both in a statistical analysis, but by coding for both it will be possible to explore which type of coding is more robust for the age factor.

How many factors should you code for? The rule is to code for as much as is practical. Similarly, make as many distinctions as you can. For example, with age in this example, I could have just coded for the age category. However, if I want to change the boundaries of my categories, I would have a hard time if I had not recorded the actual age. The three-way distinction for variants of the linguistic variable is similar:

I can always collapse two of these categories so that I only have two variants, but if I had coded only two variants I would need to recode each token manually to do so. Therefore, we *always record for more factors than we think we need*, and we *always make as many distinctions or categories as we can*, within reason (so don't record your mood, or the weather, as a factor in your coding, unless you think it has an effect!).

DESCRIBING PATTERNS

Once we have finished our coding, we count the frequency of one variant for specific factors. For example, I might count how often (aʊ) is monophthongal in my Pittsburgh sample. In order to address the constraints, transition, and embedding problems, however, we will want to count in such a way that we can find patterns. First we will want to describe the patterns, and then we will want to test whether these patterns are significantly different from data that have no discernible pattern. Let's discuss the display of patterns first. One of the primary patterns we are looking for is one in which there is a difference in variant use by age group, indicating a change in apparent time. We will discuss these patterns more fully in the chapters to come; here I simply want to provide some advice on how to display them.

In displaying a simple pattern – that is, a pattern that represents one factor group – tables are the most useful form. Table 3.2 is a table for some data on (aʊ) in Pittsburgh by age group. This table illustrates some important guidelines to follow when creating tables. First, everything should be labelled transparently. I may in my coding have used abbreviations for the (aʊ) values (see Figure 3.1), but in the table I have spelled out what is in each column and row. Because we are interested in relative frequencies, the data are represented as percentages for each factor, and I have shown through the 'Total' column that it is the rows, and not the columns, that are added to equal 100 per cent. In constructing tables of percentages, one should always show how the percentages total to 100, and also show the number of tokens each percentage represents; in this case, I have done so by placing the number of tokens in parentheses next to the percentage, although another possibility is simply to add a row of raw numbers under the row of tokens. Either strategy works.

Table 3.3 is an example of a poorly constructed table using some of the same data as Table 3.2. It is much harder to read, and moreover it looks as if the 'Mid' category might have the most 'D' (diphthong?) tokens. However, if we look at the diphthong column with the percentages in Table 3.2, we see that in fact it is the

Table 3.2 Percentage of (aʊ) variants by age category (number of tokens in parentheses)

Age category	Monophthong	Intermediate	Diphthong	Total
18-34	16% (9)	5% (3)	79% (46)	100% (58)
35-59	21% (28)	13% (17)	66% (87)	100% (132)
60 and over	34 % (37)	7% (8)	59% (65)	100% (110)
Total	25% (74)	9% (28)	66% (198)	100% (300)

42 Linguistic Variation and Change

Table 3.3 (aʊ) variants by age category (poorly constructed table!)

	M	I	D
Young	9	3	46
Mid	28	17	87
Old	37	8	65

Table 3.4 Percentage of (aʊ) variants by age and gender

Age category	Gender category	Monophthong N	%	Intermediate N	%	Diphthong N	%	Total N	%
18-34	Men	5	20.8	2	8.3	17	70.8	24	100
18-34	Women	4	11.8	1	2.9	29	85.3	34	100
35-59	Men	14	30.4	8	30.4	24	52.2	46	100
35-59	Women	14	16.3	9	16.3	63	73.3	86	100
60 & over	Men	19	35.2	4	7.4	31	57.4	54	100
60 & over	Women	18	32.1	4	7.1	34	60.7	56	100
Total		74	24.7	28	9.3	198	66.0	300	100

'Young' category – actually 18–34 years old at the time of the interview – that uses the most diphthongal tokens.

In fact, Table 3.2 shows us that there is a pattern by age, such that the oldest group uses the most monophthongal /aʊ/, the youngest the most diphthongal /aʊ/, and the mid group is in between for both of these (and also uses the most in the intermediate category).

Tables are useful for relatively straightforward patterns when only one or two factors are involved. However, a simple graph is often the best way to show patterns when two or more factors are involved (see Tufte 1986, 2003 for excellent advice on the graphics of presenting numbers). For example, consider Table 3.4, which shows what happens when gender is added as a factor to age.

With careful study, and with the help of formatting that guides the eye to compare genders in each age group, it is possible to discern that the younger two age groups show a gender difference such that men use more monophthongisation, while there is very little difference for the older age group. However, it is much easier to see this pattern with a graph, or in this case a series of graphs.

In Figure 3.2, each graph represents a separate comparison for each age category. This view makes it clear that the oldest group does not show the gender differentiation that is exhibited by the younger two categories, because the two lines are almost identical. Moreover, this presentation makes the point more forcefully than the numbers by themselves. There are other ways this could have been displayed. One display actually hides the information we are after, even though it attempts to separate things out.

In Figure 3.3, I have matched the men and women of the same generation by line type, and made all the female lines solid and all the male lines dashed. It is possible to determine that the oldest generation's lines do not cross, but it is more difficult

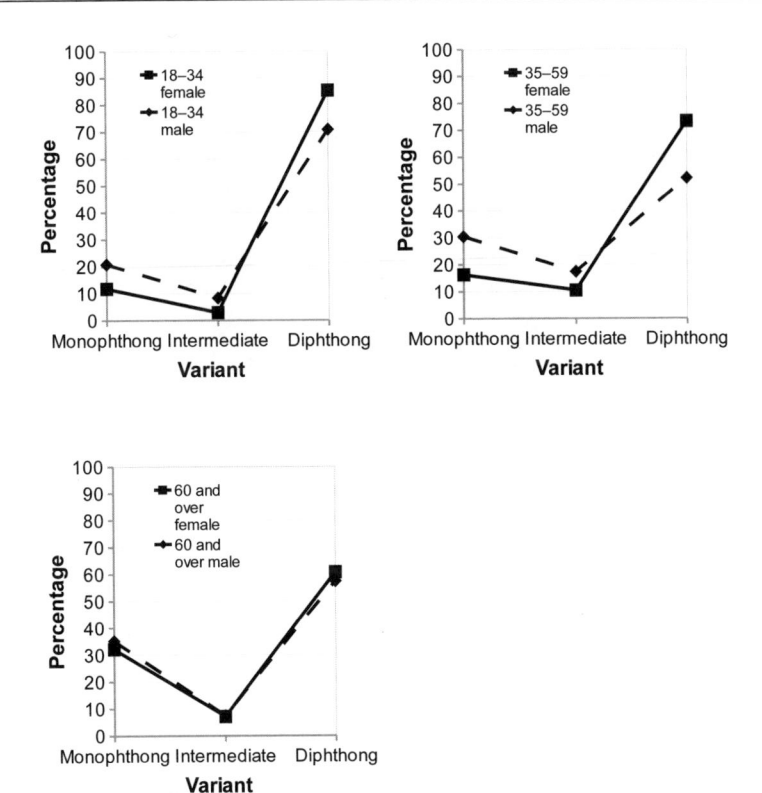

Figure 3.2 Percentage of (aʊ) variants by age category

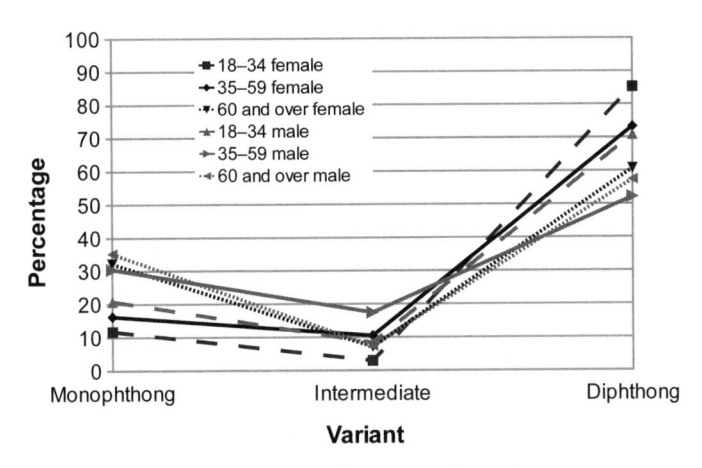

Figure 3.3 Percentage of (aʊ) variants by age and gender

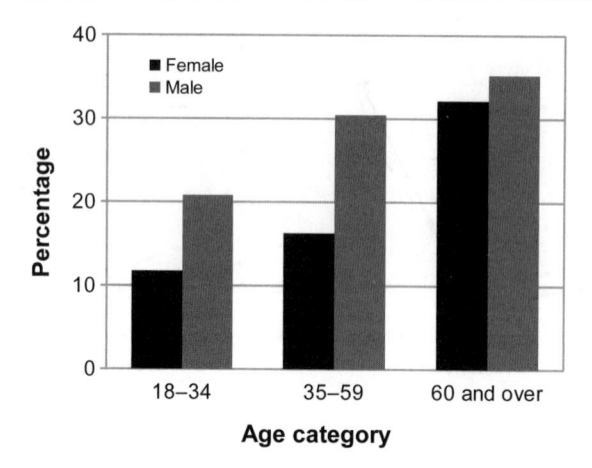

Figure 3.4 Monophthongisation percentage by age and gender (better version)

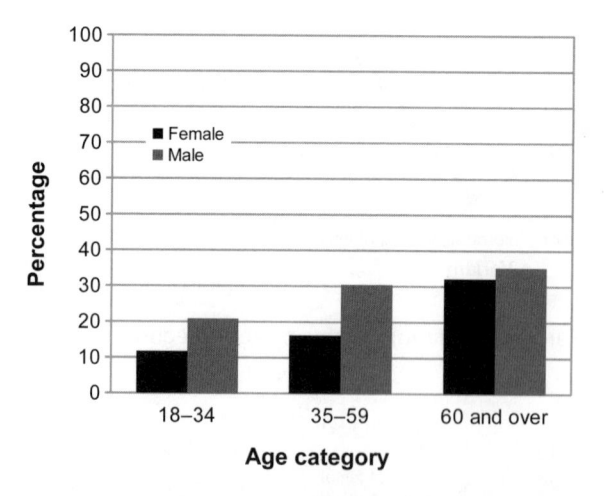

Figure 3.5 Monophthongisation percentage by age and gender (best version)

than with three separate graphs. Finally, we could simplify the chart by viewing the frequency of only one variant. In fact, if a variable has only two variants (a binary variable) then a graph showing the frequency of one of them is the best way to present our data. Traditionally, it is the 'new' or 'vernacular' variable, or the output of the variable rule, that is graphed. Figure 3.4 thus shows only the percentage of monophthongs from my data.

Figure 3.4 still shows that men are usually using more of the monophthongal variant, while at the same time showing that the gender difference is less in the oldest category. I have cheated a little bit here by not having the scale go all the way to 100%, making the differences appear slightly greater than they are. The revised graph is shown in Figure 3.5.

It should be clear by this point that tables and graphs are not dispassionate displays of objective data, but in many ways *create* the patterns that you 'find' in your data. Therefore, make sure you view your data in multiple ways. More importantly, when presenting your data in written work, choose the display that contributes best to the patterns you see in the data. For example, if I wanted to emphasise men's dominance of the use of the monophthongal variant, I would use the bar graph. However, if I wanted to point out the changes in the gender difference from the oldest to youngest age group, I would use the series of line graphs. Finally, when using tables and graphs, do not simply place the graph in the paper and assume the reader will interpret it in the same way as you. You *must* explicate the table or graph so that it fits into the patterns you want to point out in your narrative. There is nothing 'sneaky' or 'dishonest' about this; rather, you are helping the reader to understand the patterns in your data so that you can discuss them.

FINDING STRUCTURE IN VARIABILITY

Now that we have explored some ways of seeing the patterns of percentages in our data, we are going to need to ask ourselves whether the patterns we see make a difference – are they significant? There are two ways to think about significance. The first is statistical significance, which usually means something like 'This pattern is very unlikely to have come about by chance – there must be some reason why the linguistic variable patterns this way.' We will discuss this kind of significance in relative detail below.

The other kind of significance is what we might call practical significance. One important fact about statistics is that, given enough tokens or speakers of a variable, it becomes unlikely that our statistics will tell us that something is *not* significant. For example, imagine we have a hundred tokens of (aʊ) for a thousand speakers, and our sample is divided evenly by gender. We have 1,000 × 100 or 100,000 tokens of (aʊ) (we must also have a small army of research assistants!). If women have 25,330 of the monophthongal variant, and men have 26,220, then we will end up with a statistically significant outcome. But this is 50.66 per cent and 52.44 per cent respectively. This means that if we hear two people actually utter 100 tokens of (aʊ), men on average will utter one more monophthongal variant. It's very questionable whether anyone would detect this difference, so we have an example of statistical rather than practical significance.

TESTING STATISTICAL SIGNIFICANCE AND MODELLING VARIATION

This section will explain what statistical significance is, and how we model variation using statistical procedures to discover robust patterns of the orderly heterogeneity of a variable. Before we begin, we must remember that statistical tests tell us only how the variable patterns, what constraints there are on it, and how it is embedded in the speech community. Like computer programs, statistical procedures are only as useful as the user is knowledgeable, not only about statistics but also about linguistic and social theory ('garbage in, garbage out'). Before we run statistics, we need to have coded for the most plausible factors to have a large effect on the linguistic variable, and once the statistics have provided us with a numerical model of the variation, we will need to add a qualitative, possibly theoretical, interpretation to those patterns that the model presents. As noted above, it is recommended that students work thorough the relevant sections of Baayen (2008), Johnson (2008), or Tagliamonte (2006), or all three, before attempting to perform a statistical analysis on their own data.

There are several ways that statistics can be used to help describe and verify sociolinguistic patterns. One thing we want to know about our pattern is that if we find a difference between or among groups, is that difference likely to have been found by chance or not? If we had measured the *population* – every utterance, or at least utterances of everyone in our speech community – then we would know that the difference was not by chance, because we measured everything. To test for this, we need to know how likely it is that the mean of our sample is the mean we would measure if we measured the entire population. Fortunately, statisticians have discovered that if we have a certain number of observations (tokens), we can predict how likely our pattern is to be the one of the actual population. (I want to clarify here that statistical procedures work on raw numbers, although we said above that in describing patterns we must describe frequencies, *not* raw numbers. In general, though, we will always want to report frequencies.)

There are many ways to describe patterns in data. Two of the most important for sociolinguistics are the mean and the median. The mean is the average (all tokens added up and then divided by the number of tokens), while the median is the 'middle' of the data (there are as many tokens larger than the median as there are smaller). We often use these measures to compare groups and describe patterns. In fact, the data in Figure 3.5 are averages for the age and gender groups: each person in these groups will not have the exact rate in the chart, but will be slightly different from it.

So we want to know, for example, whether the difference between men and women in the (aʊ) data is one that is just because we were 'lucky', or because there is a real pattern. We do this by determining the range of values that are the most likely for the 'real' mean for each group (called the *confidence interval*), and then determining how much those two ranges overlap. If they don't overlap, or don't overlap much, then we can be sure that the rates of the two groups are actually different. To do this we need to know how many tokens we have for each group, because if we have more tokens, then the likelihood that we were just lucky is lower. The *t-test* is one of the statistical tests that makes these comparisons. This process of comparing means between groups is conceptually how most statistical tests work, although statisticians have developed many different ways of doing the equivalent of making confidence intervals and comparing them.

Another way of testing data is to look at how they are distributed, and to see if that distribution is different from what would be expected if everything were left entirely to chance. This is the basic idea behind the *chi-square* test. In this test,

Table 3.5 Observed monophthongisation in Pittsburgh by age group

	Monophthong	Intermediate	Diphthong	Total
Young	9	3	6	*18*
Mid	28	17	87	*132*
Old	37	8	65	*110*
Total	<u>74</u>	<u>28</u>	<u>158</u>	<u>*260*</u>

Table 3.6 Expected monophthongisation in Pittsburgh by age group

	Monophthong	Intermediate	Diphthong	Total
Young	5.12	1.94	10.94	*18*
Mid	37.57	14.22	80.22	*132*
Old	31.31	11.85	66.85	*110*
Total	<u>74</u>	<u>28</u>	<u>158</u>	<u>*260*</u>

you have a table of counts such as in Table 3.5. In order to decide whether this distribution has come about by chance, you work out what distribution would be expected if the data were distributed by chance (shown in Table 3.6) and find the difference between the observed and expected distributions. On the basis of the number of factors you have, you can look up the probability that the difference is significant (because these kinds of numbers are distributed in a way that statisicians can predict). In our example, the difference is significant, with a 'p value' of 0.0181, which means roughly that there's a 2 in 100 chance that our distribution could have come about by chance. This just tells you whether the distribution is significant, not what makes it significant.

A similar procedure for different kinds of data is the Analysis of Variance, or ANOVA. This is like the chi-square test in that you are trying to decide whether the pattern is not due to chance, but it is used when we have interval data (essentially, real numbers that can be expressed in integers, or counts of things) for the linguistic variable and categories for the factors. It is similar to the t-test above, but it can handle more than two groups. The test can say whether the different categories are distributed similarly or are different, and then you need to decide where the difference is.

While these tests are useful possible tools for variationist analysis, they all lack the ability to decide *which* factors are having effects on the linguistic variable. Note the number of factors in my example coding in Figure 3.1. Each of the factors could be something that makes a difference in the frequency with which (aʊ) is monophthongal. With chi-square, we could determine whether or not the distribution was significant, but not the importance of each effect. This is where the idea of modelling comes in.

The simple idea is to write an equation that uses the factors we have coded for to *predict* the rate of our linguistic variable. We then compare the prediction and the real data. The best such equation (or model, since it is a kind of 'mock-up' of the data) will give us the size of the effect of each factor. For example, let's use (aʊ) again. If we know the preceding and following phonological segment, and the age, gender, and class of the speaker, we want to be able to predict how frequently (aʊ) will manifest as [aː]. We are therefore looking for an equation like this:

([aː] rate) = constant + preceding segment value
 + following segment value + age + gender + class

So from what we've seen, we might suspect that if there is a woman speaking, the gender value will be negative, and it will be positive if the speaker is a man. It's actually much more complicated than this, of course, but this is essentially how it happens. If we have a linguistic variable that is binary, we use probabilities, and are given a probability after we multiply all the individual factor probabilities together.

As discussed in Chapter 2, this is the essence of Varbrul (also known as Goldvarb and most recently Rbrul), the dominant statistical procedure used by variationists. It works by creating a model, and then comparing it to the real data. It then changes the model slightly to see if the second model is significantly different, and if it is, it keeps this later model and tweaks it. This comparison goes on until the program can't do anything to make the model fit the data better. The output is a series of probability *weights* that tell us how important different factors are, and in what direction they change the rate of our linguistic variable.

When Sankoff and Cedergren first developed this program (Sankoff and Cedergren 1974), the statistical technique – logistic regression – was quite new. In the intervening years, the field of statistics has advanced considerably, to the point where various forms of logistic regression are usually included in major statistical packages. In fact, it can be argued that variationists should be using a more modern technique known as *mixed effects modelling*. Mixed effects modelling is a technique like multiple regression, but it models factors differently depending on their status as so-called *fixed* or *random effects*. The names 'fixed' and 'random' effects come from how they are seen in experimental methods. A fixed effect is essentially a factor that the experimenter controls, and suspects has an effect on the linguistic variable. A random effect is one that might have an effect on the variable, but the effect is not predictable in the way that fixed effects are. In general, in a variation study, our main random effect will be individual speakers (but might also be something like the lexical item), while our fixed effects will be linguistic factors and social grouping factors such as age, gender, and class. What the mixed effects model does (vastly simplified!) is factor out the effect of the *individual* speaker from the effect of the speaker's group. Mixed effects models are explained in Johnson (2008) and Baayen (2008). A Varbrul-like, stand-alone implementation of mixed effects modelling has been developed by Daniel Johnson (see Johnson 2009). All of these sources use the R statistical package, which has the advantages of being free and computer-platform independent (R Development Core Team 2009). We use these statistics to explore which of the patterns that we see in the data are significant. The meaning of those significant patterns depends on our understanding of how the patterns we found relate to those that have been found in other variation studies, a discussion of which will take up most of the rest of this book.

Part II: Variation and social relationships

Introduction to Part II

Social factors lie mostly in the realm of the embedding and evaluation questions posited by WLH: 'How are variation and change embedded in the social fabric of the speech community?' and 'How does the speech community evaluate the variables and the change?' The work of describing the embedding of variation is the central descriptive work of research on social factors, and it is how we will mainly approach these concerns in the first part of our discussion of these factors, focusing on 'canonical patterns' and challenges to them. The focus on the embedding question dovetails with the cognitive factors involved in variation, how variants are socially meaningful and useful for members of a speech community, and how those uses and meanings arise. Work on the evaluation problem will be addressed in the later chapters of this part, in terms of meanings and experimental approaches.

Labov (2001a) approaches the problem of social constraints by using sociolinguistic methods to track down the 'leaders' of sound changes – those speakers who use the most of a new variant at any one time, and whom the rest of the community appear to 'follow' in later generations. While we will review his findings, this is not the overall approach that we will take here. We will discuss the leaders, to be sure, but also the laggards, the resisters, and the clueless. The embedding and evaluation problems are about more than just the leaders, because the entire organisation of variation is embedded and evaluated in the speech community. If it were as simple as everyone following the leaders, the patterns would not be so difficult to find and organise. However, we will see that the patterns are not 'laws' of sound change, and even the principles can be fairly weak. We thus need to understand the embedding of variation in the community from the entire community's perspective, rather than just that of the 'popular kids'.

My view is that the patterns we find are the data that must be explained, and that the explanations of the embedding and evaluation questions lie in the function of language as a social communication tool, rather than simply a denotational communication tool. We thus need to understand at once how variation is used to create social meaning within a speech community, and at the same time what might motivate speakers to create and use those meanings. In other words, what are the social motivations for the linguistic decisions that speakers make, and what are the processes that make that meaning? These are the questions that will concern us in this part of the book.

Before we dive in, a word about 'identity': while I will use this term generally in the next few chapters, I believe it is not very useful as a specific explanatory term, so I will not discuss it explicitly in detail. However, most of the ways that the term is used – the component parts of its definition – are present in the chapters that follow. For example, identity can be said to be at work when we talk about accommodation, and the fact that people are identifying with another person or group of people using linguistic choices. But I think the meanings and motivations we discuss in variation can be more precise than the notion of identity, and I try to use those more specific meanings when I can. When I do use the term *identity*, I will use it as a cover term in the same sense that *variety* stands for things like dialects and languages. Thus, identities are bundles of practices or traits shared by the named group – it is how they are *identified*.

Chapter 4
Social patterns I: interspeaker variation

When variationists have discussed social factors, they have traditionally referred to patterns that predict rates of variant usage for major 'identity categories' such as age, class, sex/gender, race/ethnicity, and region. This concern is traceable to Labov's (1966) study of New York City and studies that followed soon after, such as Trudgill's (1974) study of Norwich, England. This view of the social space is generally referred to as *structuralist* in sociological theory, a usage which derives from the linguistics one, in that both refer to a system of oppositions, in which the identity of an item is dependent upon and entails *not* being something else. Structuralism in sociology refers to a view of society as having a structure of distinctions in a system. So being a man means not being a woman, and being upper-class means not being working-class; the terms are only meaningful in relation to their structural relationship to the other terms or positions in society. While this view of society has been criticised in sociology (and sociologists have criticised sociolinguistics for continuing to use this view; see Williams 1992), we will initially follow the traditional sociolinguistic view before considering challenges to it from within sociolinguistics, and examples of variationist studies that do not make structuralist assumptions, in the final section of this chapter.

Despite the criticisms, we will see that in study after study researchers have shown that one can discern patterns such that certain structural social identities in a speech community will correlate with the use of one variant over another, and that some of these patterns (at least in urban developed countries in the West) are fairly recurrent. Chambers (1995: 17) goes so far as to claim that '[c]orrelating linguistic variation as the dependent variable with independent variables such as linguistic environment, style or social categories is the primary empirical task of sociolinguistics'. It is true that correlations are the main kinds of patterns that variation researchers attempt to discover in the pursuit of answering the embedding question. Depending on how it is framed, this question could even be answered by a listing of patterns of change based on these structural social identity categories. After all, the embedding problem simply asks how a change is embedded in the speech community, and the correlations provide one answer.

But correlation is really only the beginning of our answers to the embedding question. While we might be able to find some consistent social patterns (especially if we compare similar kinds of societies) such that one of these groups tends always to pattern in the same way (for example, 'men tend to use more vernacular variants than women'), in this chapter I have organised these patterns into three *processes* by which we can group them: stratification, accommodation, and differentiation. *Stratification* is the process in which language is used differently by groups who are placed on an ordered prestige scale. Socioeconomic class is the prototype of stratification. Of course, whenever there is some kind of group division in society, there is almost inevitably a scale involved (although people don't always agree on that scale). However, the term refers to cases where stratification and value are inherent in the categories, such as caste and class (and the components of class, such as education and occupation). Stratification also inherently implies a scale in which certain kinds of speech (and the people using those kinds of speech) are valued more highly than others. *Accommodation* is the process whereby we tend to speak more like the person we are speaking to, although in the context of this chapter it will be discussed as a long-term process whereby one group shifts variable usage to be more similar to another group. Finally, *differentiation* is in a sense the opposite process to accommodation, whereby a group of speakers change their variable usage so that it is different from another group's. The difference between stratification and differentiation (as discussed initially) is that in differentiation there is not necessarily an implied consensus in the community about the value of speech for one group or another.

Even with this reorganisation, I will initially be presenting 'canonical' patterns – those patterns that tend to be taken for granted and treated as axiomatic in recent articles in variationist research (although sometimes they are taken to be axiomatic so that they can be attacked). However, there are many dimensions of challenge to the canonical viewpoints, and in the final section of this chapter I will present a number of these challenges. They point to ongoing debates that could form fruitful areas of research.

One such challenge has to do with the organisation of the speech community, and how we think about the categories we use in variationist research. The canonical view depends on a particular structural view of the speech community, and since Labov did his pioneering work in the 1960s and 1970s, social theory has gone through several important debates. One of the most relevant for sociolinguistics is the criticism of this 'consensual' structural view of society. This criticism notes that these categories may be the ones decided upon by the dominant groups in a society, and the relationships may be resisted by people in those categories. Such a view points to the fact that we are not describing patterns made up of cogs in a machine, but humans who themselves have subjective views of their society, and must have a degree of agency about the social choices they make.

STRATIFICATION

The title of Labov's pioneering (1966) work clearly focuses the variationist enterprise on stratification: *The Social Stratification of English in New York City*. It is the pattern of class stratification identified by Labov that is still the template on which many class studies of variation are discussed and understood, so it is important that we review his methods and findings before moving to more recent studies in stratification. Labov's study relied on a number of interlocking studies showing that language in New York City was stratified both in terms of production and in terms of the evaluative norms that speakers had for such speech.

The best-known of these studies, as mentioned in Chapter 1, is probably Labov's of (r) as used by employees of department stores. These stores were used as indirect measures of class, with the assumption that the salespeople in the stores were more likely to present themselves linguistically as desirable to the different clienteles. Labov identified three department stores: Sack's, Macy's, and Klein's. He then determined their class stratification by comparing prices in advertisements and the readers of papers they advertised in, and also through more qualitative measures such as the appearance of the stores (e.g., lighting, space, and organisation). He then went to each store and asked a number of workers for the location of an item he knew to be on the fourth floor. He followed up (for most respondents) by pretending he did not understand the first response and elicited a clarification. The phrase *fourth floor* contains two instances of the variable (r), in different phonological positions (pre-consonant and word-finally, respectively), so Labov recorded the amount of vocalic constriction that each worker exhibited in each of the four repetitions of the variable. In addition to a regular pattern of internal constraints (such that the *fourth* utterance was more likely to be vocalised than *floor*), Labov found that the stratification regularly patterned such that there was more 'r-lessness' in the lower-class stores, and there was the most 'r-fulness' in Sack's, the upper-class store. Labov thus found evidence that r-lessness is higher for the working class than for the upper class. He also found a pattern by age. Taking these together, Labov argued that (r) in New York City was becoming constricted, and that the change was beginning in the upper class and then moving to the middle and working classes.

The other major part of the survey was based on a sample of the population of the Lower East Side of New York City that had been generated by the Mobilization for Youth (MFY) Survey, a federally funded programme addressing 'juvenile delinquency'. The class measures were based on a ten-point scale used by the MFY survey, and serves as a good example of how class stratification is often measured. The scale is based on three indicators, each of which contributes to the number of points a person receives, as shown in Table 4.1 (Labov 1966: 216).

Thus, a person of income rank II but occupational rank IV and educational rank IV receives a score of 7, while someone with the same income rank but an occupational rank of II and an educational rank of III receives a score of 4. Education was measured on levels completed, while income was measured on relationship to the nation's median yearly income. Occupations were divided roughly into professionals, clerks and salesmen, skilled workers and blue-collar workers, and finally service workers and labourers (1966: 213). This ten-point scale was then divided further into four categories as shown in Table 4.2.

Labov interviewed a subsample of the MFY Survey sample using the methods of sociolinguistic interviewing described in Chapter 3. He analysed several variables,

Table 4.1 Class scores in Labov (1966)

Ed. Rank	Income Rank															
	IV				III				II				I			
	Occupational Rank				Occupational Rank				Occupational Rank				Occupational Rank			
	IV	III	II	I	IV	III	II	I	IV	III	II	I	IV	III	II	I
IV	9	8	7	6	8	7	6	5	7	6	5	4	6	5	4	3
III	8	7	6	5	7	6	5	4	6	5	4	3	5	4	3	2
II	7	6	5	4	6	5	4	3	5	4	3	2	4	3	2	1
I	6	5	4	3	5	4	3	2	4	3	2	1	3	2	1	0

Table 4.2 Class division in Labov (1966)

Score	Class
0-2 (sometimes 0-1)	Lower class
3-5 (sometimes 2-5)	Working class
6-8	Lower middle class
9	Upper middle class

including postvocalic (r) as in *four*, (ae) as in *bat*, (oh) as in *caught* and *dog*, the fricatives (th) as in *thing* and (dh) as in *there*. For current purposes, let us consider the analysis of (r).

Labov's hypothesis was that the rate of variation would correlate with class in a linear way, just as there had been more r-fulness in the upper-class Sack's Department store than in Macy's, and more in Macy's than in Klein's, the lowest-class store. He did not expect, for example, that the lowest class would pattern with the upper class and the middle classes together; hence the term 'stratification'. Labov indeed found clear stratification patterns for each variable. Before viewing the patterns he found, however, we must briefly address the question of style and how Labov approached it. We will discuss this topic in depth in Chapter 5.

In order to compare speech among respondents, Labov noted famously (1972b: 240) that it is not always possible to distinguish 'a casual salesman from a careful pipefitter'. So we need to control for the casualness or carefulness of speech; basically, controlling in some way for intraspeaker variation. Labov addressed this problem by assuming that more casual speech is speech in which the speaker is not paying attention to the speech itself. So the most careful speech will be when uttering a minimal pair highlighting the variable in question, because it draws attention to the variable. The most casual speech is when telling personal narratives, because attention is focused on the action in the story. The five styles discussed by Labov are therefore: reading minimal pairs, reading a word list, reading connected sentences, careful speech, and casual speech. Labov found that, in general, social class stratification appears if style is controlled for, and within each social class, styles are ordered in the same way.

Figure 4.1 Social stratification of (r) in New York interview data (adapted from Labov 1966: 240)

The analysis of (r) in this manner led to the most commonly reproduced chart in sociolinguistics, represented here as Figure 4.1 (Labov 1966: 240), which shows the percentage of r-fulness. Note that in general the lines, which represent class categories, are ordered in a linear manner, with the lower classes near the bottom.

In addition, each class uses more r-fulness as the style becomes more careful. Note, however, that in the most careful styles, the lower middle class actually uses more (r) than the upper middle class, a finding which has since been termed the lower-middle-class *hypercorrection* pattern. This pattern is hypercorrection, it is thought, because the lower middle class 'overshoots' their apparent upper-middle-class reference group in the word list and minimal pair styles. This pattern was repeated in Labov's study for the variables (ae) and (oh).

Because we are ultimately interested in the embedding of change in the community, we also wish to know whether change is occurring and if so in what direction. Real-time sources suggest that before the middle of the twentieth century, New York was mostly r-less. Apparent-time data support this; the r-fulness is a new form. Because this new form is used more by more upper-class speakers, we say that the upper middle class is *leading the change*. This pattern can also be seen in Figure 4.2, which is the percentage of r-fulness for each age and class category in the reading style.

From this figure it can be seen that the upper middle class used the most r-fulness, and that within that class the youngest used it the most (evidence from apparent time that it is new). However, notice that in the other classes, the youngest group is among the *least* likely to use r-fulness. One possible interpretation of these data is that the older members of these classes are to some extent modifying their speech as adults to approximate the upper middle class more closely, and Labov presents some other evidence that this may be the case (including the hypercorrection pattern).

58   Linguistic Variation and Change

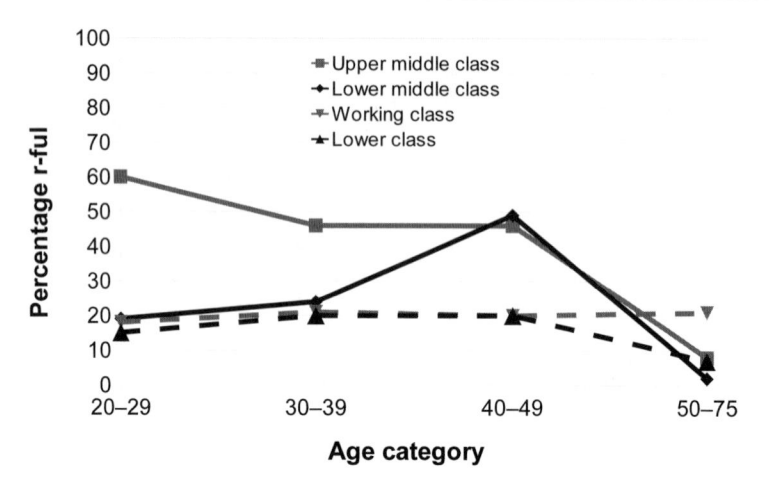

Figure 4.2   Percentage r-fulness by age and class for reading style (adapted from Labov 1966)

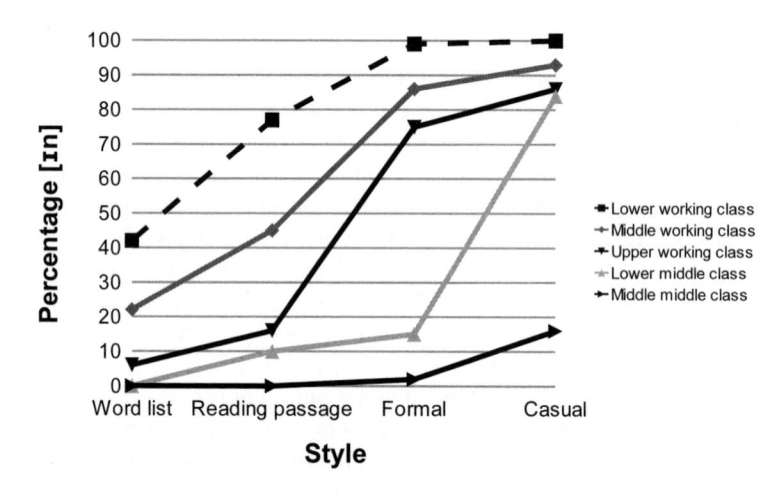

Figure 4.3   Stratification of (ing) in Norwich (adapted from Trudgill 1974: 92)

This type of change has been dubbed a *change from above*, because it seems to begin in the upper social classes, and also (it is claimed) is a variable about which speakers are aware (it is 'above the level of awareness').

Similar patterns were found by Peter Trudgill in his survey (1974) of Norwich a few years later. Trudgill also analysed a number of variables, including some that were unlikely to be undergoing change, such as (ing), and those he suspected of undergoing change. Trudgill's measure of class was similar to Labov's, and he found similar patterns of stratification. However, as shown in Figure 4.3, rather than the fairly even, linear stratification that Labov found, Trudgill found small differences within his middle-class categories, but between the lower middle classes, he found a stark separation. He also found a similar crossover pattern to that found by Labov, with the upper working class crossing over the large difference between the formal style and reading passage style, and the lower middle class crossing over between formal and casual style.

Guy (1990) suggests that these differences may not be random but related to the status of the variables in terms of awareness and meaning. This observation raises an important distinction made by Labov early on between *change from above* and *change from below*. These terms refer to 'above' and 'below' in two ways. First, they describe the so-called awareness of variables, in which variables that the community is aware of are changes from above, and variables that the community is not aware of are changes from below – changes from below the level of awareness. Awareness here is not clearly defined, although it is tied to whether or not there is style shift, and also whether or not there is any kind of overt discussion within the community about the variable. Changes from above are also thought of as changes that tend to be led by the upper classes, and changes from below are led by lower classes. There are a number of important assumptions hidden in these terms, such as what it means to be aware of a variable, and we will address them later. However, they are extremely important concepts in variationist research, because different patterns and motivations for these different changes have been found. For example, the patterns to be described in Chapter 8 for many vocalic variables are generalisations about changes from below. More recently, Labov (2007) has argued that change from above is a *change by diffusion*, which is characterised by a spread of one variant from one geographic area to another, mostly by adults, while a change from below is *change by transmission*, in which a change is under way and is moved forwards by children as they acquire the variety.

Horvath (1985) also finds class differences in her study of the vowel system of the Sydney, Australia, speech community. However, she used a different statistical method to group speakers first by whether or not they talked alike. She then identified four 'sociolects' based on four groups of speakers that the statistics program put close together. She then looked at the composition of the sociolects, and found differences for gender, age, ethnicity, and especially class. Moreover, the classes were aligned in a fairly linear fashion from one sociolect to another. Her work is important because it shows that even if we code all speakers just by their speech and not by class ahead of time, we will find a class stratification pattern.

One question we might ask is whether any components of the class measures are more important than the others. Labov (2001a) investigates this question in depth using data from his decades-long study of the many variables in the Philadelphia speech community. However, in this study he attempts to determine which components best predict the sociolinguistic variation, and he finds that of the individual indicators, including house value rather than income, occupation is often, but not always, the most robustly correlated factor of the components of the socioeconomic index. However, he finds that the combined index is the most consistent and complete predictor of most variables. In other words, occupation is the single measure that most reliably stratifies speakers, as opposed to measures of achievement or quality such as income or education. This is an important finding, because it suggests that occupation is reflecting something about people, in that it is more closely related to how they talk than income or education. We will see below that variation is closely tied to social practices, so the fact that occupation is the stratificational measure makes sense if we notice that it is the measure that is most about what people do and how they relate to people, rather than what they are or have done.

These stratification patterns appear to be fairly robust, with similar patterns in many urban centres. Nevertheless, the studies reviewed so far are all English-speaking, Anglo, urban speech communities. Can these patterns be found in other locales? To some extent, yes, as long as the societies under consideration are large urban speech communities in which there is enough diversity for something that can be called class to appear. Cedergren (1973) shows that stratification is robust in the speech in Panama City, Panama, but Bortono-Ricardo (1985) finds that in a rapidly urbanising situation such as Brasilia, Brazil, there were fewer established patterns of variation and these seemed to be developing rather than pre-existing. See also Rissel (1989), who finds a complex pattern of stratification for the assibilation of (r) in San Luis Potosi, Mexico.

All of the examples given above are phonological variables. Do similar patterns hold for morphological or syntactic variables? There is evidence that they do. Multiple negation, also referred to as negative concord, in English is one of the most sensitive variables to social class, although it is almost always a stable variable. It is the use of more than one negative marker in English sentences, such as in (1a). Sentence (1b) shows a more common use, as multiple neagtion often co-occurs with other 'non-standard' variables such as *ain't* for *am not*, and the [ɪn] form of the (ing) variable.

(1) a. I'm not getting no ketchup for you. Get your own.
(1) b. I ain't gettin' no ketchup for you.

Labov's (2001a) study of negative concord in Philadelphia shows the sensitivity of this variable to class. As shown in Figure 4.4, the lower working class uses much more negative concord than any other class. Wolfram (1969) found a similar pattern for African American speakers in Detroit, as shown in Figure 4.5.

It's clear from these studies that *stratification* – some measure of social prestige or value of a person – is a central finding in variationist work. Where there is a 'vernacular' or 'non-standard' variant, that variant tends to be used more by speakers classified at the lower end of the class or prestige structure. However, we have not explored patterns of *interaction* that have been found for stratification. Interactions are patterns in which two categories do not act independently. For example, we might find that upper-class men do something very different from upper-class women, and that this upper-class gender difference does not hold for the working class. Such interactions among sex and class and age are extremely common; once we have considered gender patterns more fully in Chapter 4 we will investigate these interactions in detail.

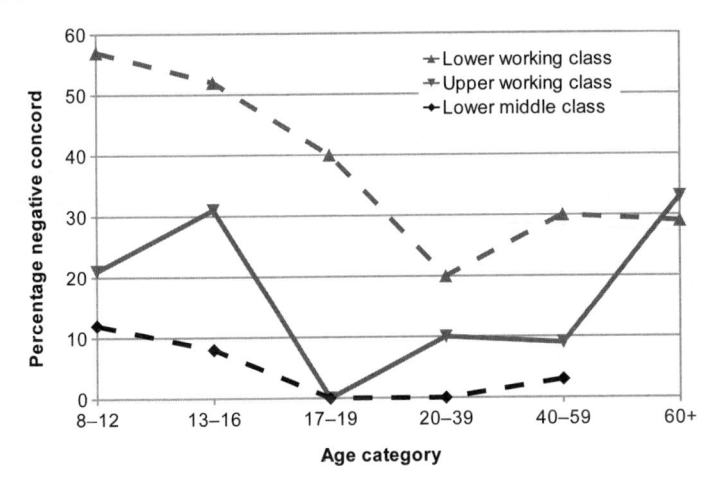

Figure 4.4 Negative concord by age and social class in Philadelphia (adapted from Labov 2001a: 107)

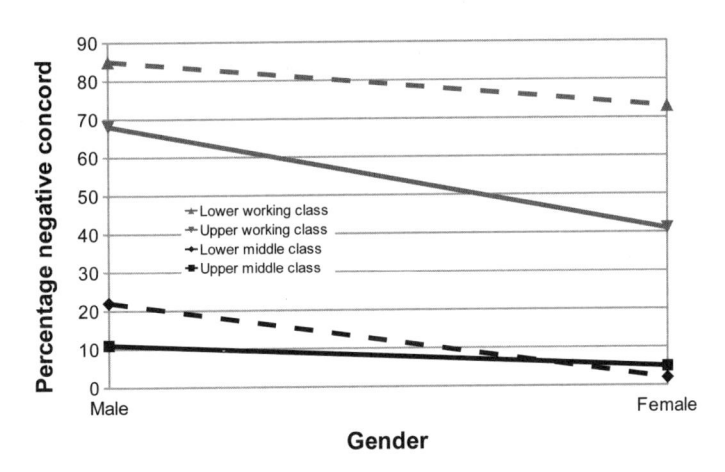

Figure 4.5 Negative concord by gender and social class in Detroit (adapted from Labov 2001a: 82; Wolfram 1969)

Even without interactions, which end of the stratification spectrum will lead a change is not entirely straightforward; that is, it is not entirely predictable from class how a change will be embedded in a speech community. Labov (1994: 300–1) argues that generalisations can be made if we divide changes in progress into our two types: change from below and change from above. In change from below, he argues, the leading class will be a low but 'interior' class. That is, the leaders will be working-class speakers but not the lowest-class speakers. However, as seen for the (r) variable in New York City, a change from above will be led by the middle or upper middle class. Labov (2001a: 188) proposes to capture this generalisation in the *Curvilinear Principle*: 'Linguistic changes from below originate in a central social group, located in the interior of the socioeconomic hierarchy.'

Another way that this stratification has been viewed is through the notion of the linguistic marketplace. Labov argues that prestige is attached to different linguistic forms; Sankoff and Laberge (1978) took this idea and connected it with the French sociologist and anthropologist Pierre Bourdieu's (1991) notion of linguistic markets. The essential idea is that ways of speaking can represent different amounts of what Bourdieu calls 'symbolic capital' in a speech community. We see then that the patterns of class stratification can represent different values of persons in some market – often the labour market. In fact, all of these stratification patterns suggest a representation of some kind of social meaning for different variants. However, the correlations do not provide the meanings; we will need to look elsewhere for those, and we will explore them in the next two chapters.

Another way of thinking about stratification is geographically. First, it has been shown that changes generally tend to originate in populous urban areas and spread from there. There are two models of how this diffusion might work: either gradually over geographic space (the wave model), or from the most populous cities and then to the second-most-populous cities, skipping over very small towns, which adopt the change last (the gravity model). The wave model is less common than the gravity model, although it has been found by Bailey et al. (1993) and Trudgill (1986: 51–3). The gravity model has been found in more cases, including by Gerritsen and Jansen (1980), Trudgill (1983), and Bailey et al. (1993). Both of these models indicate a pattern in which the urban centre, which often has the most prestige and cultural capital, is in a way equivalent to the upper-class speakers. These kinds of changes are usually represented as mechanical effects of contact rather than involving issues such as prestige. That is, because of the kinds of communication and contact that medium-sized towns have with larger ones, there is a 'natural' spread (perhaps by accommodation) from one to the other. This view would see this as a case of accommodation, which we will discuss later. However, we can also see it as a possible stratification, where people are identifying with the values, lifestyle, practices, or prestige of the larger urban centre, and not simply automomatically accommodating to it.

There have also been diffusion patterns that do not fit these models, however. Bailey et al. (1993), in addition to finding variables diffusing by the wave and gravity models in Texas English, also found one variable – the use of the aspectual marker *fixin' to* – that was diffusing in a contra-hierarchical model. That is, it was moving from smaller towns to larger urban areas. In this case, however, Bailey et al. show that the term is associated with a renewed prestige attached to the traditional southern identity. In other words, the change is able to spread in a contra-hierarchical manner because the usual prestige associations are being upended. So our view that diffusion is a kind of stratification is upheld.

Horvath and Horvath (2001, 2002) however, present more problematic data, which are also some of the most exciting in sociolinguistic geography in recent years.

Their work suggests that in a more global perspective on diffusion, these patterns do not seem to hold (note that most of what has been cited so far has been based on diffusion in relatively small areas). Horvath and Horvath analyse /l/-vocalisation in Australia and New Zealand. Either the wave model or the gravity model would predict that a change in these countries would proceed from the largest cities to the smaller, and from the larger country to the smaller. Thus, Sydney would be the centre of gravity, as would Australia. Horvath and Horvath find that neither is the case. In fact, New Zealand is the leader as far as /l/-vocalisation goes, and the smaller cities in both countries use more vocalisation. The explanation for these patterns is unclear, but they may be related to the curvilinear class pattern in which the 'interior' social classes lead changes within speech communities.

There is a second manner in which geography can be considered to be stratification. The patterns we characterised as change from above and change from below are often reflective of geographical and standardisation stratification patterns. Change from above tends to involve changes that have as their source a less 'localised' variety, perhaps even a national standard. The stratification of (r) is a good example of this pattern. R-lessness in New York, and the US more generally, was a feature of upper-class speech until after World War II. This difference in prestige can be seen clearly in portrayals of upper-class speakers in films before this time, as studied by Elliott (2000). (I suggest *The Philadelphia Story* as a particularly good example, but almost any American film before 1935 that portrays upper-class characters – particularly older patrician women – will provide examples.) After World War II, a new national 'standard' form in r-fulness developed, and it is this new, more national way of speaking that then made its way into New York, leading to the patterns that Labov found there.

In a sense, then, there is an element of variety contact happening in a case such as that of (r) in New York: a local variety and a less local variety. Globalisation, media, and mobility are thus playing an important role in the development of varieties in the developed world, to an extent probably not occurring previously. This can be seen in Pittsburgh, Pennsylvania, where I have conducted research with Barbara Johnstone. The local variant in this case is clearly being used less and less by younger generations (Kiesling and Wisnosky 2003). As we discuss in Johnstone and Kiesling (2008), however, this loss has come about just as Pittsburghers have begun to talk about the local variety as a known 'language' that they refer to as *Pittsburghese* (a process known as *enregistration*). Pittsburghers have become more and more 'aware' of the variable through its iconic use in the word *downtown*, so that the variable is usually represented by spelling *downtown* as *dahntahn*. But even as the local variety becomes more and more associated with a local identity, the everyday use of such variables is falling away. The situation is thus similar to that of (r) in New York, where the tension is not so much a local stratification between an old local form and a new local form as a stratification between a local and a non-local variant. Dubois and Horvath (1999), whose study identifies a related pattern which we will explore more in our discussion of gender, thus argue that changes from above and below should be viewed as *exonorms* and *endonorms*, respectively, because so-called changes from above are most often norms that are adopted from contact with non-local varieties. As noted above, this difference is also captured by Labov's distinction between diffusion and transmission.

CANONICAL PATTERNS: ACCOMMODATION

Stratification patterns are patterns of ordering by some kind of *prestige*, and reflect hierarchical or *power* relationships the analyst has evidence for in the speech community. However, language can also be used to create *solidarity* relationships in a speech community. In fact, these solidarity relationships may in many ways be stronger than the stratification patterns or even the differentiation patterns that we will look at later. In this section, we will explore patterns of accommodation – patterns in which speakers make similar linguistic choices for a particular variable. There are three main ways we will discuss patterns of accommodation. First, accommodation takes place among individuals in the short term, in conversations, when speakers tend to speak more like the person they are speaking to. This kind of short-term accommodation we will discuss in the next chapter. Second, we find that over longer stretches of time, people make more enduring adjustments to speak in ways similar to other people whom they regard as close friends, otherwise known as their *social networks*. Finally, when large groups of people come into contact, such as in cases of large-scale migration, we find that in general the members of the groups end up speaking in ways that are similar to each other and eventually form new varieties known as *koines*.

Although Labov discussed the role of network integration in his study of Black Americans in the Harlem neighbourhood of New York City (1972a), Lesley and James Milroy (Milroy 1980) were the first to use network analysis in a large-scale sociolinguistic survey. They showed that we can correlate speakers' variable use depending on the kinds of social networks that they are in. Drawing on sociological studies of networks, the researchers characterised networks in two dimensions. First, networks can be measured in terms of *density*, such that dense networks are those in which people have connections, or *ties*, to many other people in the network. Figure 4.6 shows the difference between a low-density network (left) and a high-density network (right). Each point represents a person; networks are often represented from the perspective of a single person, or *ego*, although that is not necessary. In Figure 4.6 the ego is represented by a star.

Density can be calculated numerically in a number of ways, but the most common is a network strength scale of some sort, which is a composite of a number of measures such as the number of ties. Within a network, we can also measure the different kinds of ties that people have to each other. For example, we may measure a network by whether somebody names somebody else as a friend, or we may measure whether they have other connections such as whether they work with them or are part of the same family or live in the same neighbourhood. The number of different kinds of ties is a measure of the *multiplexity* of the network, such that multiplex ties or networks are those that have many such connections. Multiplexity

Social patterns I: interspeaker variation   65

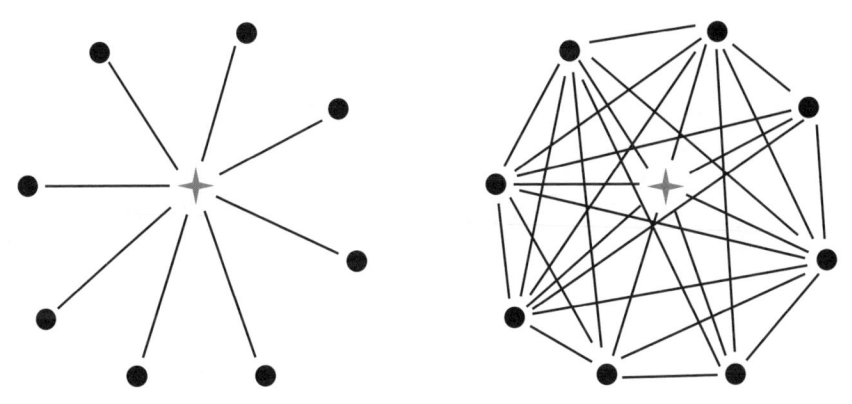

Figure 4.6   Low-density (left) and high-density (right) networks

is usually represented by drawing more lines or thickening the lines between each person.

Milroy (1980) showed that the kinds of networks that speakers are in can predict variable usage, such that dense and multiplex networks tend to be correlated with the use of a local, or vernacular, variant. Milroy performed her research in three neighbourhoods of Belfast, Northern Ireland: Ballymacarret, Clonard, and the Hammer. She was interested in the different patterning of a number of variables in these three areas, which were characterised by different network patterns. Ballymacarret was a stable community with network ties intact. In addition, in this neighbourhood, men tended to have more dense and multiplex networks than women. The Hammer had lost the industry that made it a stable working-class community, and hence all networks were less dense and multiplex than in Ballymacarrett. Finally, in Clonard, there was a similar loss of the traditional neighbourhood, with the exception that in Clonard more industry still existed. One of the variables Milroy investigated was the backing of the vowel /æ/. Figure 4.7 shows the scores for age, gender, and neighbourhood from Milroy's data.

In general, and especially in Ballymacarrett, men tend to back more than women. Milroy shows that men, especially in Ballymacarrett, also have more dense and multiplex networks. She argues, then, that the pattern is reflecting differences in networks as much as gender. An analysis of another variable – the deletion of /ð/ intervocalically in words such as *mother* represented by (th) – shows this correlation quite closely, as seen in Figure 4.8.

This network effect even suggests why the young women use more backing in Clonard: Milroy found that they have higher network scores. Since Milroy's work, many more studies have shown that strong network ties, however measured, are often correlated with greater use of local or vernacular variants.

Cheshire (1982) measured the integration of young boys and girls into a peer-group network and found that those who were more integrated used more local morphosyntacic variants. She determined that the 'core' members of an adventure-playground group used more 'vernacular' variants than those who were 'secondary'

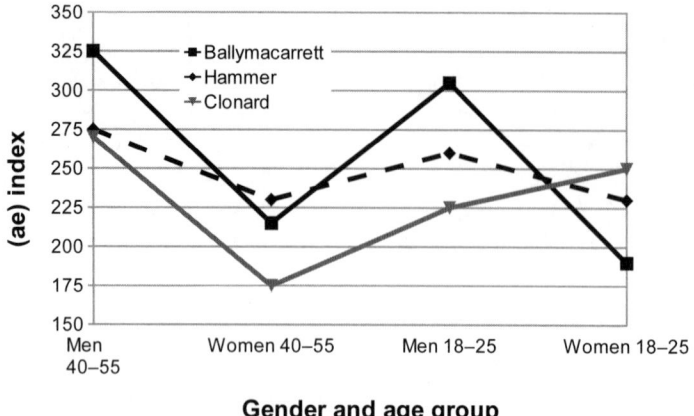

66 Linguistic Variation and Change

Note: The (ae) index score was based on the total for all (ae) tokens, with each token receiving one to five points, with five the most retracted or 'non-standard'.

Figure 4.7 (ae) variation in Belfast neighbourhoods by gender and age (adapted from Milroy 1980: 124)

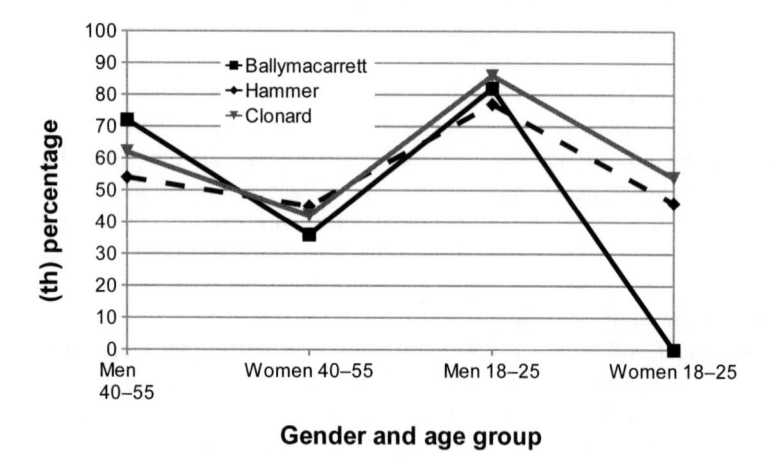

Figure 4.8 (th) variation in Belfast neighbourhoods by gender and age (adapted from Milroy 1980: 128)

or 'peripheral'. Network status was determined from two criteria. The first was similar to Milroy's measures, obtained by asking the kids whom they spent the most time with. Second, Cheshire devised a 'vernacular culture index', which was based on social practices and aspirations such as carrying weapons, clothing style, job aspirations, crime participation, fighting skill, and swearing (note that this prefigures Eckert's study of variation and social practice, which we will discuss below, as Cheshire is essentially noting that linguistic variation can be correlated with other social practices, although she does not use this terminology). The core members all showed the most vernacular practices and were also named the most frequently by others in the network. The core members were most likely to use three non-standard morphosyntactic variables: -s on present tense verbs in non-third person singular contexts (e.g., *I just lets her beat me*), *what* used as a complementiser (*Are you the little bastards what hit my son over the head?*), and *never* used in a narrow sense to mean essentially *didn't this time* (*I never went to school today*). Cheshire thus began to show what network strengths measure – the strength with which a person is socially integrated into the local practices of their community.

It is important to note that network strength is not universally predictive of vernacular language. For example, Salami (1991) studied the effect of networks on the use of six phonological variables in the variety of Yoruba spoken in Ile-Ife, Nigeria. For two variables, network strength had a significant effect. However, when Salami tested whether network strength had an effect separately for men and women, he found that the networks correlated only with the variables for the women. Thus, network does not have a consistent effect across all groups in every study. Dubois and Horvath (1999) find a similar pattern of different network effects by gender, and we will discuss that work more fully below. Network patterns are thus useful and often predictive of variation, but this effect can often be very complex, and is not a universal tendency.

Network analyses point to the complex relationship between accommodation and stratification in variation studies. This relationship is highlighted when we ask whose language is accommodated to. That is, are there some speakers in a network who are the real innovators, and others in the network who are accommodators? Eckert's (2000) and Labov's (2001a) work suggests there are. Labov (2001a: 354) shows that within the neighbourhood blocks making up his study of Philadelphia, there are central actors, or 'stars', who have the greatest influence on their network (and also often have the most connections outside the network). Eckert (2000), in her study of an urban high school in Detroit, Michigan, shows that certain individuals become, as she calls them, 'sociolinguistic icons'. These icons are the reference points to which other students accommodate (or, in many cases, don't accommodate). If stratification represents differences in the prestige attached to variants, as claimed by Labov and others reviewed above, then these icons have a kind of prestige, and represent a more local way that stratification is replicated. More importantly, it is not only membership in a dense or multiplex network, but a particular position in the network, that is important in predicting an individual's use of a variant. Labov's (1972a) study of Black Americans in Harlem, mentioned above, is another example of this effect, although from a different perspective.

One of the best general pieces of evidence that accommodation is an important force in linguistic change comes from the third type of accommodation situation mentioned above: the studies of koines, which are generally discussed as new dialects that form from a mixture of previous varieties (the term derives from the Greek *koine*, the word for a variety that became the lingua franca form of Greek around 300 BCE).

Importantly, this work also points to accommodation by way of network structure. Bortoni-Ricardo (1985) investigated the process of urbanisation in Brazlandia, Brazil, near the capital Brasilia, and the influences on speakers adopting features of the most vernacular Brasilian Portuguese variety, known as Caipira. Bortoni-Ricardo was interested in measuring the difference in how *insulated from* or *integrated with* the urban milieu the rural migrants were. In other words, did the migrants stay with other rural migrants when they moved to urban areas, or did they move into new, more urban networks? For this study, Bortoni-Ricardo had two network measures. The integration index was a complex measurement of network strength, while the urbanisation index was a measure of the urbanisation of a speaker's network. The latter measure attempts to capture how much the people in a speaker's network engage in urban cultural practices. As such it is similar to Cheshire's vernacular culture measure. Bortoni-Ricardo analysed four variables, but we will focus only on the reduction of /ʎ/-vocalisation, in which words such as *mulher* 'woman', normally pronounced [muʎɛr], are pronounced as [mujʲɛ]. Similarly to the results of Salami, Milroy and Milroy, and Dubois and Horvath, Bortoni-Ricardo found that although the urbanisation index had predictive effect for both men and women, the integration measure was different for men and women. For the men, she found that both indexes correlate positively with /ʎ/-vocalisation, but for women, it was only the urbanisation index that predicted /ʎ/-vocalisation. Investigating further, Bortoni-Ricardo found that for men, the two measures were positively correlated with each other, meaning essentially that the indexes were measuring similar social aspects, while for women, the indexes were negatively correlated, meaning they were measuring *opposite* aspects. Bortoni-Ricardo explains this result with the observation from her ethnographic analysis that a strong integration measure for women is more likely to be due to dense networks composed of other rural migrants (and family members), while when men have strong networks, these are not necessarily made up of other migrants. So we again see that accommodation, through a measure of networks, operates to affect linguistic choice, although other measures would be needed to operationalise the kinds of networks involved.

Kerswill and Williams (2000, 2005) also provide convincing evidence of this network effect in another study of migration and dialect contact. This study focuses on the development of a koine in the 'New Town' of Milton Keynes, which was created in the late 1960s, and was located in the countryside between two main modern dialect areas of England. This study has been extremely important for informing our knowledge about dialect contact and variation in general, especially since the design included young children around age four and older children around age twelve. For their network analysis, Kerswill and Williams focused on the fronting of the /oʊ/ vowel as in *goat*. They used a four-point scale of fronting for their analysis (from 0 to 3). While Kerswill and William did not perform a formal network analysis with network scores as Milroy or Bortoni-Ricardo did, their qualitative look at several of the older children who were in the forefront of the new dialect forms is revealing. The researchers concluded (2005: 94) that 'the main factor is the child's orientation towards the peer group. All the high scorers

'... are very well integrated into a (mainly school-centred) group of friends; they are sociable and are often cited as friends by other children. By contrast, the low scorers are somewhat distanced from their peers.' Kerswill and Williams also confirmed that this network effect was far stronger than any connection between the speech of the caregivers of the children and their scores; indeed, Kerswill and Williams found no correlation between the speech of the caregivers and that of the older children (the youngest children were still clearly influenced by their caregivers' speech forms). These results suggest that it is the children with more dense and multiplex networks who are more involved in creating the 'new' variety in Milton Keynes.

So it is pretty clear that we can predict who will be the movers and shakers in variation: those people who are more central to social networks. Moreover, subgroups or speech communities with more dense and multiplex networks will be more likely to be affected by the norms in this group than those who have looser networks. We might ask, then, whether we might be able to explain the class differences we find through network differences – perhaps working-class speakers are more likely than upper-class speakers to have more dense and multiplex networks – or, for that matter, whether any pattern we discuss can be explained in terms of networks. Milroy and Milroy (1992) explicitly address the issue of the relationship between class and networks. They cite work (Fischer 1982; Cochran et al. 1990) that shows that 'Generally speaking, middle-class networks (consisting largely of weak ties in Granovetter's [1973] sense) are larger, less kin- and territory-oriented and perceived as more supportive. Mewett (1982) examined the relationship between class and network from a different perspective, arguing that class differences in small communities begin to emerge over time as the proportion of multiplex relationships declines' (1992: 16).

Labov (2001a: 334–56), however, compares regression analyses for ongoing changes in Philadelphia vowels both with and without a network measure. He finds that the network measure adds to the amount of variation the model explains, but it does not replace the other factors such as gender. So, while there may be some correlation between network strength and class, it looks as if they are accounting for linguistic variation in different ways.

Labov (2001a) and Milroy and Milroy (1992) both find support for another finding of the Milroys in Belfast, however, in the role of what they call *weak ties* in the diffusion of linguistic changes. Weak ties are the opposite of the *strong ties* found in dense multiplex networks. These weak ties are ties of acquaintance – for example, the parent of a schoolmate of one's child seen three times a year, or a co-worker who works in the same office but with whom one shares cordial greetings and occasional small talk in the lunchroom. Following the sociologist Mark Granovetter (1973) the Milroys argue 'not only that groups linked internally mainly by relatively weak ties are susceptible to innovation, but also that innovations between groups are generally transmitted by means of weak rather than strong network ties' (Milroy and Milroy 1992: 9). Labov finds that the leaders of linguistic change in Philadelphia are characterised by being central in their own networks and are 'not limited to their local networks, but have intimate friends in the wider neighborhood' (2001a: 360).

In sum, let's review the ways that social networks have been operationalised in the sociolinguistic literature. These have all been productive in predicting who will use how much of a particular variant. These measures include:

- **Density** (the number of ties) and **multiplexity** (the number of different ties linking two people, or an aggregate of that for a network). Both correlate with vernacular variants, such that more dense and multiplex networks lead to more use of the vernacular. Group members accommodate to each other more readily if they all know each other in multiple ways.
- **Weak and strong ties**. While dense and multiplex networks reflect strong ties that correlate with vernacular use, weak ties are theorised to promote the diffusion of a linguistic change. Group members are more likely to accommodate to people who have status in the group.
- **Identity of the network**. Finally, there is evidence that the kinds of ties are not the only predictor. Bortoni-Ricardo's (1985) data show us that the norms that are accommodated to within a network can depend on who is in that network (migrants or non-migrants in Bortoni-Ricardo's case).

In general, then, it is fairly clear that accommodation is one of the basic processes of variation: people tend to talk like the people they are talking to. They talk more like people they are predisposed to like, and people they are otherwise close to socially, but they also like to 'borrow' from people they don't know well. Of course, if this were the only process in affecting variation, we would all speak alike. Therefore in the next section we will investigate the canonical patterns of *differentiation* that exist in tension with accommodation and stratification.

CANONICAL PATTERNS: DIFFERENTIATION

While we can find differentiation in many situations involving variation, there are three main social domains in which differentiation has been found: geography, race and ethnicity, and gender. In each of these domains, we find that some difference in identity or place leads to speakers making different linguistic choices from other speakers, sometimes even other speakers they talk to every day. We might assume that differentiation is just the flip-side of accommodation – since we can't accommodate to everyone, we must end up with some group differences. In the case of geographical differentiation, this is often the case. That is, when there is a difference in language or variety across boundaries such as mountains or rivers, we are not surprised, because it is pretty clear to us that there are fewer opportunities for accommodation across these kinds of boundaries (although less so in the last century). But there are some mysteries that suggest the answer is not so easy, such as why geographical boundaries seem to be stable for generations, even without clear physical boundaries.

Britain's (1991) study of the English Fens provides us with a view into how such boundaries develop, change, and are maintained. The Fens are an area of southern England to the north of London, abutting the coast of the North Sea. They sit on a

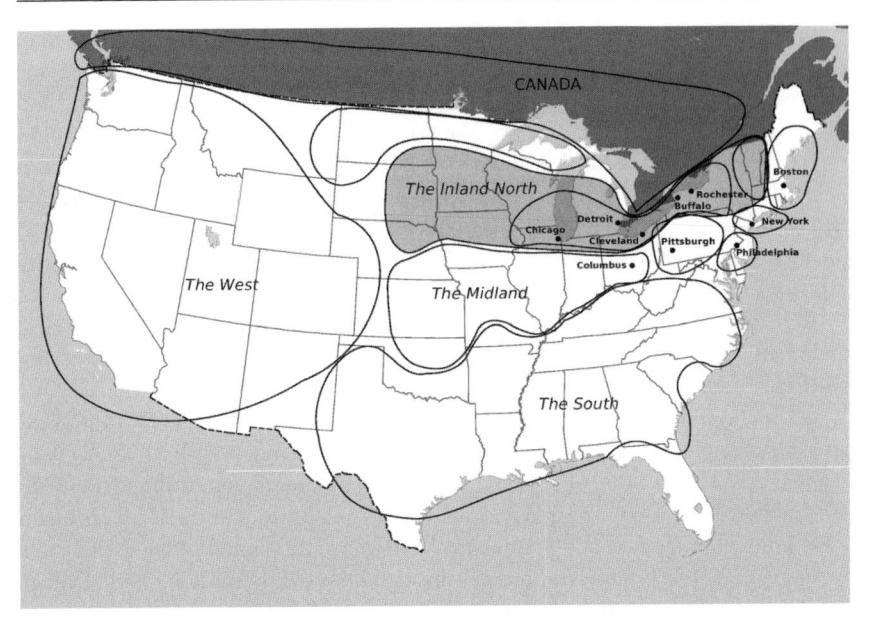

Figure 4.9 Major dialect areas of North America (based on Labov et al. 2006; http://commons.wikimedia.org/wiki/File:StatesU.svg)

political boundary between the counties of Norfolk and Suffolk (together known as East Anglia), and other counties to the north and west. The land was a marsh until a few hundred years ago, when it started to be drained and become productive farmland. One can understand why, over the thousands of years preceding this, differences developed in the English spoken to the east and west of the Fens. Nevertheless, a boundary has been maintained up to the present day, even with newer variants arising in the different dialect areas. Britain shows that there is very little interaction between people on either side of the dialect boundary, whilst few people live in the boundary area, and transportation networks favour local and north–south routes rather than east–west connections between the two major towns of the area, Wisbech and King's Lynn. The links between the populations in the east and west are therefore weak, and this is one factor leading to their differentiation. However, given the discussion of weak ties in the previous section, we might expect that in fact there would be some accommodation between the two areas. The difference is that there are also, as Britain puts it, 'local rivalries and negative stereotyping of each other's residents' (2004: 612). So there is what we can loosely call an ideological or identity differentiation that reinforces the physical and social practice differentiation, and probably helps to enforce these latter separations.

Some boundaries, though, are still somewhat mysterious. In North America, there are vast expanses of the continent that essentially share a variety, separated by thousands of miles. For example, Chicago, Detroit, Cleveland, Buffalo, and Rochester all share a dialect region (Labov et al. 2006), as shown in Figure 4.9.

Pittsburgh and Columbus, however, which are both closer to Cleveland than Cleveland is to Chicago, are in quite different dialect regions, with little in the way of rivers and mountains in between (in fact, the topography between Cleveland and Columbus is mind-numbingly flat). We thus find a maintenance of differentiation on a large scale, without a clear indication of how this happens through a break in networks or accommodation. It thus appears that differentiation is not something that is automatic on the basis of geography, but incorporates a dimension of social practice (e.g., where and with whom one works), and an ideological or identity dimension.

A view of race or ethnicity presents a similar and starker picture of ideological and identity differentiation: we find people living near each other and often working with each other, and part of similar networks or at least engaging in many weak-tie links, but nevertheless speaking quite differently. The case of AAVE is the most striking example of this, although we will see that other situations have similar consequences. AAVE is a case of both uniformity and differentiation. It shows uniformity in that it is a variety that is very similar across many cities in the USA, although with some phonological and grammatical variation. This similarity points to some sort of supraregional norm or process –through both communication and ideology – that allows this to be described as a single variety in most cases (see Wolfram and Schilling-Estes 1998; Green 2002). But for the purposes of our discussion of differentiation, the remarkable fact about AAVE is that it shows so much difference from non-Black varieties spoken in the same cities and towns.

Wolfram (2000) provides an overview of research that gives an example of how this simultaneous differentiation and accommodation can take place. He summarises a number of studies of communities in Hyde County, North Carolina, reproduced in Figure 4.10, that show older speakers using more local Anglo-American features and younger African American speakers increasing in the use of some linguistic variants associated with AAVE.

Wolfram writes, 'African American speakers are diverging from their Anglo-American vernacular cohorts as local dialect features are being replaced by a more widespread, common-core set of AAVE features. In effect, the ethnic marking of speech in Hyde County seems to be superseding its regional locus' (2000: 343). He notes that some of these changes may be due to expanded mobility for younger speakers, so they are exposed to AAVE whereas the older speakers were not. However, expanded mobility by itself does not produce this difference – the speakers still must orient themselves to these new variants, and make choices to adopt them in their own speech.

Of course AAVE is not the only example of such ethnic differentiation, and immigration is not always the only cause. People generally come into contact when they move in large groups from place to place. African Americans were brought into contact with White Americans because they were forced to migrate as slaves; this history and later histories of segregation and discrimination contributed to the patterns of AAVE. The other two main ways that ethnic groups come into contact are through voluntary migration and through colonialism. The former is the more

Dialect feature	Elderly Hyde Anglo-American	Elderly Hyde African American	Young Hyde Anglo-American	Young Hyde African American	Urban AAVE
Phonology					
Prevocalic CCR in *bes' egg*	–	■	–	■	■
Postvocalic *-r* in *year*	■	■	■	–	–
Backed /aɪ/ in *time*	■	■	+/–	■	■
Unglided /aɪ/ in *time*	–	–	+/–	+/–	+/–
Front-gliding /aʊ/ in *town*	■	■	–	+/–	–
Lowered /er/ in *bear*	■	■	–	–	–
Raised unglided /ɔ/ in *caught*	■	■	+/–	+/–	–
Fronted /o/ in *coat*	■	■	■	■	–
Morphosyntax					
NP 3rd pl. subj. verbal *-s* e.g., *The dogs barks*	■	■	+/–	–	–
Pro 3rd pl. subj. verbal *-s* e.g., *They barks*	–	■	–	–	–
3rd sing., *-s* absence e.g., *The dog go*	–	■	–	■	■
Habitual *be* verb *-ing* e.g., *Sometimes the dog be barking*	–	–	–	■	■
Copula absence e.g., *She nice*	–	■	–	■	■
Was regularisation e.g., *The dogs was nice*	■	■	■	■	■
Weren't regularisation e.g., *It weren't nice*	■	■	+/–	–	–

Figure 4.10   AAVE features in five communities (adapted from Wolfram 2000: 342)

common, and happens quite often. In these cases, as perhaps originally for AAVE, there is an added complication that aspects of the ancestral language may have an 'interference' or 'transference' effect on the language. This language contact phenomenon, especially among second-generation members of the ethnic community (i.e., the first to be born in the new country), has been documented to some degree (see Clyne et al. 2001), although it is often difficult to show without any doubt that a second-generation speaker uses particular variants because they are bilingual. That is, it is almost impossible to show that someone who speaks a language 'defectively' does so because of their bilingualism. Indians have long migrated to South Africa, and those who migrated were generally not native English speakers. Mesthrie (2002) finds that, as English is spoken more and more by Indian South Africans, a variety (Indian South African English or ISAE) seems to be developing, and many of the features that it exhibits are clearly 'transference' features from Indian languages (migrants hail from all over India and speak a number of languages). Examples are consonants showing retroflexion, the insertion of the copula after a *wh*-word in indirect questions (as in *Do you know what's roti?*), and a more common use of the partitive construction than in non-Indian varieties (as in *He's got too much of money*). Mesthrie (1996, 2002) provide a more extensive list.

One of the most complex situations when it comes to differentiation and language is that of the migration of Spanish-speaking groups to the United States. It is important to understand that Spanish has been in the United States about as long as English – indeed, in Texas and the southwest of the USA it has been spoken longer, since these parts were originally Spanish colonies and later part of Mexico – and that the USA has territories, such as Puerto Rico, where Spanish is the dominant language. However, there has always been a steady flow of migrants to the USA, particularly to California, the southwest, and the core cities of the north and northeast. Variation in the USA is complex, due to English–Spanish contact as well as contact among many different Spanish varieties, including Mexican, Puerto Rican, and other Caribbean varieties, as well as Central American varieties such as Salvadoran and Guatamalan. There is thus the possibility of an English variety arising, and also the possibility of a koine of several varieties of Spanish. Fought (2006: 74–5) provides an excellent list of the variety of codes that Latino Americans might have as linguistic choices. Chicano English, which is spoken by Mexican Americans in the west and southwest, is the most widely spoken, and shows features of 'interference' (see Fought 2003). In addition, this variety seems to be maintained for identity reasons in a similar manner to AAVE.

We might predict that, just as Indians in South Africa have created something of a common language of identity in ISAE, so Latinos in the USA would create a kind of koine variety of Spanish as they began to identify as Latinos and not specifically Mexicans or Puerto Ricans. Indeed, there is some evidence that something like this may be happening in New York City. Otheguy et al. (2007) found suggestive evidence that the use of personal pronouns was becoming more similar between speakers from six Latin American countries. On the other hand, Ghosh-Johnson (2005) shows that in Chicago, there is absolutely no accommodation going on because there is an antagonistic relationship between Puerto Ricans and Mexicans. In fact, there is differentiation both in the Spanish spoken by the groups, and in whether Spanish is spoken at all.

All of these examples show that ideologies about groups and identity differentiation are important ways that language variation patterns socially – how it is embedded in the speech community. In some cases, we may even want to argue that different races/ethnicities are part of separate speech communities, although this takes a fairly narrow view of what a speech community is. The question, of course, becomes why we might find this pattern, and especially whether we can suggest that it is 'just' speaker accommodation. Le Page and Tabouret-Keller (1985) argue that in a sense this is accommodation, not necessarily convergence with the current interlocutor, but convergence with and divergence from imagined speakers from the speech community. In this view, Black speakers will diverge from White speech in order to assert or perform their non-White identity.

The effects of ideology and identity are even clearer when it comes to gender variation. Gender is at once the most obvious and the most puzzling of social factors affecting variation, and it has some effect almost universally. It is paradoxical because of what Labov (1990) calls the pattern of intimate diversification, which refers to the fact that men and women interact and share networks in many cultures, but that they continue to act differently depending on their gender. Gender differentiation is probably the most recurrent social pattern in sociolinguistics. That is, if a speech community shows any social differentiation at all, then there is likely to be some gender differentiation. Along with class stratification and accommodation in networks, gender differentiation creates the main patterns that a theory of variation and change has to be able to explain.

Because gender has such a robust effect, it will not surprise readers at this stage in the book that Labov has identified some principles for gender differentiation. I will introduce these and then some of the studies that support them. Labov's first formulation of these principles comes from his article focusing on gender patterns (Labov 1990), in which he catalogues a large number of changes to support the principles. He makes a distinction again between stable variables and those involved in change, and between changes from above and changes from below, for those undergoing change:

> Principle I. For stable sociolinguistic variables, men use a higher frequency of 'non-standard' forms than women do.
> Principle Ia. In change from above, women favour the incoming prestige form more than men do.
> Principle II. In change from below, women are most often the innovators.

This leads to what he calls the gender paradox, in that women lead in both changes from above and changes from below.

The greater use of vernacular variants by men was found in one of the first studies of variation, that of the (ing) variable by Fischer (1958). His study of school children in New England found that boys used more of the [ɪn] variant than the girls. He also found a difference between so-called 'typical boys' and 'model boys', an issue we will return to later. This pattern has been repeated in study after study of this variable (Labov 1966; Wolfram 1969; Trudgill 1974; Houston 1985; among others). A good example is Trudgill's (1974) Norwich study, as shown in Figure 4.11.

Negative concord (NC) is another variable that often shows this pattern of gender distinction, as well as the class stratification discussed earlier. Eckert (2000) found a strong effect for gender for this variable, with men using more NC than women, as shown in Figure 4.12. ('Jocks' and 'Burnouts' are other social categories in the school, as explained below.)

Labov (2001) found similar results for Philadelphia. However, Fought (2003) found that gender has no difference for NC in her study of Chicano English in Los Angeles, even though there were gender differences for other variables in her study.

Principle Ia states that women lead changes from above. Labov's (1966) study of (r) in New York is again our most canonical example. However, there are many

76 Linguistic Variation and Change

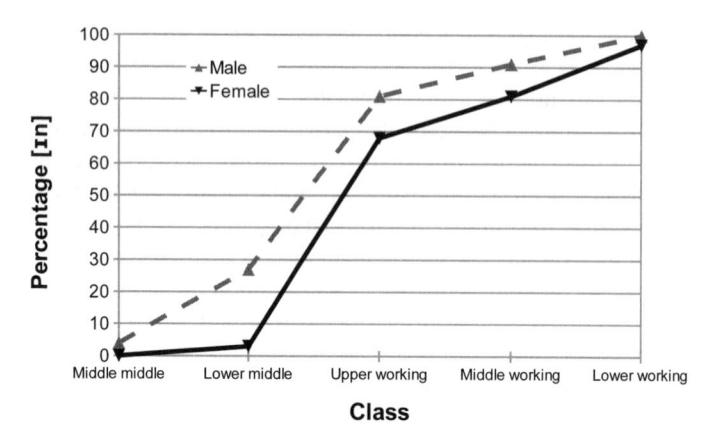

Figure 4.11 [ɪn] use in Norwich by gender and class (adapted from Trudgill 1974: 94)

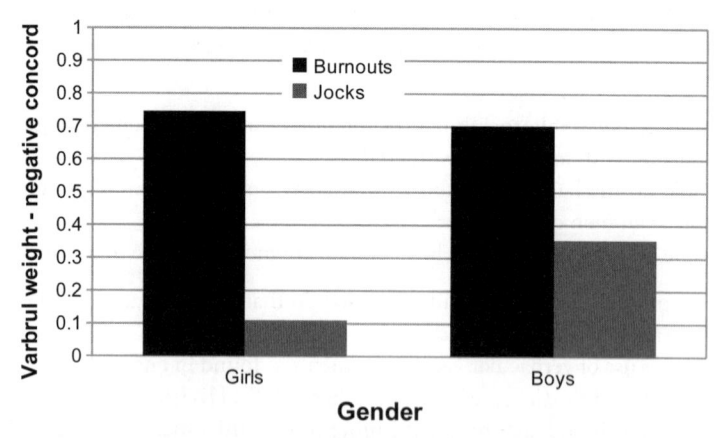

Figure 4.12 Negative concord in Detroit by gender and school category (adapted from Eckert 2000: 113)

other studies that show this same pattern. In Pittsburgh, /aʊ/-monophthongisation is clearly used more by men than women, and the age trend is to use less monophthongisation, as shown in Figure 4.13. Thus, we can say that women are leading in this change from above.

Principle II states that women lead in change from below. Again, there is ample evidence for this pattern, although there are more studies that run counter to this than to the other gender principles. Labov (1990) suggests that the first observation of this pattern was by Gauchat in the Swiss French village of Charmey. Quantitative support for this pattern can be seen in a number of studies (see Labov 1990, 2001a). A good example is Labov's (2001a) regression analyses of the vowel changes in Philadelphia. Out of fourteen vowel variables undergoing change, eleven show

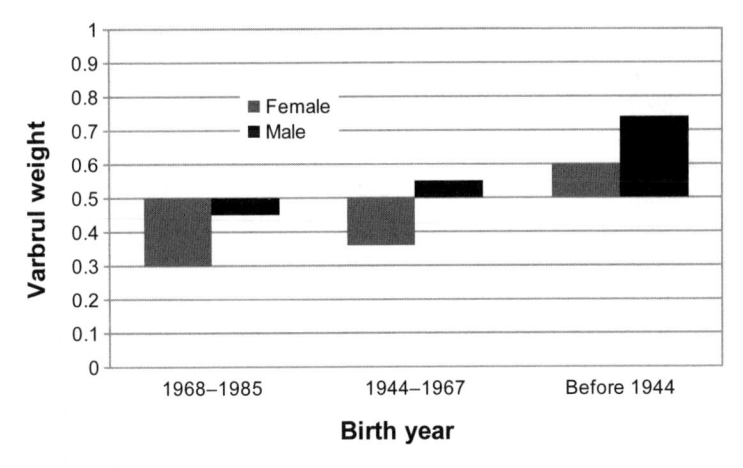

Figure 4.13 /aʊ/-monophthongisation in Pittsburgh by age and gender, 2005

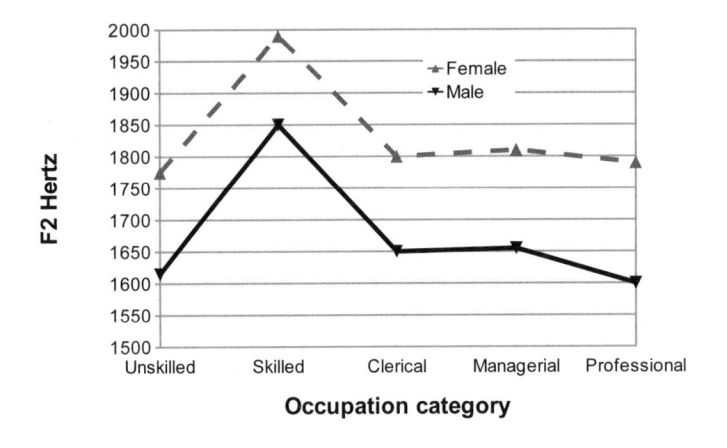

Figure 4.14 /oʊ/-fronting in Philadelphia by gender and occupation (adapted from Labov 2001a: 298)

that women are in advance. An example of the pattern, including class measures, is included in Figure 4.14. This shows the fronting of the nucleus of /oʊ/ in open syllables (higher F2 values indicate a fronted vowel), which is the canonical pattern that Principle II predicts.

These patterns are described by Labov as the *gender paradox* (2001a: 293): 'Women conform more closely than men to sociolinguistic norms that are overtly prescribed, but conform less than men when they are not.' It is worth unpacking this statement somewhat, and the assumptions contained in it, as a prelude to our discussion below of the challenges to the canonical patterns. First, the statement is formed in terms of what women do, which gives an impression that men are the

Table 4.3 Summary of canonical variation patterns

Social category \ Type of variable	Stable	Change from above	Change from below
Social Class	Local or vernacular variant used more by lower classes	Led by UC speakers, with a possible stylistic 'hypercorrection' by LMC or UWC	Led by 'interior' social classes such as UWC or LMC.
Sex/Gender	Vernacular variant used more by men.	New variant used by women more than men.	New variant used more by women than men in each social class.
Age	No regular pattern by age; vernacular may be used more by adolescents, and possibly older speakers	Younger speakers consistently use one variant more than older speakers; linear or curvilinear relationship.	Younger speakers consistently use one variant more than older speakers.
Race/Ethnicity	The majority or dominant group is seen as using the standard variant.	Changes are led by the majority or dominant group.	Changes are led by the minority or subordinated group.
Geography	Vernacular variant is often the local variant, some are vernacular in a number of places	Likely to take place either in several places at once, or the source will be a regional or national standard.	Spreads from older, working class regions in urban areas to less dense areas.

norm against which women should be measured, and that men are acting statically and women are acting in reaction. However, there's no reason this paradox could not be formulated in terms of men, who may seem just as paradoxical: they don't conform as much as women to overtly prescribed norms, but they do conform to non-overtly prescribed norms. In fact, this behaviour seems more paradoxical, because we would think that people who don't follow overt norms might require more explanation than those who do. Next, note that the language of change from above and below is represented in terms of norms that are 'overtly prescribed'. However, in his discussion Labov never explains exactly what it means to be overtly prescribed, and the exact mechanism of overt prescription. This topic will formulate much of our discussion in the challenges to the canonical patterns. Finally, we will need to pick apart what it means to *conform*: is this purely a quantification issue, or should we be more sensitive to how a variable is used in particular speech situations?

This discussion of gender brings the outline of canonical patterns to a close. Table 4.3 provides a summary of the canonical patterns, framed in terms of correlations for class, gender, age, race/ethnicity, and geography (age and geography have not been discussed explicitly). Patterns of differentiation do not fit so easily into this chart, but I have attempted it. Note that there should be a proviso that for race and ethnicity, we might find that a change in one group is rejected by another; that is, they diverge completely into what we might want to call two completely different speech communities.

The patterns discussed in this chapter thus far are those that one finds in most accounts of sociolinguistic variation. I call them canonical because in the academic discourse of variation and change, these studies and patterns loom large, and serve as reference points for newer studies. It is the equivalent in English literature of discussing a work suggesting an Oedipal complex and referring to *Hamlet*. While these are important and in some cases replicable and enduring findings, we also need to realise that we do find new data constantly, and that these patterns and the ways they have been formulated have been challenged.

CHALLENGES TO CANONICAL PATTERNS

We have seen that there are three main overall social patterns of variation: stratification, accommodation, and differentiation. Another way of thinking about these patterns is the kinds of motivations that have been suggested for each pattern: prestige, solidarity, and difference. So variationists have argued that in patterns of stratification, some kind of social prestige is attached to one variant and some kind of stigma to another. In accommodation patterns, speakers are motivated not by the prestige or stigma of the particular variant, but by solidarity with other speakers in their networks. Finally, patterns of differentiation are theorised to arise because speakers want to contrast their identity with a certain group (and at the same time identify with another group). The difficulty with these divisions is that at any time, a variant might be used for any of these purposes, or have any of these kinds of meanings. We will explore meaning and motivation extensively in the chapters to follow. In the rest of this chapter, however, we will explore some of the ways the patterns described above turn out to be more complex than at first imagined.

There are four ways that the canonical patterns have been complicated and challenged. First, in many studies researchers have found complex interactions among social variables. For example, we might find that men and women show different rates of a variant in one class, but no difference in another. Second, new studies are sometimes performed that provide counter-examples to the canonical patterns. Third, we find studies that rethink or refine the analytical terms used (such as class, age, ethnicity, and gender). Finally, we have to acknowledge studies in which there is no pattern where we would expect it. It would be convenient if research fell neatly into these categories, but in fact many studies challenge canonical patterns in more than one way. So for the rest of the chapter, we will review a few important studies that have led to a rethinking of some of these canonical patterns.

The first of these challenges some assumptions made about the concept of class. Rickford's (1986) analysis of class in the Guyanese village of Cane Walk leads to a questioning of how class is thought of in variation studies. The studies in the canonical tradition, such as Labov's New York City study, take a view of class – and indeed the speech community overall – that is a consensus, functionalist view (Durkheim 1933; Parsons 1964). This understanding of class is a *consensus* one in that it posits that variants used by the upper classes are valued by both the upper and the lower classes; even though the latter do not use these variants as much, the consensus view assumes that the lower classes concur with the view of their value. It should be noted that Labov argues that this is the case on the basis of the hypercorrection pattern and on 'subjective reaction tests', which explicitly ask speakers to make judgements about variants. The understanding is *functionalist* in that it views each class stratum as having a functional role in the workings of society. By contrast, a conflict view (Marx and Engels 1867; Weber 1947; Collins 1975) argues that people from different classes (such as the capitalist and proletariat classes) have different economic interests in society, and these are often in conflict. Such a view suggests that in fact working-class speakers may want to resist the prestige that is symbolised by the variants used by upper-class speakers because the working classes have no stake in that prestige system.

Rickford was able to demonstrate this conflict clearly. First, he realised as he did ethnographic work in Cane Walk that the kind of class measurements that variationists had used previously would fail completely there. The class system was much simpler, and was articulated by almost all of his informants. One class was the estate class, which was the larger group of speakers who did the hard physical labour on the sugar plantations for which the village had been built. The second class was the non-estate class, which was composed of 'drivers and field foremen on the sugar estate, and clerks, shopowners and skilled tradesmen who may have little if anything to do with the sugar estate' (1986: 217). Rickford found dramatic differences in the rates of usage of the first person, which varies between the Guyanese Creole *mi* and the English *ai*, as shown in Figure 4.15.

Here we see a sharp increase in the use of *ai* as we move from individuals in the estate class (EC) to the non-estate class (NEC). Rickford notes that

> contrary to what a thoroughly functionalist view might assume – that the EC speakers don't use standard English because they can't (through limited education, contact with speakers, etc.) – many EC speakers use creole rather than standard English as a matter of choice, as a revolutionary act, as a means of emphasizing solidarity over individual self-advancement and communicating political militancy rather than accommodation. (1986: 218)

The denizens of Cane Walk were quite aware of this linguistic difference, and the contrasting evaluations of the different variants. So while Rickford is careful not to throw out the idea of consensus in some communities altogether, we do need to question whether all uses of a variable are going to be evaluated on the class continuum in the same way as they are in the somewhat artificial situations in which speech is gathered for most sociolinguistic studies.

There is a third model: that of hegemony, articulated by Gramsci (1971). This captures both the conflict and the consensus models, arguing that the working classes do value the speech of the upper class, because they have been conditioned to believe that what is in the interests of the upper classes is in their interest, whereas in actuality it is not. It is worth noting that we might say that the EC speakers of Cane

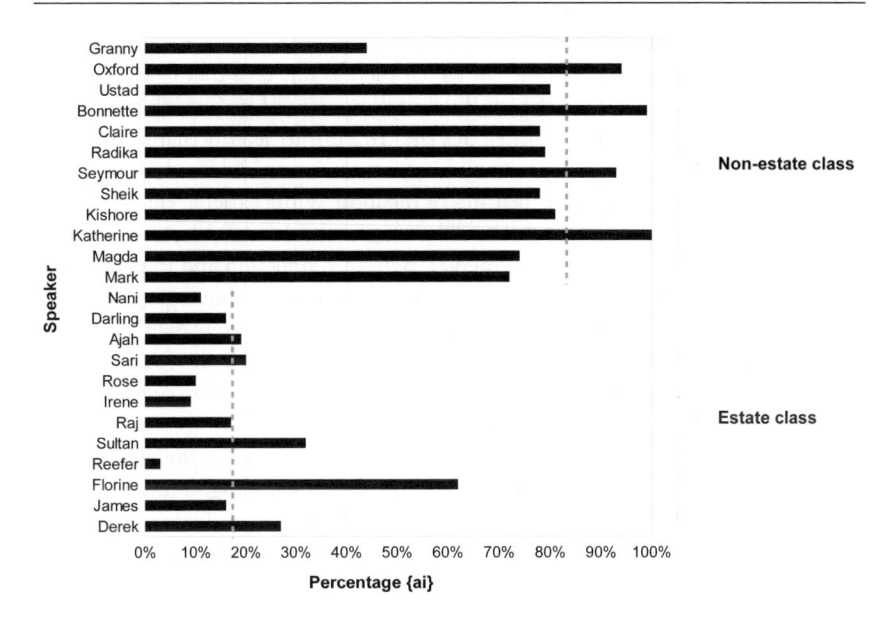

Figure 4.15 Amount of English *ai* used by individuals in Cane Walk, ordered by class (adapted from Rickford 1986: 218)

Walk had more of a conflict orientation because their situation was so clear, and the elites dominated not through hegemony but through raw economic and physical force. One of Rickford's main points, however, was not that the consensus models were necessarily wrong, but that they are culturally constructed and variable, and that views of class and the canonical patterns surrounding those views should not be seen as universal, and especially not as timeless.

Others have shown that not all variables are differentiated in situations where we might predict it. The identity-and-ideological dimension of race differentiation is most clearly shown in a recent study by Maeve Eberhardt in Pittsburgh (Eberhardt 2009a, 2009b), in which two different variables behave differently depending on how much each has ideological associations with race. Eberhardt was interested in whether the African American community in Pittsburgh was adopting any features of the White variety (as the older Hyde County African Americans did) or whether they were orienting more towards AAVE. She chose two phonological variables to investigate, both present in the local White variety but absent in all descriptions of AAVE. One was /aʊ/-monophthongisation, described earlier in Chapter 2, while the second was the so-called low-back merger (LBM), also referred to as the *cot–caught* merger because words in these two classes are pronounced the same and speakers cannot hear any small differences in their pronunciation, even when they are present (see the discussion in Chapter 8). The LBM is present in several varieties in North America, including Canadian English, the Midlands of the USA, and the West of the USA.

Pittsburgh, like most US cities, shows patterns of housing segregation by race, although neighbourhoods that are now mostly monoracial were not always that way. In addition, unlike other cities in which there is one area that is identified as an African American neighbourhood, Pittsburgh has several such neighbourhoods, which are also somewhat distinguished by class. This history led Eberhardt to suspect that there might have been enough contact and interaction to lead Pittsburgh African Americans to use some linguistic features of the local White variety. The analysis of of the LBM supported this hypothesis: all but one of the African American speakers that Eberhardt analysed showed the merger, both in production and in perception. This result suggests that in fact the two groups' varieties are converging, and that there is less difference in Black and White varieties in Pittsburgh than elsewhere. However, when Eberhardt analysed /aʊ/-monophthongisation, she found that *no* African American speakers showed evidence of monophthongisation, suggesting the opposite conclusion of that for the LBM.

The key to the difference is the status of these two variables in the community. Using the canonical terms we have discussed above, monophthongisation is a change from above the level of consciousness, while the LBM is not. In fact, monophthongisation is the subject of lots of talk by White Pittsburghers, and appears on T-shirts, mugs, and representations of localness in local media. Moreover, when Eberhardt asked speakers about this feature, many knew what she was talking about and explicitly identified it as a 'White thing.' On the other hand 'the low-back merger is not the subject of metalinguistic talk in the city, nor does it appear in representations of the local dialect, nor generally does it feature in performances of local speech' (2009a: 207). The distinction of the two variables shows quite neatly that the resistance of African American speakers to monophthongisation is not a mechanical effect such as limited contact or networks, because for the variable that is less salient in the speech community, there is no such resistance. The difference in African American and White monopthongisation rates in Pittsburgh is thus due to identity and ideological factors.

Penelope Eckert has similarly taken on the way variation is conceptualised, as well as challenging the notion of conformity used by Labov. Her work shows a rethinking of how interactions among class and gender undermine the canonical patterns. In fact, Eckert and McConnell-Ginet (2003: 292) argue that the notion that women's speech is more standard is a 'hall of mirrors'. Before we explore how Eckert addresses this claim, we should also note that her study of variation in a high school near Detroit, Michigan, particularly as it is presented in her (2000) book, has revolutionised how variationists think about the social categories they investigate.

One of Eckert's important innovations is that the social categories she uses in her analysis are based on those that are relevant to the speakers she is studying. In addition, the categories formed by interactions (e.g., 'White working-class woman') are seen not as additions, multiplications, or combinations of the interacting categories, but as unique categories on their own terms. Thus, Eckert found that in a number of ways the school resolved itself into two social poles – *jocks* and *burnouts*. The jocks were students who were aligned with the corporate, college-bound culture of the school, and participated more in school activities, while the burnouts were

Table 4.4 Percentage of negative concord among Detroit high school students

Jock Girls	Jock Boys	Burned-out Burnout Girls	Other Burnout Girls	Burnout Boys
2	19	50	40	45

primarily oriented towards concerns outside school. Eckert shows that a number of social practices and norms define the poles of these groups: how widely students cuff their jeans, which students go cruising into Detroit on the weekends, take illegal drugs, drink alcoholic beverages, etc. She argues that linguistic variation is a social practice like these others, used to create personal styles in the same way as dress and activities. Note that while there is some correlation between 'jock' and 'middle-class' and between 'burnout' and 'working-class' (determined by measuring parents' class in the canonical manner), Eckert finds that class measures are not as robust as the locally relevant jock and burnout categories.

Eckert's linguistic variables were mostly the vowels of the Northern Cities Shift (see Chapter 8), but she also analysed the use of negative concord. Table 4.4 shows the percent of negative concord for the particular categories and gender groups (Eckert and McConnell-Ginet 2003: 295).

Here we see that there is a big difference for gender in the jock category, but almost no difference in the burnout category. In addition, Eckert identified one network cluster of girls she calls the 'burned-out burnouts' who exemplified the practices of the burnout category in the extreme, including language. Their average percentage use of negative concord is 50 per cent, the highest in Table 4.4.

Even using more traditional class measures, Labov (2001a) finds similar patterns for some variables. For example, for (ing), he finds a big gender gap in the middle classes, but almost no difference in the working classes. The pattern is even more striking in the 'change from below', the raising of /æ/ before /s/. Figure 4.16 shows that in the lower occupational groups, women use more raised variants, while in the upper occupations, this pattern is reversed and men use more.

Doxsey (2005) found a similar pattern. She analysed the loss of the traditional /ai/-monophthongisation in a small town in coastal Alabama. She found that, while women were in the lead for this change for the middle and upper classes, the reverse was true for the working class.

I checked to see whether there were any patterns like this in Pittsburgh. The results are shown in Figure 4.17, and provide another example of this gender crossover pattern that challenges the generalisation that women are more conservative or standard. Here, education is taken as a class measure. In general, men use more monophthongisation than women, but in the lowest educational group, the use of monophthongisation by women increases far beyond that of men.

So for the changes from below, the generalisation we can make, if any, is that women tend to be at the extremes of the status spectrum, and it is this more general pattern that needs to be explained rather than the conformity or standardness of women.

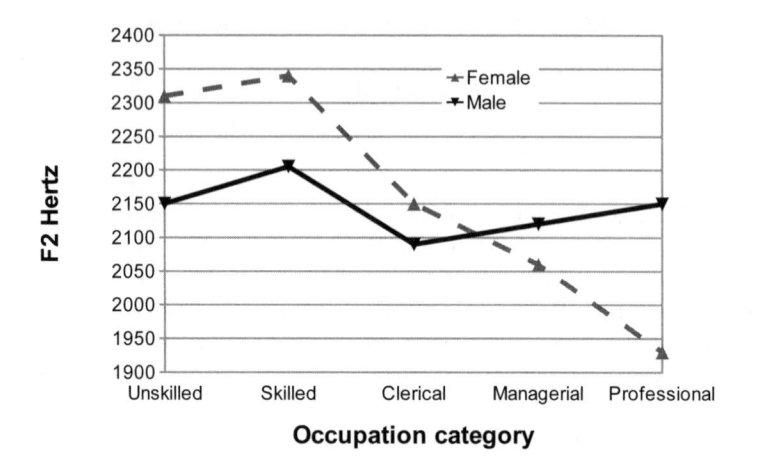

Figure 4.16 (ae)-raising in Philadelphia by gender and occupation (adapted from Labov 2001a: 298)

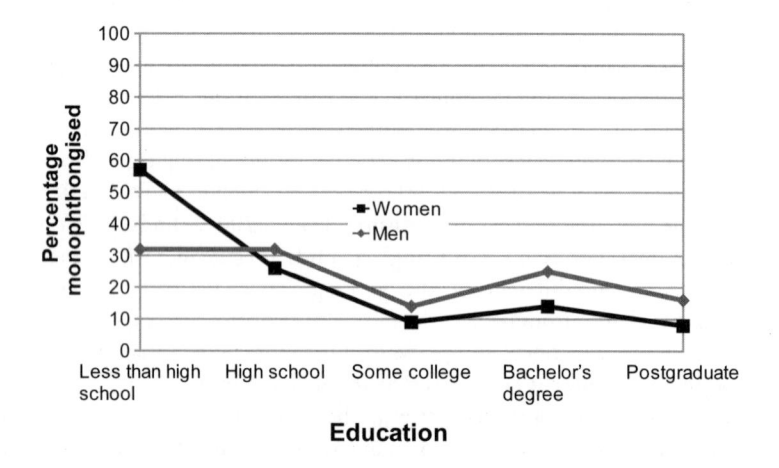

Figure 4.17 /aʊ/-monophthongisation in Pittsburgh by gender and education

Eckert also prefigures Labov (2001a) in differentiating variables in terms not of whether they are changing or not, but of what stage of change they are in. Eckert (1989: 262) shows that the differences in gender appear only in the older, more established changes in the set she is studying (the Northern Cities Shift, described in detail in Chapter 8), while the newer changes are differentiated along jock–burnout lines. Here again, our simple categories of change are complicated in ways that lead to a more sensitive understanding of the embedding of variation in the speech community.

Two more studies challenge how we think about stratification and the relationship of gender to it. Sidnell (1999) performed ethnographic research in a village in Guyana, and analysed the gendered use of the same variable as Rickford. He found that men tended to use the more standard *ai* variant more than women did. He argued that this difference had to do with the fact that when women used *ai* too much they ran the risk of seeming 'uppity', and so they avoided it. Haeri (1997) found men using more of a standard variant as well, but for different reasons. The variable she investigated was the *qaf*, in Cairo, Egypt, where there are really three relevant varieties: colloquial Arabic, Modern Standard Arabic, and Classical Arabic. Classical Arabic is not spoken outside religious and education settings, but it makes a distinction between a /q/ (a voiceless uvular stop) and /ʔ/ (glottal stop). This distinction has been lost in modern Arabic, and both phonemes have merged in the glottal stop. However, the use of /q/ in the correct environments carries prestige, and men use it more than women, which is the opposite of what is predicted by Labov's Principle Ia. We thus find a number of further challenges to the idea that there is a single kind of prestige variant that can easily be correlated with gender or class.

Another innovation in Eckert's work is how she groups her speakers. Her work introduces the concept of the *community of practice* (introduced in Eckert and McConnell-Ginet 1992), which is generally smaller and more coherent than a speech community. Jocks and burnouts form different communities of practice, because they engage in different practices and have different norms in many social domains. Eckert (2000: 35) explains the concept:

> A Community of Practice is an aggregate of people who come together around some enterprise. United by this common enterprise, people come to develop and share ways of doing things, ways of talking, beliefs, values – in short, practices – as a function of their joint engagement in activity. Simultaneously, social relationships form around the activities and activities form around relationships . . . It is not the assemblage or the purpose that defines the community of practice; rather, a community of practice is simultaneously defined by its membership and the shared practice in which that membership engages.

This concept provides a level of organisation for the creation of norms that is similar to social networks, although it is focused on the group rather than the individuals in the group, and the meaning and practices represented by social network ties. It is thus a very useful concept for mediating networks, communities, and the kinds of social categories discussed above (class, gender, etc.). Eckert's methods have inspired a number of similar studies in the USA (Mendoza-Denton 2008), the UK (Moore 2003; Lawson 2009), and Denmark (Maegaard 2007). Fought (1999) is another study with a similar orientation, although it does not use the community of practice terminology, as is Cheshire's (1982) study of working-class adolescents in Reading, England. Cheshire found that the degree of engagement in 'vernacular culture' was an important predictor for a number of variables. Her vernacular culture is a good example of a community of practice, as the kids oriented in this way engaged in practices stereotypically associated with the working class.

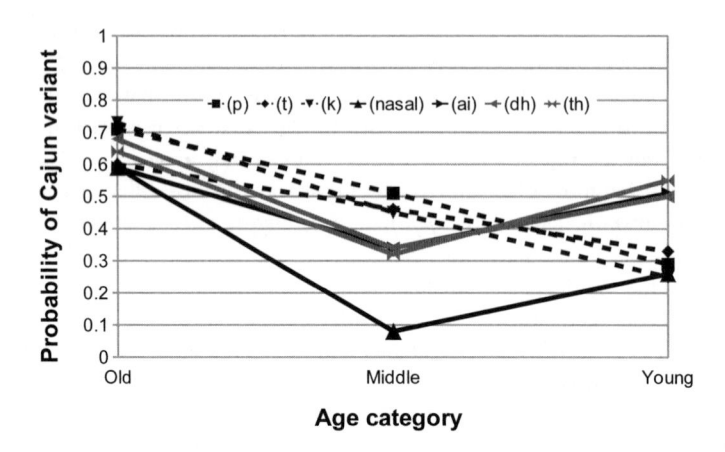

Figure 4.18 Cajun English variants by age (adapted from Dubois and Horvath 1999: 293)

Dubois and Horvath's (1999) article on the use of Cajun English variables in Louisiana, USA, offers some important critiques of and innovations to almost all of the canon: they question the notion of change from above and below, and even the idea of a stable variable, and of course the gender pattern outlined by Labov. Like others, they show the importance of a deep understanding of the community being analysed, but they show how the local history and culture can produce a complex interaction of social factors that suggests generalisations about these social factors are premature. Their study focuses on two sets of variables, which can effectively be treated as two variables for the most part. The first is the non-aspiration of voiceless stops, which I will call (ptk). The 'Cajun' variant shows a lack of aspiration where standard American English would be predicted to have it (e.g., not as the last element in a consonant cluster). The second variable is the replacement of /θ/ and /ð/ with dental stops – (th) and (dh); heavy nasalisation – (nas); and the monophthongisation of /ai/ – (ai). Their data are in general split into three generations. These variables give two different age patterns, shown in Figure 4.18.

The first pattern is shown only by (ptk), and shows a steady decrease over the three generations. The other variables show a v-shaped curve, in which the use of non-standard variables drops off considerably in the middle age group, and then increases in the final one. This overall picture is only background to the important distinctions Dubois and Horvath find for gender and network. For (ptk), there is a clear gender difference as women lead the change towards the non-Cajun use of the variable. For (nas) and (ai), there is no gender difference in the two oldest groups, but in the youngest generation, the men use more of the Cajun variant than women, as shown in Figure 4.19.

A similar but even more complex pattern takes place for (dh) and (th). Here we find a gender difference, but it interacts with network, which Dubois and Horvath characterise as 'open' or 'closed', with closed networks being more locally and Cajun

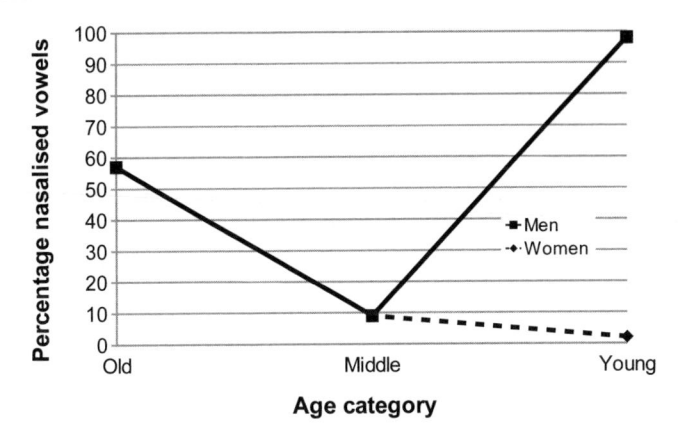

Figure 4.19 Nasalisation in Cajun English by gender and age (adapted from Dubois and Horvath 1999: 294)

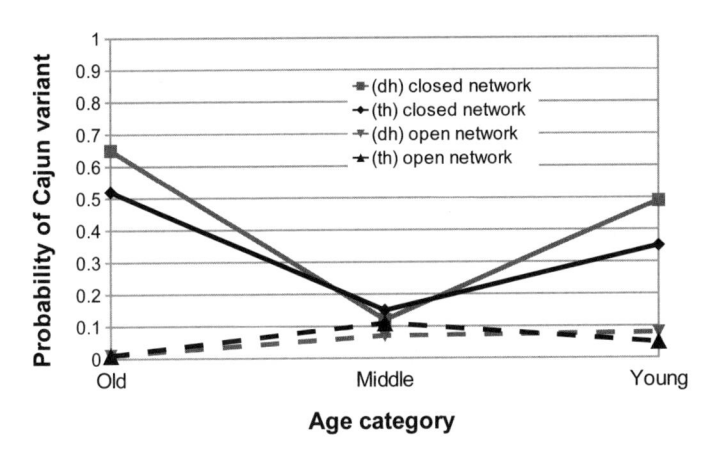

Figure 4.20 (dh) and (th) stopping by Louisiana women, by age group and network type (adapted from Dubois and Horvath 1999: 295)

focused. The status of the network is important for the women but not for the men. The men show the familiar v-shaped age pattern for both kinds of networks (with the exception of the (dh) open network, who show a linear increase), while for the women it is only those in closed networks who show this pattern. See Figure 4.20, which shows the rates of the two variables for women in both open and closed networks.

Dubois and Horvath go on to show how these network and gender patterns are related to the linguistic markets and social practices the speakers engage in. They argue that the v-shaped age pattern is related to the status of the Cajun identity in Louisiana. For the middle-aged group, it was highly stigmatised when this age cohort was young, as was the language, but the younger generation has grown up during a 'Cajun Renaissance'. The gender effect is the result of the Cajun identity being attached more to male Cajunness than to female Cajunness – it takes the shape of outward Cajun performances and cooking that is traditionally male. The linguistic marketplace is also an explanation for the network pattern. An open network generally means that the speaker is employed outside the home or small town, and has contact with non-Cajuns. For men, this contact may increase their use of Cajun variants, which have become a valuable commodity, especially in the tourist industry. But since femininity is less attached to Cajunness, the women use fewer Cajun variants.

Dubois and Horvath also argue that we need to use more precise terms than 'change from above' and 'change from below'. These researchers identify changes as either adoption or innovation. Adoption occurs when the incoming variant is a norm from another speech community. In the Cajun case, the aspiration of stops is an adoption. Another example would be the retroflex /r/ in Labov's (1966) study. Dubois and Horvath suggest that this process is 'a fundamentally social phenomenon with a linguistic dimension' (1999: 302). Innovation, on the other hand, is 'a fundamentally linguistic process with a social dimension' (1999: 302), and concerns changes that originate from within the speech community. This language is similar to Guy's (1990) distinction (which parallels work in language contact; see Sankoff 2004) among spontaneous change, borrowing, and imposition; Dubois and Horvath essentially collapse the distinction between borrowing and imposition. It is also similar to Labov's (2007) distinction between change by transmission and by diffusion. Dubois and Horvath use this distinction more productively, however, to line up historical events with the adoption and recycling of the variants, where recycling refers to the reuse of variants that were on the wane, such as all the non-(ptk) variables.

In Newcastle-upon-Tyne, England, there exists a similarly complex pattern for stops, although in this case they are either glottalised or replaced by a glottal stop, as explained in Chapter 2. Milroy et al. (1994) show that glottal replacement is a change that is expanding across the UK, and that in many places it is women who use it more. These authors provide evidence that this is the case in Newcastle. However, there is another variant there, which they refer to as glottalisation, and this is used more by the local men. There are interesting parallels here with the Cajun example, as we can think of glottalisation as a (fairly old, and local) innovation, whereas glottal replacement is an adoption. We might be tempted to generalise, then, that men are more likely to recycle older innovations, but there is probably not enough evidence to make such a broad claim. As Dubois and Horvath show, we need to take into account the local history and practices of the speakers to determine the status of the variables and to provide an explanation for the patterns we find.

What have these challenges taught us about the ways we should view social patterns of variation and change? Can we still make generalisations? Yes, there a number of ways we can still make them; one of the reasons I have organised this chapter as I have is that we can make better generalisations when we use more abstract terms such as stratification, accommodation, and differentiation. At the most abstract, we can note that these are three basic patterns, and in some senses, they form general explanations on the dimensions of power and solidarity, or status and friendship. Some variables display power or prestige. Prestige and power are imprecise words, however, so we are better off operationalising this idea for each study by noting that prestige or power represents some level of worth in a social marketplace, and that such a marketplace is not always accessible to everyone in the same way. Thus Cajun men operate in a different linguistic marketplace from Cajun women, and jocks and burnouts may similarly be operating in different markets. This perspective may carry over to many gender differences, as men and women have different orientations not just to the economic marketplace, but also to what Eckert calls the heterosexual marketplace. In other words, a valuable straight man performs social practices, and symbolises them linguistically differently from a valuable straight woman. The embedding of variation in society is thus likely to pattern at least partially by these different kinds of markets. Other variants are related to accommodation and solidarity. But this accommodation is not necessarily automatic. We tend to talk the way people we like do, and hope that by doing so we will make others like us. The key to understanding this pattern is to determine which variables and variants are more or less imbued with market value.

As Dubois and Horvath argue, 'Since the 1960s, urban language surveys have designed samples of speakers using the social categories of age, sex, social class, and ethnicity in order to ensure that the sample includes all types of relevant people in a speech community. The real problem comes in using these same categories in the interpretation of results' (1999: 289). In other words, describing patterns in terms of these categories is not an explanation. Explanations for social patterns come from understanding what variants symbolise for different speakers in a speech community, how history, ideologies, and practices imbue the variants with meaning, and why a variant is a desirable way of speaking for those speakers who use it. So these patterns trace people's and communities' lives – their practices, networks, markets, and ideologies about language – and the explanations will need to relate to these lives, and their everyday use of variation. In a way, the work that we might consider to be the beginning of the variationist canon – Labov's study of Martha's Vineyard – takes this perspective, as we learn about the young man who moved to Boston but wanted to come back to the island, and how his mother noticed a change in his speech after he had been back on the island for a while. What we need, then, is to look more into the process of how speakers use variables to create social meanings in their daily interactions, and this is where we go in the next chapter.

Chapter 5

Social patterns II: intraspeaker variation

As we search for patterns of variation and change in the speech community, one of the challenges is how to represent the fact that individual speakers use different ways of speaking in different situations. In most of our discussion to this point, we have considered speakers in speech communities to be single 'data points', often with one value for the rate of use for a particular variant, or even the rate of use for a group of speakers based on class, race, gender, etc. However, it is axiomatic that there are no speakers who speak exactly the same way all the time. This *intraspeaker variation* is also structured in the community, and points us to explanations for the larger patterns discussed in the previous chapter. So in this chapter we will review the kinds of intraspeaker variation patterns that have been found and various explanations for such patterns, before moving to explanations for both kinds of social patterning in the next chapter.

INTRASPEAKER PATTERNS, COMMUNITY PATTERNS, AND STYLE

As noted in the previous chapter, even in his early study of New York City, Labov was concerned with intraspeaker variation. In that study, followed by later works by others such as Trudgill (1974), Labov shows that we can correlate measures of *attention paid to speech* with rates of use. This within-speaker variation is an important fact that variation studies must address, for a number of reasons. First, as we have seen Labov pithily summarise it, we do not want to compare 'a casual salesman to a careful pipefitter' (1972b: 240) and conclude that the patterning of their overall variation is the same. If our goal is to discover how variation is embedded and constrained in a speech community, we need to know the effect of both identity and speech event, and we need to be able to separate the two. Thus, it is argued, we need a method for comparing a careful lawyer with a careful factory worker. The second reason such studies are important is that the overall patterning can indicate the distribution of the values attached to the variants in a speech community. Labov argues, for example, that the consistent rise of (r) constriction in more careful speech for all speakers suggests that this is the prestige variant, on the assumption that when people pay attention to their speech, they are likely to shift to what is

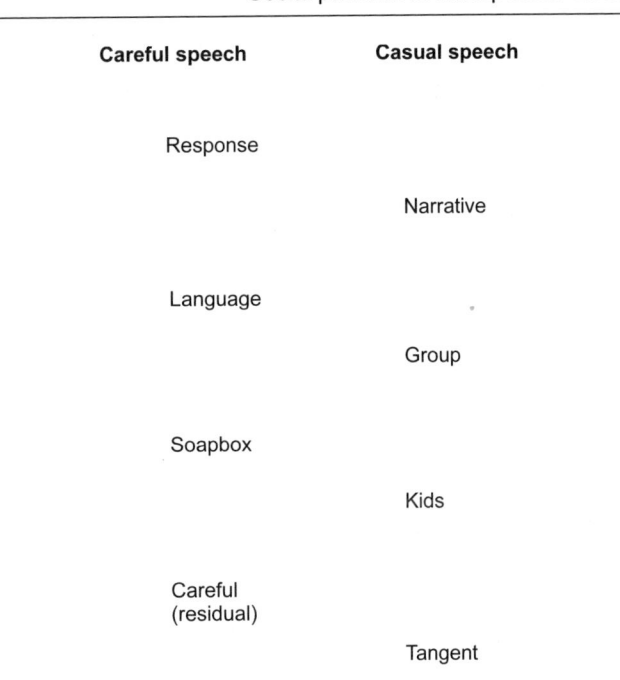

Careful speech	Casual speech
Response	
	Narrative
Language	
	Group
Soapbox	
	Kids
Careful (residual)	
	Tangent

Figure 5.1 Labov's decision tree for coding attention to speech (after Labov 2001b: 94)

the most prestigious (although this is an assumption, and it has been challenged by some recent research, most notably Schilling-Estes 1998, discussed below). Finally, intraspeaker variation can provide a window on the linguistic organisation of the speech community: it forms another dimension of norms about which kinds of speech should be used in what kinds of situations. This understanding of intraspeaker variation takes us beyond the casual–careful continuum and suggests that variation is embedded and constrained in the speech community by other kinds of speech norms in addition to identity and prestige.

Labov's work in this dimension displays a characteristic focus on objectivity, and his approach to individual variation – which he calls style – is no exception. He developed a coding scheme in the form of a decision tree (shown in Figure 5.1) that allows a coder to put each token of a variable into a style category.

As we saw in the discussion of Labov's study in the previous chapter, there was a correlation between the class pattern found in the speech community and the direction of style shifting: more 'careful' styles were correlated with the highest classes. This pattern is probably the most prototypical in variationist sociolinguistics studies, and is an important finding and insight into the embedding of variation in the speech community. Since Labov's development of this method, however, the sub-field of *sociolinguistic style* has developed considerably. In the rest of this section, I provide a review of the canonical studies of style; that is, how it is normally presented in texts and how most sociolinguists probably think about it. I also provide a short explanation of some of the recent challenges. The remainder of the chapter is a reorganisation of the subject of intraspeaker variation, which I believe provides a way of integrating the interspeaker and intraspeaker patterns, addressed in the next chapter.

Before we address the canonical patterns of intraspeaker variation, we should clear up the ways that the term *style* has been used in variationist studies in sociolinguistics, because different researchers have conceived of it in different ways. Each conception is perfectly valid but it is important to be aware of these conceptions because they can cause confusion if they are not kept separate. The first is simply intraspeaker variation, as discussed by Labov: what is the type of speech situation (or what does the speaker understand the speech situation to be), and how do they shift from one type of situation to another? A more recent view sees style as being like style in fashion: a set of speech practices (such as variables) that pattern together to provide a certain kind of style, much as different clothes and accessories can be combined to create different kinds of styles depending on their combination. This latter concept of style is discussed by Eckert (Eckert and Rickford 2001: 123) as 'a clustering of linguistic resources', such that the clustering leads to some social meaning or even a group identity (such as 'Valley Girl' or 'New York Jew'). Of course these two views can be combined to some extent, so that we might find that variables pattern together in different speech situations (or when people are more or less 'careful'), but it is possible to separate them, and most researchers do not discuss them both under the title 'style'. It is also for this reason that I will be clear when discussing the two as either intraspeaker variation (Labovian style) or variable co-occurrence (Eckertian style).

Intraspeaker variation (IV) under the term 'style' has been the subject of less research than interspeaker or group variation, for the simple reason that originally IV had been measured to facilitate the study of interspeaker variation in the ways noted above. But over the years the theorising of IV as style has been the topic of a number of theoretical statements that connect it to interspeaker variation. Reaction to Labov's 'attention to speech' model of IV criticised two main things. First, it modelled only a single dimension of IV; people change the way they speak for other reasons in addition to how much attention they are paying to speech. Second, paying attention to speech can have different effects depending on how speakers are paying attention to it. For example, Schilling-Estes (1998) shows that speakers sometimes produce speech that is *more* vernacular when they are paying attention to it. It has become clear that while attention to speech produces the regularity that Labov observes, this is a pattern that requires explanation rather than an explanation in itself. Note that this means we still need to be able to explain why Labov's measures produce the regular patterning that they do.

Allan Bell (1984, 2001) was one of the first to argue for a rethinking and theorisation of style based on whom the speaker is talking to. He articulated an 'audience design' (AD) model following the accommodation theories of Giles et al. (Giles 1973; Giles et al. 1973, 1991; Giles and Powesland 1975) and the division of different types of hearer by Goffman (1981). In essence, style shifting in AD is accommodation to the addressee, and to a lesser extent to other participants in a speech event, such as overhearers and possible eavesdroppers. The usual direction of shift is convergence towards the speech of audience members. However, speakers may initiate shifts in which they diverge from their audience in order to dissociate from this audience and converge with a non-present reference group. The primary direction of shift, nevertheless, is responsive or accommodative. Bell argues, especially on the basis of data from radio announcers on different radio channels, that speakers also accommodate to a 'referee', or an imagined, idealised addressee. Finally, he suggests that speakers do not always simply follow the speech of another, but may initiate a change in the chosen referee. But it is not clear how this explains the regular patterns that Labov finds for attention to speech; presumably we would say that Labov is detecting a subtle change in the referee.

The 'acts of identity' model for IV focuses more on this idea of the referee, although that is not the term used in this model. This approach is articulated by Le Page and Tabouret-Keller, who developed it to address patterns in creole languages in the Caribbean. They argue that

> the individual creates for himself [*sic*] the patterns of his linguistic behaviour so as to resemble those of the group or groups with which from time to time he wishes to be identified, or so as to be unlike those from whom he wishes to be distinguished . . . speech acts are acts of projection: the speaker is projecting his inner universe, implicitly with the invitation to others to share it . . . By verbalising as he does, he is seeking to reinforce his models of the world, and hopes for acts of solidarity from those with whom he wishes to identify. (Le Page and Tabouret-Keller 1985: 181)

This view is of course similar to the referee design of Bell, but it is more focused on the speaker and their alignment with different groups who might form referees. As Coupland (2007) points out, it is also vague as to what is meant by 'projecting' and 'wishing to identify with'.

We thus have three axes upon which IV is explained. One is a language-focused axis, with a formal-to-casual continuum, which implicitly posits that speakers are either 'naturally' speaking their one vernacular, or 'unnaturally' speaking another variety imposed upon them. Second, we have a hearer-focused axis, with speakers changing their speech depending on their interlocutor, real or imagined. Finally, we have a speaker-focused axis, so that a speaker accomplishes an 'act of identity' regarding herself or himself, essentially making a statement about identity when using certain variants.

All of these motivations suggest that there is essentially one overriding motivation for speakers to change the kinds of choices they make about language. But sociolinguistics and related disciplines – especially in linguistic anthropology – have found a wide range of ways in which speech is connected with non-linguistic contextual factors. Therefore, in the rest of this chapter, we will explore the various constructs that can be used to explain such shifts. I believe that all have a role to play, especially depending on the native understanding of language forms in a speech community. That is, in some communities identities may be important; in others it may be that addressees are more important. Nor are all of the motivations necessarily separable (a change in addressee may in fact change the kind of identity one wishes to 'project'). In the end we want to be able to explain the patterns of linguistic organisation that we find, on the basis of what the speakers themselves do and know. If we realise that speakers understand themselves to be *being someone and doing something related to other social actors*, we will be able to move towards an explanation for the social patterns of variation.

REGISTER, SPEECH ACTIVITY, SPEECH EVENT, GENRE, FRAME

In addition to the identity-focused and audience-focused motivations for IV, another way to organise IV is to find differences in the way speakers use variables depending on how the speaker perceives 'what is going on'. This 'what is going on' can be and has been variously conceived of as *register, speech activity, speech event, genre,* and *frame*. These are all terms for ways of thinking about or describing recurring practices that include speech, and can conceivably be used to compare intraspeaker variation. All the terms come from the insight that talk in a speech community is not an endless, undifferentiated flow, and most of this talk is different from the sociolinguistic interview upon which so many sociolinguistic data are based. Speakers in the community have a sense of what differentiates situations, and can articulate to some degree what is appropriate and what is not in each of those speech situations. This organisation of speech events includes terms used by variationists to describe different kinds of speech: formal–informal, casual–careful, standard–vernacular. While variation studies have normally considered speech only in terms of these continua, let's look at the different terms introduced above and how they can be used with these more common terms.

All of these terms – register, speech activity, speech event, genre, and frame – represent different ways of noticing structure or norms in a speech community. Let's begin with register, which for our purposes will be very similar to a style. A *register* is a set of connected linguistic practices that are associated with a group of speech situations in a speech community, or with an institution in a speech community. We might speak of a more formal style of English, where we use grammar that is more complex (i.e., more embedded clauses), words that are more Latinate, and pronunciation that is more fully articulated. Registers might be more specialised, such as the one a doctor uses to talk to her colleagues. We thus might think of the standard–vernacular continuum often assumed in variation studies as a register continuum to the extent that the speech community recognises these kinds of shifts in regular ways. The attention-paid-to-speech definition of IV assumes that when people pay more attention to how they are speaking, they move their register 'up' to the more standard. But note that this view assumes that there is an understanding – an *ideology* – in the speech community that organises registers in terms of standard and vernacular. While this organisation of speech may seem obvious to many students, this obviousness is precisely what makes it an ideology. Other registers can be imagined. In fact, in English churches there is often another register that is even more formal and sounds more like an older form of English than the standard register. In the next chapter, we will expand the idea of register following the work of Asif Agha (2007).

A *speech activity* is a recognised, repeatable activity in a speech community which has speech as an important part of its definition. Lecturing is a speech activity that students are familiar with, and one that often happens in classrooms, but aspects of lecturing – such as a long turn at talk, complex phrase structure, or explaining in detail – can be used at times when they are not so appropriate. In fact, younger students will probably recall recent instances of telling their parents that they should not lecture them. A *speech event* is an instance of an event that is speech-focused. It can be thought of as a particular token of a speech activity: *a* lecture, *a* class meeting, *a* conversation, etc. The speech event is the focus of an approach to language and culture known as the *ethnography of speaking* or the *ethnography of communication*, articulated first by Hymes (e.g., Hymes 1972); a book-length treatment is Saville-Troike (2003; see also Kiesling forthcoming). The ethnography of speaking has as its general goal an articulation of the emic (or insider) knowledge that a speaker needs to have to be *communicatively competent* in a language, and thus tries to represent how speakers think about the kinds of speech events and the language used in them in their speech communities. Common components of the speech event as discussed by Hymes are the setting, participants, ends (goals and outcomes), act structure, key (the 'tone, manner or spirit'; Hymes 1986: 62), instrumentalities (channels – spoken, signed, written – and forms of speech: variants), norms of language (e.g., turn taking, who may speak when), and genre. Speech activities are fruitful ways through which to organise an analysis of variation in a community from speaker to speaker.

Genre, also part of the ethnography-of-speaking framework, is a tricky concept, partly because the term is used in so many ways in different traditions. In Hymes's use, it is very similar to speech activity. He gives examples such as 'poem, myth, tale, proverb, riddle, curse, oration, lecture, commercial, form letter, editorial, etc.' (1986: 65). Importantly, he argues that 'genres often coincide with speech events, but must be treated as analytically independent of them', and notes that 'the sermon as a genre is typically identical with a certain place in a church service, but its properties may be invoked, for serious or humorous effect, in other situations' (1986: 65). Genres thus have formal characteristics that can be transported from one speech event to another. Note that some of the ways that Labov codes for attention paid to speech are based on what speech activity or genre is going on – thus, 'soapbox' style is a speech activity very similar to lecturing. In addition, both participants and norms can encompass the kinds of information discussed under the acts-of-identity and audience-design approaches to style.

Frames (Goffman 1974) are explicitly centred on the ongoing interaction, and how speakers are orienting to 'what is going on'. 'Frame' is a term not used in the ethnography of speaking, but is related to the notion of genre and speech event. One of the important facets of approaches using framing is that they posit that the speech we use is not just a reaction to the frame, but in fact the linguistic choices are used by speakers to indicate what they think the frame currently is, or to shift the frame. One of the best-known examples of this sort of interactional analysis is Tannen and Wallat's (1982) analysis of a paediatrician, who juggles three frames at once. One frame is the examination of the child, which is indicated by the doctor's use of 'motherese' features such as exaggerated intonation. A second frame is the reporting of findings to the child's mother, for which the doctor uses more complex language, but also indicates her authority by using speech activities such as explaining. Finally, the doctor is recording the interaction for a training video, and when she addresses this audience (for example, describing what she sees when looking in the child's ear), she uses specialist medical terminology (which may be characterised as a register).

Coupland (2007) among others also points out that *voicing* can be the motivation for making different linguistic choices in an interaction. In interaction, we often voice others, either directly (using quotatives such as *said* or *like* in English) or indirectly (by changing voices slightly). Mikhail Bakhtin (1981) in fact argues that all speech reproduces echoes of previous voices, but here I simply want to point out that speakers will often talk 'as if' they are someone else, and not just in a story. For example, if I use a full name address term (like 'Scott Fabius Kiesling') I am likely to be voicing my mother. Thus, IV may be sensitive to changes in voicing as well.

The point of reviewing all of these concepts is that in each one, various social practices go together: how we sit or stand, where we do what, when we talk, and of course how we talk. They thus represent a way that variation is embedded in the speech community. Note that for all of these concepts, there is a tension between *iterability* and creativity. Iterability is the repetition of a form in the same context: that is, we notice that in the activity of lecturing, for example, certain kinds of speech are repeated over and over again. We may even say that there is a community 'rule' or 'norm' that requires the use of this kind of speech. However, this iterability can also be used creatively, as when a snippet of the lecturing activity is inserted into a different speech event, such as an argument.

The reader may have noticed that I have not in this section yet cited any quantitative studies that use any of these concepts as factors. The reason for this is simple: there aren't very many. The lack of such studies is mostly related to the methods of sociolinguistics, which rely on sociolinguistic interviews. Researchers have assumed that speakers are essentially engaged in a single speech event. While this is true, it may be a speech event that speakers are not very familiar with (I haven't been interviewed very many times in my life). This fact means that we may be able to find different frames or activities that the speakers are engaging in during the interview.

One early work that focuses on something similar to speech activity is Hindle's (1980) study that tracked one speaker, Carol Meyers. These recordings were made by Arvilla Payne, who recorded Meyers in three situations: (1) at work; (2) at home with her husband and Payne (whom Meyers lived with at the time); and (3) at a regular bridge game with friends. Hindle finds a significant difference in vowel production for most vowels for the three situations. Hindle also coded Meyers's speech

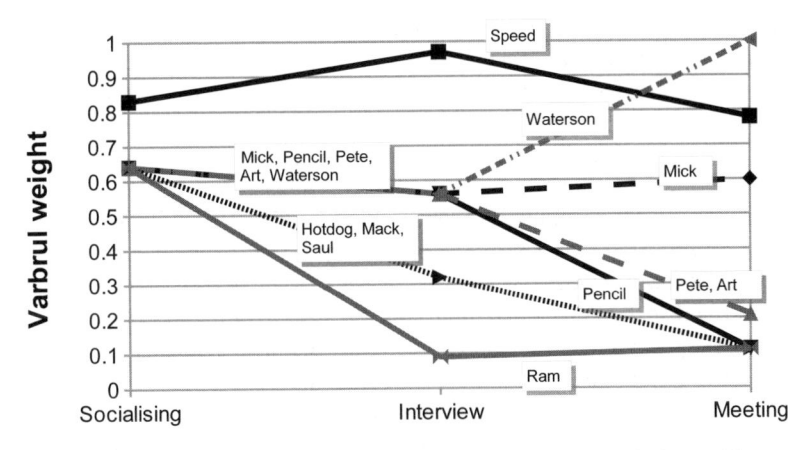

Figure 5.2 [ɪn] use probability by speaker and speech event (adapted from Kiesling 1998: 81)

on the basis of *key:* businesslike, serious, light, excited, complaint, and residual. Here he finds a significant difference in tense /æ/ between complaint and all other keys, suggesting that (æ) is fronted in this key, which is also the direction of the change in Philadelphia. It is clear from these data that Meyers is using the variable in order to express a key (or *stance*). (See also the discussion of Hindle's work in Labov 2001a: 438–42.)

Schilling-Estes (1998) takes this view when she notes that her interviewee, Rex, repeatedly 'performs' a short set monologue at different points during the interview. This monologue demonstrates some of the well-known features of the local (Ocracoke, North Carolina) variety, which begins 'It's high tide on the sound side.' The feature in question is the raising of /aɪ/, a feature widely known throughout the island to be part of the local variety. Schilling-Estes shows that the important variables in this 'performance register' are as regular and structured as in the rest of the interview, and that they shift Rex's speech significantly away from the standard; it fact, it is the speech for which Rex shows the most raised /aɪ/, even higher than conversations with his brothers. This finding suggests that attending to register and activity are central to understanding the embedding of variation in the speech community.

In my own research I have also attempted to use some of the concepts for how to understand speech events. In my first research project on language use in an American fraternity (an all-men's social club at a university), I was able to record speech in a number of different kinds of speech events, which I eventually grouped into three broad speech activities: socialising, interview, and meeting. This division was mostly tied to the kinds of events I had recorded: meetings of the fraternity were easy to record, as were interviews, but the different kinds of socialising (parties especially) presented a challenge. As shown in Figure 5.2, I was able to determine the rates of variation for the (ing) variable for ten men in the fraternity in these three speech activities ('Varbrul weight' is discussed in detail in Chapter 3; here it is enough to understand that values over 0.5 favour the use of the [In] variant).

There are a number of interesting properties of the patterns in this figure, but the most striking is the one that shows the men using similar rates of variation in the socialising situation, but markedly different rates in the meeting and interview situations. In order to explain this, I appealed to the fact that the men were creating a variety of *stances* with respect to me or their interlocutors in the interview and meeting activities, but that they were fairly consistent in their stances in the socialising activity (we will explore stances in more depth in the next section). The important point is that the IV is much more complex here than on a monodimensional attention-to-speech model, and more importantly that this representation shows the actual embedding of variation in the speech community.

In another project with Maeve Eberhardt (Eberhardt 2006; Kiesling 2009), I again focused on speech activity. Eberhardt recorded a conversation among eight women, with each woman wearing her own microphone. We have analysed several variables, but the most telling is Eberhardt's (2006) analysis of (ing) in the conversation. We first coded each token in the conversation for speech activity, and after combining some we used two categories: social and informational. This time, there is much more agreement about the direction of the shift in (ing) use, with the exception of one participant, Marcie. Eberhardt shows that Marcie takes very different stances from the others in situations of giving information. The point is that the concepts used above can be used to code sociolinguistic data, and in the end can point to important patterns of variation in the speech community. As noted, there is little research that explores the variation patterns of speech activities, frames, genres, voices, etc., but there is every indication that these are valid constructs that speakers rely on to make linguistic choices. The problem is making reliable coding mechanisms, a project that is still in its infancy, and could prove to be a fruitful area of research.

STANCE AND IDENTITY

We have entertained a number of possible motivations for speakers to make linguistic choices. But what are speakers actually *doing* when they make choices (whether conscious or unconscious) about what variant of a variable they use? Conversations (and other speech events) are social practices, because they relate one person to another in some way. This relationship-indicating function of language is one suggested by many of the patterns we have seen in this chapter and the previous one: power (stratification) and solidarity (accommodation, audience design, and acts of identity) are the most general motivations for speakers to choose one way of speaking over another. But we have mostly been considering these dimensions of power and solidarity from a wide perspective, inferring their meaning from large patterns of use. In actual conversations, in the moment-to-moment give and take, it is more likely that speakers tend to be more concerned with what is happening *now* in *this particular conversation*.

One possibility that has been entertained by sociolinguistics is whether the *topic* of an interview or conversation has an effect. The results here are inconsistent. One problem is that it is notoriously difficult to provide a reliable definition of topic, and that the coding of topic may be such that topics not relevant to the speakers or the variables being measured are coded for. A study by Schilling-Estes (2004) provides an example of the effect of topic, and manages to avoid the pitfalls. Schilling-Estes analysed the use of six phonological and morphological variables as used by two men from different ethnicities. The speech event was an interview of a Lumbee (American Indian) by an African American researcher in North Carolina. The variables were all characteristic of African American English or Southern American English. Schilling-Estes finds that for some topics, and for some variables, the topic makes a difference, especially in whether the two men converge or diverge in their use of a variant. For example, for the feature of r-vocalisation (r), the two show more difference in use in sections on race relations than in topics about family and friends. In a sense, it is the racial topics that make a difference. Of course, simply noting the correlation does not really explain the motivation for the difference. In her qualitative analyses of different topics, then, Schilling-Estes shows that this result is not simply due to whether the men are aligning more to ethnic harmony or to difference, but that they are orienting to each other and the ethnic categories in complex ways. Thus, while we may find that changing topics is a way to find quantitative patterns in interactions, it is still a *measurement* rather than an *explanation*. It is how a speaker relates to a topic, and how that topic mediates the relationship between interactants, that are the engine driving the variation patterns. Schilling-Estes thus also suggests that what speakers are doing in conversation is creating relationships in their talk, this time simultaneously with the topic of the talk and the people in the interaction, sometimes in complex and interconnected ways.

A term increasingly used to discuss this creation of relationships is *stance* (Jaffe 2009). Stance is another term in sociolinguistics that can be defined in a number of ways. For example, are we taking an aggressive stance (linguistically putting up our fists, standing tall) or an uncertain one (linguistically shrinking and curling defensively)? There is thus an intuitive understanding of stance, and in fact when people describe others they have met and the conversations they have had with them, I think they are more likely to describe a stance than whether the speaker was accommodating, or even whether they were a young Black woman or an old White man. We will define stance in two ways: as *a person's representation of their relationship to their talk* (their epistemic stance – e.g., how certain they are about their assertions), and as *a person's representation of their relationship to their interlocutors* (their interpersonal stance – e.g., friendly or dominating). Epistemic and interpersonal stance are often related: someone who is being patronising (interpersonal stance) is usually expressing the fact that they are very certain (epistemic stance) about what they are saying, but they are also expressing something about that knowledge with respect to their interlocutor, namely that the interlocutor does not have the same knowledge. The term 'representation of' in the definition is intentionally unspecified, because researchers have found that almost any linguistic feature can be and is used to represent stance. Moreover, it is not any one linguistic feature that creates a stance, but the co-occurrence of the features, within a specific interaction, that creates the specific utterance. However, we can use variationist methods to show what kinds of general stances a person takes when using a linguistic variant, and we can use qualitative analyses to understand and interpret them.

Stance can be used to explain a number of the IV patterns we have already seen. For example, Schilling-Estes (2004) shows that it is not the topic of conversation that drives the divergence or convergence of her two speakers, but the stance they take to that topic, and how it relates to or mediates their interpersonal relationship. In the conversation, there are two sections on race relations, and it is in the second that Schilling-Estes finds more convergence. She argues that there is more convergence because the speakers orient to race in a less personal and local way in the second section, so that they are not talking about themselves so much as about more abstract ideas and groups. As their stances to the topic of race relations change, then, so do their stances to each other, and this change in stance is partially constructed through the rates of variation.

One of the most important studies in the audience-design and accommodation literature is Coupland's study of one travel agency assistant called 'Sue' in Cardiff, Wales (Coupland 1980, 1984; see also his criticism of his study in Coupland 2007: 70–3). He finds two patterns that are important. First, he coded Sue's talk into four 'contexts', which were very much like speech activities: casual, informal and work-related, client, and telephone contexts. He measured Sue's variation in five variables that had local and more 'standard' variants, and found a clear pattern of using the local variants the most in casual contexts, and decreasing through informal, client, and telephone contexts. Here we could argue for stance as a factor, as one often takes a different stance to people depending on speech activity and who is in it: a 'casual' context implies a 'casual', friendly stance. More important for audience design is the fact that Sue changed her use of at least one variable, t-voicing, depending on the rate of voicing of the client with whom she is speaking. Figure 5.3 shows Bell's representation of Coupland's data, in which we see Sue approximating the productions of people in different classes in the client context.

Bell interprets this as evidence for audience design overall, but we need to remember that this is in the context of a client–server relationship, one that the server wishes to maintain. Thus we would expect Sue to accommodate, because that's the stance that is required in other ways: she accommodates to the clients' wishes by definition as an 'assistant.' Other instances of interaction, in which different stances are taken, may not be so 'accommodating'. So it is partially the 'audience' that is important in IV, but it is the stance that the speaker takes with respect to that audience that is the real explanation for the variation. (In fact, we might note that with the highest-class speaker, Sue accommodates the least, so she may be taking a quite different stance to them, for example if she thinks they are too demanding and she resists somewhat.) Similar is Trudgill's (1981) comparison of his production of t-glottalisation with that of the people he interviewed. He found that his production of (t) tracked his interviewees' very closely. Again, though, in this speech

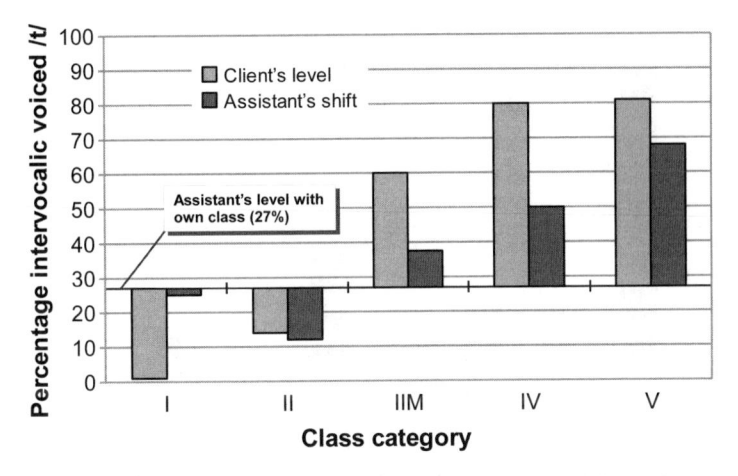

Note: The light grey bars represent the mean for clients, and the dark grey bars represent the difference between Sue's mean when speaking to someone of her own class and the mean when speaking to clients of that class. I = highest class, V = lowest class.

Figure 5.3 Sue's mean rate of /t/-vocalisation when speaking to clients of varying classes (adapted from Bell 1984: 165)

situation the point is to develop a rapport with the speaker and make them feel as comfortable and 'casual' as possible, and one way to express this solidarity could be through linguistic accommodation, as shown by Schilling-Estes. One would expect that Trudgill did not accommodate quite so readily in an undergraduate classroom.

Another important study in IV, already mentioned in Chapter 3, is Rickford and McNair-Knox's (1994) study of Foxy, an African American teenaged woman from East Palo Alto, California. They analyse two interviews with Foxy, one done by McNair-Knox and her teenaged daughter Roberta, both African American, and one done by a 25-year-old White postgraduate student at Stanford University. The variables they measure are all associated with AAVE. For all of them, Foxy uses a higher rate of the AAVE variants with the African American interviewers than with the White interviewer. However, different topics do not always have the same effect. For example, school topics have some of the highest rates of AAVE variants with the African American interviewers, but some of the lowest rates with the White interviewer. But the researchers also note stance differences in the two interviews, characterising the interview with McNair-Knox and Roberta as being 'livelier and more informal' with 'more give and take' (1994: 242); *livelier* and *more give and take* are clearly characterisations of stance. So the interviewer has an effect on the *stance* that Foxy takes, and it is arguable that it is this stance of solidarity or alignment that Foxy is using the variants to create.

Finally, as noted above, I used stance to explain the differences in the way the fraternity men used (ing) in the meeting, with some men taking a stance that created

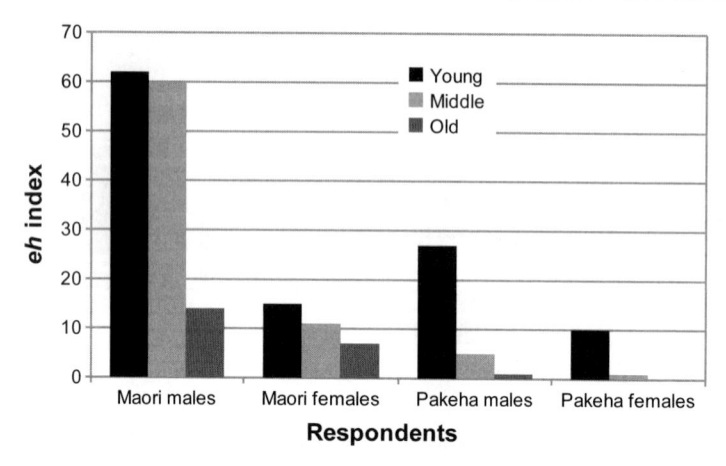

Figure 5.4 Use of *eh* by ethnicity and gender (adapted from Meyerhof 1994: 373)

a power hierarchy between them and the other men, and other men creating a more affiliative, solidary stance, or a stance resisting the power 'claimed' by the others (Kiesling 1998, 2009). It was the latter who used the most if the [ɪn] variants. Similarly, recall that Eberhardt (2006) found that one woman in the meeting actually used more [ɪn] in situations of explaining. Eberhardt was able to show that she took a very different stance when explaining, which was self-deprecatory and played down the importance of what she was saying.

A number of studies show that linguistic variants are used to create stances without explicitly appealing to the notion of stance. As an example, let's take Miriam Meyerhoff's study of the discourse particle *eh* in New Zealand English (Meyerhoff 1994). *Eh* is a particle that is added to the end of an utterance. Creating a variable context for discourse features can be problematic. In this case, it is not clear what restrictions there are for *eh*: end of sentence, clause, or utterance. Meyerhoff thus took the approach of creating an '*eh* index' by calculating the number of *eh*'s per minute of talk. Meyerhoff found mainly that *eh* was being used more by younger speakers, and that ethnicity and gender played a significant role in its adoption. She found that Maori men used *eh* the most, but that young Pakeha women seem to be adopting it (*Pakeha* is the New Zealand term that means roughly 'Anglo'), as shown in Figure 5.4. In her analysis of why these patterns might occur, she shows that *eh* functions as a 'positive politeness' marker. Without going into Brown and Levinson's (1987) politeness theory too much, positive politeness is a set of strategies that show appreciation for an interlocutor's self-worth, or 'positive face'. They are strategies that suggest a solidary stance, and this is in effect how Meyerhoff analyses them, in slightly different terminology, using examples from discourse. She also argues that it is the Maori men and some Pakeha women who would be likely to value such stances, thus tracing the quantitative pattern back to the stance functions of *eh*.

We have considered a number of ways of describing patterns of variation and the way that variants co-occur with a large number of axes of the sociocultural world humans inhabit: stratification (power), accommodation (solidarity), differentiation, and various aspects of speech events and identity. For the most part, however, I have put off a discussion of how to explain these patterns. The discussion of stance and interaction began to bring us closer to explanations about why we find the kinds of social patterns we do. We have discussed the effects of these patterns, and couched them in some meaningful terms such as power and solidarity. But in order to explain what is happening with these patterns we need a theory about how variants convey meaning for speakers and how these speakers' everyday decisions about such meaningful variants lead to patterns that they themselves might not even be aware of. This is the issue taken up in the next chapter.

Chapter 6

Meaning and social patterns

In the previous three chapters, we have explored the different kinds of social patterns found in the variationist literature. In the realm of interspeaker variation, we have found patterns of stratification, differentiation, and accommodation. These patterns are also found among the patterns of IV and the various ways that have been proposed to measure this: attention to speech suggests stratification, while audience design suggests accommodation. Finally, we find that speakers are often aware of very subtle linguistic patterns, and we find that attitudes and reactions to variants create predictable patterns as well. All of these patterns are simply that: patterns of correlation that point to how the variables are embedded in the speech community, how they are transmitted, and how they spread. At the end of each chapter, in areas focusing on more recent advances in these topics, we find a move towards more explanation that focuses on how speakers create meaning through their patterns of variation. This focus gets us to the heart of how variation and change are embedded in the speech community: how they are used meaningfully by speakers to do social work.

In this chapter, then, we explore some of the ways 'social meaning' has been theorised in sociolinguistics, and how it can be applied to the patterns we have seen in the previous three chapters. We will first discuss how this meaning works and some terms that help us discuss it, especially *indexicality*. Second, we will explore theories about how indexical meanings come about and change, how they become embedded in the speech community. We will revisit a few of the studies and explain how these indexical explanations can be applied, before considering how 'identity' is used as an explanatory concept and how it relies on the more general types of meaning discussed throughout the chapter.

INDEXICALITY: MEANING IN THE SOCIOLINGUISTIC VARIABLE

How do variables mean? In other words, when a speaker makes a choice between two variants, would that utterance have been understood differently if the speaker had made another choice? Of course, according to the original definition of the sociolinguistic variable – two or more ways of saying the same thing – there is no meaning difference. But that definition refers to a particular kind of meaning, which is called a *symbol* and is characterised by arbitrary, referential, and denotational meaning. In other words, two words can refer to the same thing (like *pop* and *soda*), and we could invent a new name for the same thing that is totally unrelated, like *spenada* (which I just made up). The word (or, more generally, the *signifier* or *sign*, which could be a morpheme, word, picture, etc.) has an *arbitrary* or *conventional* connection with the *referent* or *object*. This is the kind of meaning we are used to thinking about. Another type of sign is the *icon*, which is a sign that resembles its object. A common example of this is a traffic sign that shows people crossing the street at a pedestrian crossing. In spoken languages some words are *iconic*, in the sense that they sound like what they refer to, such as *buzz* referring to the sound made by a bee. In signed languages there is even more iconicity, but these signs are not literally icons, because there is a always some conventionalisation involved (for example, the British Sign Language sign for bicycle is a hand motion that resembles the motion of feet on pedals, but this motion could be all sorts of other things as well). Finally, there is the category of sign called an *index*. This type of sign is one that is inherently or directly connected to its referent. A non-linguistic example is a human footprint: the footprint is directly connected to the human who made it, and we infer from it that a human has been present. In language, deictic words such as *this/that, here/there*, and *now/later* are indexical because their meaning is directly connected to where the referent is with respect to the speaker (*this/that*). where the speaker is (*here/there*), or when they are speaking (*now/later*). (Note that deictics also have symbolic meaning, in that the relationship of *here* to the speaker – in close proximity – is arbitrary; these kinds of words are sometimes called 'shifters'.)

It may be clear at this point that indexical meaning is the meaning we are after when we are talking about sociolinguistic variation, although there is an element of symbolic meaning as well. Let's take the pronunciation of /r/ in English as an example. If we hear an /r/ articulated in a constricted, alveolar way, there are a number of ways we might interpret it. If we live in New York City, we have probably heard lots of people pronounce /r/ this way, and we may remember something about those people: we may remember the situation, what was going on, whether they were friendly, their age, whether they were dressed well, had authority, etc. The list, in its particulars, is endless. The next time we hear /r/ pronounced this way, however, this memory surfaces as a kind of indexical meaning for /r/, because we make an inference that there is a connection between how a speaker pronounces /r/ and other facts about them. We have direct indexical experience.

We can also have a mediated indexical experience, in which case the meaning of the variant takes on aspects of a symbol. By *mediated* I mean that someone points out to us the relationship between the variant and its indexical meaning. Ways of speaking (like pronouncing /r/) and who uses those ways of speaking may be noticed by speakers in a speech community, and perhaps even talked about and imitated, and they thus become more and more conventionalised. Even if I have never been to New York, I may have heard or read about someone discussing /r/-pronunciation there, and if I later visit I may already have formed an opinion that a vocalised

/r/ is more working-class (at which point hearing the billionaire Mayor Michael Bloomberg talk about [nuwyaːk] might be surprising!).

Labov (1972b) used the terms *indicator*, *marker*, and *stereotype* to discuss this distinction, although he used different criteria. For Labov, an indicator is a variable that has a social pattern, but one that the speakers are not yet *aware* of. That is, some people speak one way, others speak another way, but no one in the speech community has yet noticed the difference. Moreover, Labov defines an indicator as showing no regular IV pattern (or style-shifting, as he calls it). A marker shows IV shifts, and there is a subconscious awareness of the social group patterns of language. Finally, the stereotype is a variable that everyone in the speech community is aware of and can talk about. Labov developed these categories to discuss the possible ways that a linguistic change travels through a speech community, beginning as an indicator, moving through being a marker, and sometimes becoming a stereotype.

Michael Silverstein (2003) brings these ideas and insights into a more general theoretical construct, which he calls the *indexical order*. The indexical order categorises indexes as to their relationship with what Silverstein calls the *metapragmatic function*. 'Metapragmatic' parallels the term *metalinguistic*, which is the use of language to discuss language. Metapragmatics is the use of language to represent pragmatics, here roughly understood as how speakers use language (also known as 'rules of use'). It is an idea very similar to awareness, but Silverstein is interested not in what is purported to be 'in the heads' of speakers, but in how metapragmatic discourse is circulated throughout the community. So for a first-order indexical the connection between, for example, a category of speaker and a variant might be present as a demonstrable correlation, but there is no metapragmatic function in the community that imbues it with the indexical meaning connecting the way of speaking to the type of speaker. Indexes become second-order as the metapragmatic function makes the correlation between the type of person and way of speaking more meaningful. As the index becomes more fixed into the metapragmatic function, we say that it is becoming *enregistered* – becoming a recognised index in the speech community. Finally, there can then develop a third-order indexical in which the meaningful correlation of the second-order indexical becomes the subject of yet another metapragmatic function.

There is one more set of ideas to discuss before moving to an exampl: the distinction between *presupposing* and *creative* indexes. An index is used in a presupposing sense if it follows the 'rules of use'. To put it another way, assume that a linguistic form is used in a particular situation; for instance, in the classroom in front of students I call a fellow professor 'Dr Paulston'. If I use this form of address in another classroom, I am following expectations that in a classroom we use 'title + surname' with instructors. It is thus a presupposing use of the address term 'title + surname' (which is an index). I can also use this address term creatively, however. For example, suppose that I am speaking casually with this same colleague at an informal lunch. The corresponding presupposing address term would be 'Christina' in this case. However, if at some point this colleague makes a point that reveals my younger, more inexperienced (or naïve) status, I may respond by saying something like 'I understand now, Dr Paulston', in which case I am using the 'title + surname' address form *creatively* to index her status as instructor. That is, she is not really currently in her instructor role, so in a sense my use of 'Dr Paulston' *creates* that role and speech event. This distinction is important because the move from one level of indexicality to another requires repeated and noticed creative indexing of the linguistic form.

Johnstone et al. (2006) provide an excellent example of these concepts and the process by which a variable moves from first- to third-order indexicality, and how this idea relates to Labov's terms. Johnstone et al. analyse the ways in which /aʊ/-monophthongisation (aʊ) in Pittsburgh became enregistered as a variable that can mark someone as being a Pittsburger. Table 6.1 represents this process (in the third column), and its relationship to Silverstein's orders of indexicality and Labov's indicator, marker, and stereotype. The 'n+1+1-th' level for Silverstein (a formula that is challenging to unpack!) is the order that is always 'lurking', and once people notice the enregistration they might move that enregistration further such that the use of an indexical is expected in order, for example, for someone to claim to be a Pittsburgher.

One of the most important insights in this schema is the representation of the contest or dialectic relationship between the different orders of indexicality. Johnstone et al. illustrate this concept by presenting the words of Pittsburghers of different generations. Most telling is the comment by Dottie X., a Pittsburgher born in 1930, who notes about *yinz*, which in Pittsburgh is a second-person plural pronoun, that 'everyone said it, so I never thought anything of it or something like that. But now, people are like, "Yinz!", and I'm like, "Well so what?"' (Johnstone et al. 2006: 88). For younger speakers, the term *yinz* is indexical of a particular kind of Pittsburgher, a fact which has been enregistered to the point where a stereotypical working-class Pittsburgher is known as a *yinzer*. For Dottie, though, there is a tension between the fact that she said *yinz* when she was younger but didn't notice it and the fact that it is now such a noticed index of a particular Pittsburgh identity.

EXPERIMENTAL EVIDENCE FOR MEANING

Beyond the correlational evidence, and evidence from people talking about language, what evidence is there that people attach such indexical meanings to these sometimes subtle differences in language? Since before Labov performed his study in New York City, linguists and social psychologists have used experimental evidence to show that meanings are indeed attached to different ways of speaking. The most common technique in this field is known as the 'matched guise' technique, pioneered by Wallace Lambert in the late 1950s and 1960s (Lambert 1967). In studies focusing on the perception of speakers of French and English in Quebec, Canada, Lambert and associates played Canadian English, Canadian French, and Continental French voices to Quebecers, and asked them to rate the speaker on a number of personality traits using a *semantic differential*, a scale representing antonymic qualities. For example, does this person sound more or less intelligent,

108 Linguistic Variation and Change

Table 6.1 Orders of indexicality and Labovian variable types for (aʊ) in Pittsburgh

Silverstein (2003)	**Labov (1972b: 178-180)**	**in Pittsburgh**
'*n*-th-order indexical': A feature whose use can be correlated with a socio-demographic identity (e.g. region or class) or a semantic function (e.g. number-marking). *N*-th-order accounts are 'scientific' (p. 205), i.e. could be generated by a cultural outsider such as a linguist. The feature's indexicality is 'presupposing': occurrence of the feature can only be interpreted with reference to a pre-existing partition of social or semantic space.	**'indicator'**: A variable feature which shows no pattern of stylistic variation in users' speech, affecting all items in the relevant word classes. Speakers are not aware of the variable. The variable is 'defined as a function of group membership' (p. 179), or, as its use spreads in subsequent generations, group membership and age.	**first-order indexicality**: At this stage, the frequency of regional variants in a person's speech can be correlated with whether he/she is from southwestern PA (especially from Pittsburgh) working-class, and/or male. But for socially non-mobile speakers in dense, multiplex social networks, these correlations are not noticeable, because 'everybody speaks that way.'
'*n*+1-th-order indexical': An *n*-th order indexical feature that has been assigned 'an ethno-metapragmatically driven native interpretation' (p. 212), i.e. a meaning in terms of one or more native ideologies (the idea that certain people speak more correctly than others, for example, or that some people are due greater respect than others).The feature has been 'enregistered', that is, it has become associated with a style of speech and can be used to create a context for that style. Its indexicality is thus 'entailing' or 'creative.'	**'marker'**: A variable feature which shows stylistic variation, i.e. speakers use different variants in different contexts, because the use of one variant or another is socially meaningful. Speakers are not necessarily aware of the variables or their social meanings, however.	**second-order indexicality**: Regional features become available for social work; speakers start to notice and attribute meaning to regional variants and shift styles in their own speech. The meaning of these forms is shaped, for many by ideologies about class and correctness, though regional forms can also be linked with locality by people who have had the 'localness' of these forms called to attention, and there are more idiosyncratic linkages as well. Note that not all features will acquire second-order indexical meaning for all speakers.
'(*n*+1)+1-th-order indexical' 'For any indexical phenomenon at order *n*, an indexical phenomenon at order *n*+1 is always immanent, lurking in the potential of an ethno-metapragmatically driven native interpretation of the *n*-th-order paradigmatic contextual variation that it creates or constitutes as a register phenomenon' (p. 212). In the case of Labovian 'stereotypes', '*n*+1st order indexicality has become presupposing . . . replacing an older *n*-th order indexical presupposition' (p. 220)	**'stereotype'**: a variable feature which is the overt topic of social comment; may become increasingly divorced from forms that are actually used; the form may eventually disappear from vernacular speech.	**third-order indexicality**: People noticing the existence of second-order stylistic variation in Pittsburghers' speech link the regional variants they are most likely to hear with Pittsburgh identity, drawing on the increasingly widely circulating idea that places and dialects are essentially linked (every place has a dialect). These people, who include Pittsburghers and non-Pittsburghers, use regional forms drawn from highly codified lists (such as popular 'dictionaries' of Pittsburghese) to perform local identity, often in ironic, semi-serious ways.

From hearing the speaker's voice, what kind of person do you think the speaker is:

1.	intelligent	_:_:_:_:_	unintelligent
2.	high social status	_:_:_:_:_	low social status
3.	biased	_:_:_:_:_	fair
4.	self-confident	_:_:_:_:_	not self-confident
5.	reliable	_:_:_:_:_	unreliable
6.	likeable	_:_:_:_:_	hateful
7.	conservative	_:_:_:_:_	open
8.	having character	_:_:_:_:_	not having character
9.	conversable	_:_:_:_:_	uncouth
10.	ambitious	_:_:_:_:_	unambitious
11.	humorous	_:_:_:_:_	humourless
12.	superstitious	_:_:_:_:_	not superstitious
13.	obliging	_:_:_:_:_	unsociable/eccentric
14.	selfish	_:_:_:_:_	not selfish
15.	sincere	_:_:_:_:_	insincere
16.	not religious	_:_:_:_:_	pious
17.	diligent	_:_:_:_:_	careless
18.	impolite	_:_:_:_:_	courteous
19.	discontent	_:_:_:_:_	content
20.	not having leadership	_:_:_:_:_	having leadership
21.	arrogant	_:_:_:_:_	modest
22.	short	_:_:_:_:_	tall
23.	good-looking	_:_:_:_:_	ugly
24.	kind	_:_:_:_:_	unkind
25.	informal	_:_:_:_:_	formal

Figure 6.1 Sample Likert scale response sheet for a matched-guide experiment

ambitious, or friendly? The scale is presented as a *Likert scale*, so that a response sheet might resemble Figure 6.1.

Lambert et al. grouped the different traits into three different sets – competence, personal integrity, and social attractiveness – and calculated the average rating of each set. They found that there was a somewhat complex interaction between the language background and gender of the respondent and the language and gender of the stimulus voice, or *guise:* English-speaking respondents overall rated women more favourably in French, and men in English. The English speakers also rated the French female voice as more intelligent, ambitious, and self-confident than the

English female voice. The French Canadian respondents in general actually rated French guises with lower values, with the exception that the French Canadian women rated the French guise as better than the English. The finding that the speakers of Canadian French rate French Canadians lower is a significant and interesting insight, and one that has often been repeated in matched guise studies.

Matched-guise-type studies have been performed with different kinds of sociolinguistic variables or sets of variables. Labov (2001a: 206–20) performed a similar study in Philadelphia based on four vowel variables and one consonantal variable, but had responses based on two traits only: job suitability and friendliness. All the stimuli for this 'subjective reaction test', as Labov called it, were taken from different Philadelphians interviewed for his study, and showing different values for vowels undergoing changes. The job suitability scale asked speakers what job the person was most suitable for, with *television personality* as the highest and *no job at all* as the lowest. Labov found a strong reaction from ninety-nine Philadelphians: when listening to guises with the most advanced tokens (in terms of the changes ongoing in Philadelphia), speakers downgraded the speaker's job suitability. Labov argued that these results showed that all speakers evaluate variation in a uniform manner. He also asked for each one 'If you got to know this speaker well, how likely is it that she would become a good friend of yours?' We might expect that these answers would go in the opposite direction from job suitability, because in other studies, such as Trudgill's (1974) in Norwich, there was evidence that there was some kind of value attached to the newer variants. But Labov found that the friendliness scale went in the same direction, but had less effect.

This study points to a danger of the matched-guise method: the experimenter chooses ahead of time the possibilities for how a speaker may respond. Thus, the respondents in Labov's question were responding to two specific questions, which were whether the person they were listening to was suitable for certain jobs or would be their friend. Listening to the speech of television personalities (who tend not to be locally based) suggests that any deviation from speech that is not local to any region will get a negative response. Labov's results are thus not surprising. In other words, while it might be true that this task measures television job suitability, what if people don't usually actually evaluate people on whether they would be good television personalities, or whether they will be friends? Their criteria are likely to depend on the speech situation and what they already know about the person. For example, if the respondents were asked whether they thought the voices could be potential spouses, would they get a different answer? The task is thus already structured for meaning, and for one that might not be the relevant meaning for the community. This is only a problem when we make the jump in interpretation from job suitability to overall evaluation of a person as positive or negative. The matched-guise technique is important in that it shows without a doubt that linguistic variants *do* index speaker categories, but we must remember that these results derive from a decontextualised experimental task and realise that the meanings detected are shaped by that very task.

In addition, note that all of the stimulus voices in Labov's experiment are women's. Given the different reactions for men and women found by Lambert, we might wonder what effect gender or other social characteristics of the stimulus might have on a respondent. A number of studies show that what a listener knows about a speaker before they hear anything leads to different indexical interpretations of that speaker. Two studies show this particularly clearly, with each *priming* participants in different ways. *Priming* refers to giving the experiment participant information that may bias their response in the experiment. Niedzielski (1999) primed speakers indirectly, by writing identifying information on the top of a response sheet. Her experiment took place in Detroit, Michigan, which borders Canada. Both areas show evidence of 'Canadian raising' in the diphthong /aʊ/, in which the /a/ element is pronounced higher. However, this pronunciation has a second-, and possibly third-, order indexicality in Detroit of being Canadian and not Detroit; in fact, Americans often perform this stereotype with the phrase 'out and about' pronounced [uːt] and [əbuːt]. Niedzielski played a token of a Detroit speaker pronouncing *house* for respondents, as well as tokens that she had manipulated to be 'ultra-low' and 'canonical', which had the same formant values as the /aʊ/ in Peterson and Barney's (1952) descriptive study of American English. Respondents simply had to match the stimulus *house* with the examples they had heard before; however, they were 'primed' indirectly because the answer sheet had either 'Canadian' or 'Michigan' printed in red at the top of the page, although Niedzielski did not tell respondents what this label referred to. The respondents matched the (raised) token correctly 60 per cent of the time when using a 'Canadian' answer sheet, but only 11 per cent when using a 'Michigan' answer sheet. This result indicates that when the respondents thought that the speaker was Canadian, they were more likely to report hearing the token as raised, conforming to their metapragmatic views. So even in this very subtle way, Niedzielski was able to tap into the ethno-metapragmatics of Detroiters. Hay et al. (2006) replicated the experiment with vowel stimuli in New Zealand and found a similar result, lending support to the effect as real and not limited to the special circumstances of Detroit.

Strand's (2000) and Strand and Johnson's (1996, cited in Strand 1999) studies of the effect of social identity knowledge on perception are even more striking. The first set of experiments focused on the perceptual boundary between /s/ and /ʃ/ in American English. Naslund (1993) showed that American women tend to use a more fronted /s/ and men a more alveolar pronunciation. Johnson and Strand (1996) tested to see whether listeners perceived this boundary differently depending on the speaker. They first determined the gender stereotypicality of four voices, from stereotypically feminine to stereotypically masculine. Then for each voice they created stimuli that varied in regular increments from *sod* to *shod*. They played these stimuli in random order for participants and asked them to categorise the word as *sod* or *shod*. They found that the boundary was significantly different for every different voice, as shown in Figure 6.2, with the stereotypically male voice changing from /ʃ/ to /s/ first, then the non-stereotypical male, and so on so that the stereotypical voices were furthest apart.

Johnson and Strand took this insight further, and added a video component to

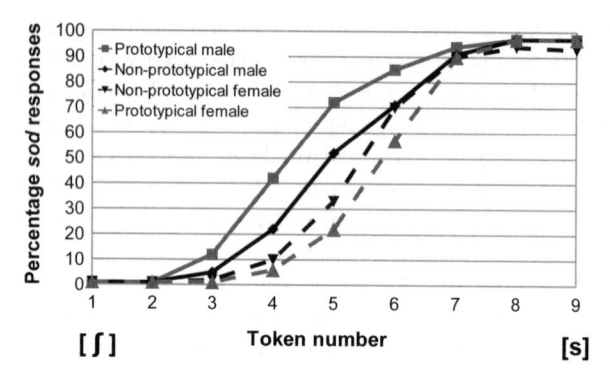

Figure 6.2 Perceptual boundaries between /s/ and /ʃ/ by gender stereotypicality (adapted from Strand 1999: 92)

the experiment. First they measured reactions to faces to determine ones that were stereotypically male and female. They then video-recorded these people saying *sod* and *shod*, substituted the pronunciations of the audio from the first (1996) experiment, and repeated the test from the first experiment with the video. They found that the boundary for the stereotypically female faces shifted for the same audio stimuli. Strand (2000) shows that a mismatch between the stereotypicality of face and voice leads participants in her experiments to take longer to repeat a word, indicating that they have to process non-matching video and audio information longer. These studies together, as pointed out by Strand (1999: 93), 'indicate that higher level, relatively complex social expectations might have an influence on such low-level basic processes as phonological categorisation of the speech signal'. In other words, indexical meaning (at least for gender) is not something that is added on after the signal has been processed or 'decoded', but is used to aid in the very decoding. Indexical meaning is thus much more deeply embedded in speech than we might think.

Campbell-Kibler's (2007, 2008, 2009) sophisticated matched-guise-type studies take all of these aspects into account to shed light on how people use variation to create opinions about the people they are listening to – how variants index social traits. Campbell-Kibler's work in general shows that other variables and other ways that speakers think about the speaker affect the way they interpret the indexicality of a particular linguistic variable. Campbell-Kibler focused on the (ing) variable in English, and used extracts from sociolinguistic interviews as stimuli. However, she digitally manipulated these stimuli so that both the [ɪŋ] and [ɪn] variants appeared in recordings that were otherwise exactly the same. We therefore know that any difference between the two ratings is due to this one variable. Campbell-Kibler's method addressed some of the problems of the matched-guise technique. First, she performed several group interviews before she ran the experiment to elicit qualitative responses to the different stimuli recordings. This allowed her to narrow the qualities she put on her semantic differentials. Second, she included lists of identity

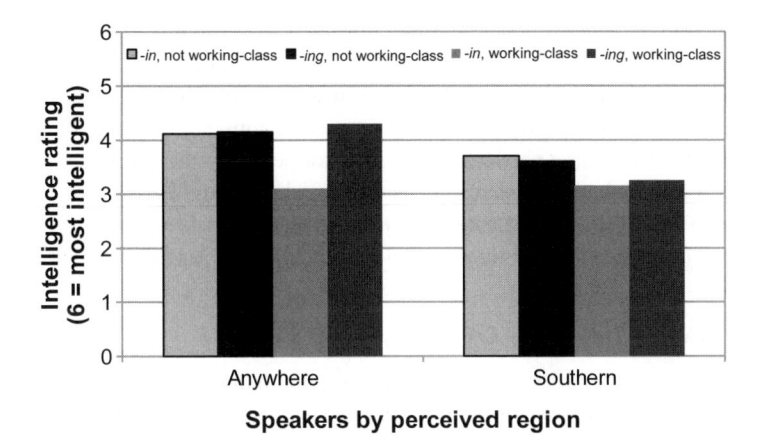

Figure 6.3 Perception of intelligence by perceived region (adapted from Campbell-Kibler 2009: 148)

traits such as age and regional and class backgrounds, as well as other kinds of identity traits like *jock* or *annoying*. Finally, she asked about what kind of speech activity the respondents thought the speaker was engaging in and the stance the speaker was taking. The stimuli included young speakers from California and North Carolina, in the US Southern dialect area, and had respondents from the same places.

The general results show that the meaning of a variant is highly sensitive to other factors. Campbell-Kibler has explored the differential effects in different reports. One effect was *perceived region*, or where respondents thought the speaker was from (which might not match where they were really from). Campbell-Kibler (2009) found that the effect of (ing) changed depending on how the respondents categorised the speaker in terms of class and perceived region. As shown in Figure 6.3, if the speaker was not perceived as working-class, there was no difference in whether or not the speaker was heard as intelligent. If they were judged to be from the south, they were heard as less intelligent overall (this is not a surprising finding given US stereotypes about the south). However, if they were not heard as being southern, and they were judged to be working-class, the (ing) had a large effect. Of course, (ing) plays a part in the judgement of class and region, but the matched-guise test shows that the (ing) variant switch makes a significant difference only in this one case. Campbell-Kibler has shown that the effect of (ing), even with some core meanings, can be shown to differ depending on the topic of the recording, but that the topic did not have a consistent effect across all speakers and respondents. Perhaps most interesting is the result that for one speaker, respondents thought that the [ɪŋ] variant actually made her sound less intelligent. Campbell-Kibler was able to use the interview materials to understand that many listeners thought that this speaker was seen as using [ɪŋ] to sound more intelligent than she was – she was using it 'inauthentically'. Other speakers and topics produced different responses.

The complexity of Campbell-Kibler's work is in itself instructive. It shows that while there may be some vague central meanings to different variants, they are realised only in particularly contexts and that these contexts interact to create a unique meaning in each interaction. Of course, it also means that previous interactions with a speaker or in a particular situation will colour our interpretation of social meanings of the same particular variant. Most generally, however, the perceptions taken together show that we can detect indexical meanings beyond the correlations between variant and identity category or other social variables. We next turn to theoretical understandings of the wider social processes that lead to these indexicalities.

INDEXICAL WEBS, CYCLES, AND FIELDS

We have seen that indexical meanings of variants change over time, and that change in meaning is important in the ways that changes become embedded in the speech community. The vast majority of linguistic changes never become third-order indexicals, but they are important in explaining how change works. Most importantly, it returns us to the origins of norms in speech communities, or the local *ethno-metapragmatics*, in Silverstein's terms. Johnstone et al. show that (aʊ) becomes a third-order indexical when the speech community comes into contact with *exonorms*, in Dubois and Horvath's (1999) terminology. Recall that they showed how some Cajun variants lost favour in Louisiana, and then reversed as the culture began to value Cajun social practices, including some Cajun ways of speaking. The non-Cajun variants were in this case exonorms, and their appearance (especially in schools) moved some of the Cajun variables from first- to second-order indexicality. The polarity of this indexicality was for the most recent (male) generation reversed such that Cajun-ness became valued, and these variants then moved towards being third-order indexicals. In other words, the Cajun way of speaking was in a sense 're-enregistered'.

This indexical cycling of enregistrations and tensions among norms are central processes in sociolinguistic variation and change. We can see it in the different patterns discussed in Chapter 3. For accommodation, the first possibility is that there is no indexical value at all, and people follow a predisposition to mimic the talk that they encounter. Eberhardt's (2009a, 2009b) finding that African Americans in Pittsburgh have the low back merger (LBM) suggests that the distinction between the two phonemes that are merged does not have an indexical value for the African American Pittsburghers. However, accommodation may also come into play when there is an indexical value, for example one in which there is a standard–vernacular metapragmatic relationship (as for Sue, the travel agent whose speech was analysed by Coupland 1984; see above in this chapter). Differentiation is something that will generally occur for variants with indexicality at the second-order level at least. The avoidance of /au/-monophthongisation by African American Pittsburghers in Eberhardt's study shows that they associate monophthongisation with White speakers, and it is clear that this variable has reached third-order status. Stratification is dependent on not only the metapragmatics of the speech community, but also the way groups are valued and organised in that speech community. We have evidence that for working-class speakers in Pittsburgh in the early twentieth century, monophthongisation was a first-order index, and may have been so for upper-class Pittsburghers as well. However, as the variable moved up the indexical order, its indexicality also acquired the values attached to the identities with which it was indexed, and fitted into a more basic metapragmatics in which there is 'good speech' and 'bad speech'. We find in stratification, then, the conflicting orientations to the metapragmatics of 'standard language', with the upper class oriented more positively and the middle and working class oriented (mostly) negatively.

Dennis Preston (1989; Niedzielski and Preston 2003) has investigated how people organise their metapragmatic representations of language, or what he calls 'folk theories' of language. In one task, he asked speakers from Michigan, USA, to rate the different US states on how correct and how pleasant the inhabitants' speech is, and then repeated the experiment with speakers in Alabama, a southern state. He found that the Michiganders rate their own state (and those close by) as speaking more 'correctly', but that they don't distinguish states very much on 'pleasantness'. The Alabamans are just the opposite, showing less difference for correctness and more for pleasantness. We thus have experimental evidence that people orient differently to the values of pleasantness and correctness in their metapragmatics. The different cultural reasons behind these differential values for Michiganders and Alabamans are interesting and important, but for now the most important aspect of this finding is that the orientation to 'standard' language is neither consistent nor 'natural'.

'Values attached to language' have also been referred to in the literature as *language ideologies*, which are beliefs about language and its use that are taken as natural and not open to question. That there is a 'correct' way of speaking is itself an ideology, largely tied up with ideologies about class. Lippi-Green (1997) identifies this 'standard language ideology' in the USA, and Mugglestone (2003) and Agha (2003, 2007) both discuss how the ideology of Received Pronunciation (RP) in the UK was enregistered in the nineteenth and twentieth centuries. Although standard language ideologies are the most obvious, we can find alternative ideologies and enregistrations, such that, for example, using RP is to be avoided so that one is not perceived as being too posh. In Pittsburgh, there is a clear ideology of language attached to some forms of the local dialect that connects these forms with geography rather than class.

The meanings of a variant are thus intimately tied to the social structure and cultural values of the speech community, and of course we have seen that variation is in fact a part of those structures and values. As noted above, we find that there is a repeated change of meaning of variants, sometimes in concert with social change (as in the case of the revival of Cajun variants), but sometimes being recruited to support the status quo in a new way, as in the case of (r) in New York. Moreover, work in perception and in studies on stance shows that the indexicalities of variants are not only not fixed, but vague and contestable, as shown by Campbell-Kibler and Preston. How can we represent, then, the way that choices of variant make social meaning?

```
                        UNEDUCATED
                            |
                         EDUCATED


RELAXED ——— FORMAL              EFFORTFUL ——— EASYGOING/LAZY


              ARTICULATE / PRETENTIOUS
                         |
              INARTICULATE / UNPRETENTIOUS
```

Figure 6.4 Indexical field of (ing) (adapted from Eckert 2008a: 466)

As Silverstein points out, these indexicalities are always both creative and presupposing: they rely on previous use for meaning, but are being used in a new situation and thus creating new indexicalities. Even when used in a way that exactly follows the 'rules of use', indexes reinforce that meaning and are thus re-creative. Eckert (2008a) argues that we should think of the indexicalities not as a single meaning, but as indexing a range of potential meanings which she calls an *indexical field*, which she defines as 'a constellation of meanings that are ideologically linked' (2008a: 464). Importantly, however, 'this field is not a static structure, but at every moment a representation of a continuous process of reinterpretation' (2008a: 464). For example, from a large number of studies of (ing) and Campbell-Kibler's studies, Eckert suggests that the indexical field of potential meanings for (ing) is as represented in Figure 6.4.

The indexical field is an important way to think about indexes, because it frees us from viewing their meaning as relatively fixed and monodimensional, which has been a surprisingly tenacious idea in sociolinguistic variation. We might want to expand on the idea, however, and give some structure to the fields. That is, can we represent the connections between forms and indexicalities? Can we represent the connections among indexicalities? For example, Eckert's (ing) field in Figure 6.4 has four indexicalities for the [ɪŋ] variant: *educated, formal, articulate/pretentious*, and *effortful*. First, note that some of these indexicalities are traits of individuals (such as *educated* and *articulate*) while others are more akin to stances (*formal*) or both (*pretentious*). In creating meaning, speakers are likely to use associations among the indexicalities to create new meanings: for example, a person who sounds educated could also sound more articulate since there is an ideological connection between these two.

Ochs (1992) proposes a similar process in which indexes are *indirect*. She argues that gendered particles in Japanese originally had stance indexicalities such as *rough* and *refined*, which were then indirectly indexed to the genders that were rough and refined (men and women, respectively). The connections among non-linguistic indexes we can more generally call secondary indexes, with primary indexes being the connection between the linguistic item and the concept. So, in Preston's work, southerners in the US are seen by northerners as speaking less correctly, but southerners are also stereotypically and ideologically seen as more rural and less intelligent, just as there is a connection between using less correct language and being less intelligent. So the connection between correctness and intelligence is a secondary index, while the connection between southern speech and correctness is a primary index. Of course, we may not always be able to tell which is the primary index, but it is important to realise that by indexing one quality or stance of a person, we are inserted into a complex web of indexical meanings that can be foregrounded or backgrounded in actual use. There is thus an interaction between the indexicalities in the relatively more durable, but not unchangeable, indexical field and the meanings created in interaction. We can then see indexical changes as constantly ongoing dialectical processes working in many directions at once, as new meanings are accreted to the variant, either through secondary indexicalities, or through new creative primary indexicalities.

DIMENSIONS OF SOCIAL MEANING IN LANGUAGE

Now that we have some terminology to represent meaning in variation and an idea of some of the more general and abstract processes that drive change, let's take a brief look at some of the actual indexicalities that variants take on, and the semantic relations among them. Since Labov's (1963) study of Martha's Vineyard, *identity* has been seen as a motivation for variable choices. Labov showed that speakers with a more English islander identity were more likely to use centralised diphthongs than those who were more oriented to the mainland or less oriented to the English identity. We have also seen the 'acts of identity' model for style, in which speakers *identify* with certain groups by using language associated with that group. While much of variationist research has taken such groups to be the classic 'census' categories such as age, gender, class, ethnicity, etc., more recent research into social personae have suggested that such categories are experienced in more specific and local forms.

As discussed in Chapter 4, Eckert's (2000) analysis of the Detroit area high school she called Belten High has been pioneering in this regard, and has set the template for a number of other studies that have similar general findings. Eckert's ethnographic work in the high school revealed that the social world was ideologically organised around the opposition between *jocks* and *burnouts* and by gender. The jock and burnout categories were defined by the social practices engaged in by the students and secondarily by their social networks. Thus, jocks were not necessarily athletes (as suggested by the label), but engaged in social practices officially sanctioned by the school, while burnouts engaged in more resistant and non-school activities, including leaving the school cafeteria at lunch, 'cruising' in cars into the Detroit urban centre, and smoking and doing drugs. Eckert found that language was also important to the jock–burnout distinction, although that effect was slightly different for each vowel variable that Eckert investigated. The important point is that the jock and burnout labels were ideologically recognised and practice-based categories that were indexed partially by the different vowel variables. Zhang (2005, 2008) shows that a similar process is at work in the kinds of personae that speakers in Beijing create. Eckert's work has inspired a number of studies that elucidate further the details of how locally relevant, practice-based, and ideologically recognised personae are related to larger patterns of variation. These studies include Moore's (2003) study of a secondary school in England, Podesva et al.'s (2001) study of the varying personae of a gay man in San Francisco, Lawson's (2009) study of masculine personae in Glasgow, Maegaard's (2007) study of variation in a multi-ethnic high school in Copenhagen, Denmark, and Benor's (2001, 2004) study of the use of /t/ among Orthodox Jews in Philadelphia. All of these studies show how variation is used by speakers to align themselves with personae in communities of practice which can be understood as local ways of experiencing larger social categories such as class and gender. These personae are in a sense made up of stances (Kiesling 2009; Eckert 2008a: 455), such that there is a secondary indexicality between the personae and the stances that the speakers take up. Bucholtz and Hall (2004) refer to this process as *stance accretion*. We have already seen how variation can index stances.

We thus have three abstract levels of social organisation that are related dialectically and interact to produce indexical meaning and change in such meaning. The largest is that of the groups traditionally coded for by variationists (age, gender, class); the middle level is that of communities of practice and the ideologically relevant personae that they are inhabited by; and finally there is the level of stance. These levels interact in both the interactions in which variables are used and over longer stretches of time as a change expands through a speech community. We have seen numerous examples of such a process. Eckert shows that the oppositional stances that the burnouts take are related to their use of variants that are used more towards Detroit's urban core. This three-level view gives us a fairly good understanding of how variation and change are embedded in the speech community and spread through it. The actual path of a change is still very much a mystery, but it looks as though, as a change becomes older, its meanings become more diffuse and vague. New generations will also reinterpret the meanings, and they will expand as they are used in wider contexts. As well, in order for speakers to create a distinctive persona, they will need to advance a change further. But this view of the 'transmission' of changes is speculative. In the next chapter, we will explore what is known about how children acquire variation.

Chapter 7

Acquisition of variation

HOW IS VARIATION LEARNED?

Although the question of how variation is acquired is a central one – it is the transmission problem for WLH – surprisingly little work has been done on exactly how children acquire variation, and what patterns they show as they develop their linguistic systems. While not non-existent, studies of the acquisition of variation are fairly rare compared to the studies of adult speakers. Labov (2001a) proposes a model of transmission that has language learning in the early years – from the caregiver, who he notes is usually female – as central, so it is important to uncover the processes and constraints in this transmission process.

There are several crucial questions we must answer:

1. When do children begin acquiring variation? Do they have a 'categorical' period and then start to vary, or is there variation from the beginning?
2. When does the influence of peers take over and what form does that influence take?
3. To what extent is variation changeable over the lifespan?
4. Do children acquire all constraints for a variable (social and structural) at the same time?
5. What do children actually hear from caregivers?
6. Does what children do with language actually reflect the input they hear?
7. How do children learn social constraints? Is it through overt talk, implicitly, or both?
8. Are all variables acquired in the same way and at the same speed?

We will consider these questions as we view four different developmental stages: early childhood, the emerging peer group, adolescence, and adulthood.

EARLY CHILDHOOD

Children's production from early on is necessarily variable, in fact more variable than adult speech. Much of this variability, however, is probably part of the learning process as children refine their linguistic systems and in fact narrow the variability.

120 Linguistic Variation and Change

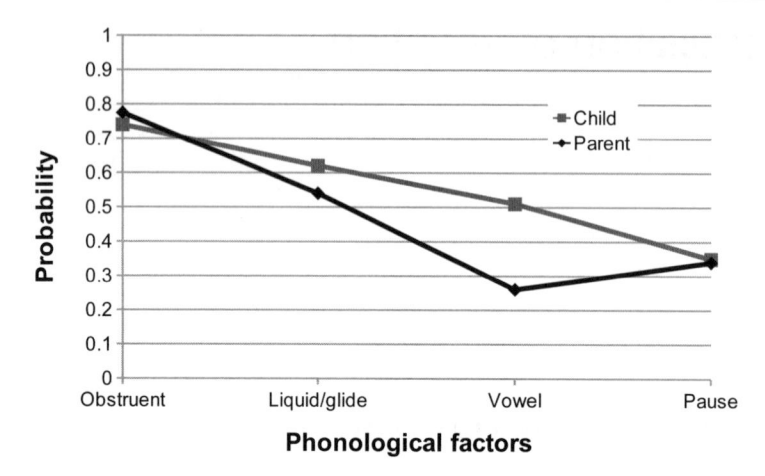

Figure 7.1 Coronal stop deletion (CSD) by age and following environment (adapted from Labov 1989: 93)

One of the challenges of studying childhood variation is determining what part of the variation is developmental – related to the process of acquisition – and what part is part of the system they are acquiring. If a longitudinal view of individual children is taken, then the difference will appear over time. However, little work of this sort has been done.

Despite these difficulties, it is clear from the research so far that children learn variation as an integral part of the language acquisition process. The earliest age that has been reliably reported is about three, and the studies that have been performed show that some fairly complex patterns of variation already appear. A classic early work in this area is Payne's (1980) study in a suburb of Philadelphia. She found that the young children in her corpus whose parents were native to the area had acquired the complex pattern of /æ/-tensing characteristic of the area, but that those with parents from other dialect areas had not mastered it. Thus, it appears that early exposure to phonemic categories is crucial in acquiring at least this complex system (or it may be that such complex patterns need lots of input to form).

Roberts (1997) analyses the variation patterns for coronal stop deletion (CSD) among 3- and 4-year-old children in Philadelphia, and finds that they have mostly acquired the following environment and morphological constraints. The results for following segment are shown in Figure 7.1. It can be seen the children closely match the adult pattern, with the exception of the vowel category, which diverges slightly.

Labov (1989) shows that the structural constraints on CSD and (ing) are already present in the speech of a 7-year-old boy in Philadelphia, and also shows that the relevant constraints are present – including the grammatical conditioning of (ing). Foulkes et al. (1999) similarly showed that children aged between 2 and 4 were learning the complex glottalisation patterns in Newcastle-upon-Tyne, England. Kerswill (1996), however, working in a dialect contact situation, shows that fairly young children are active in creating the new dialect. In other words, they are already deviating from the language of their caregivers and towards a new community norm. This result suggests that even at a young age, if children have contact with other children, these peers will have some influence on the development of variable patterns. However, a later analysis (Kerswill and Williams 2005) shows that the youngest (4-year-old) children have the closest correlation with their caregivers, while older (8- and 12-year-old) children correlate less with their caregivers, showing that there is an influence of caregivers that is greater at the younger stage than at the older.

One of the most important recent studies in this area is Smith et al.'s study (2007) of 2-to-4-year olds. They discover how two different variables in Buckie, Scotland, are acquired in different ways. They recorded caregiver–child pairs in natural settings, and then measured rates of variation for two local variables. One was of (ʌʊ), the use of [u:] for a set of words where the standard has /aʊ/, as in *out* or *house*, while the other was the use of verbal *-s* in third person plural contexts. Both variables are represented in the phrase in the title: *My trousers is fa'in doon*. Note that it is only the second token of (ʌʊ) in the title that shows [u:]; this is because there are lexical constraints on this variable. Smith et al. show that the structural constraints on both variables are present in children from a young age. We might predict that in general, the more regular constraints and patterns seem to be adopted at an earlier age, while more complex, specific, and abstract patterns show up later; but this is not always the result.

Smith et al. also show that the caregiver has a different effect on the children's use of each variable. They found a very significant effect for both structural and social patterns for (ʌʊ), but no such effect for (-s). Moreover, the caregivers' patterns matched that of the wider community (which Smith et al. also had data from) for (-s), but they found that the caregivers used less [u:] for (ʌʊ) than the community when speaking to their children. So for some variables caregivers adjust their child-directed speech, while for others they don't. It remains to be discovered under what condition each occurs, but it is a reasonable hypothesis that it is related to the indexical status (first- or second-order) of the variable; (ʌʊ) is a more stereotyped feature of Scottish speech than plural -s.

In addition to the structural patterning at a young age, the social use of variation is also present at this age. Labov (1989) shows regular intraspeaker patterning for CSD and (ing) for a 7-year-old in Philadelphia. Such patterning is difficult to detect, since most young children's speech is not collected in extended interviews with opportunities for different forms of speech activity. Smith et al.'s study is again important in this regard. They coded their data by speech activity: *play, teaching, routine,* and *discipline*. For (ʌʊ), they found a stunning correlation between caregivers and children, as shown in Figure 7.2.

The figure shows that the caregivers have a regular intraspeaker shift between roles in which they are creating a clear authoritative persona (teaching and discipline) and ones that create less difference between them and the child. Most importantly, the children match this difference exactly. This result hints that the early acquisition of

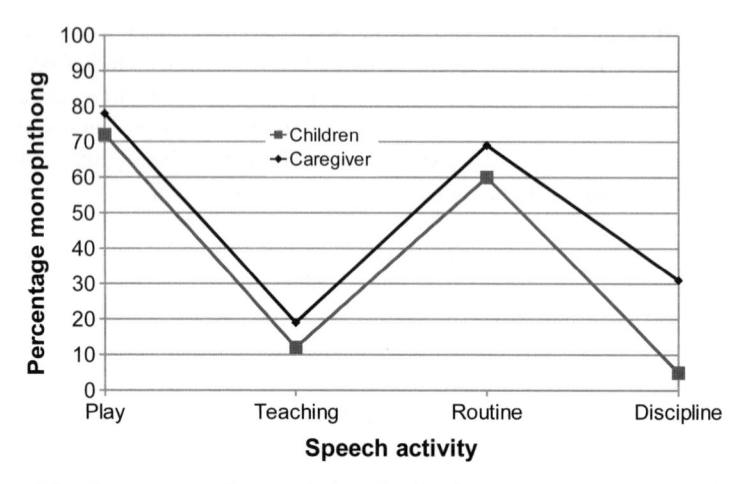

Figure 7.2 Percentage of monophthongisation by speaker and speech activity (adapted from Smith et al. 2007: 75)

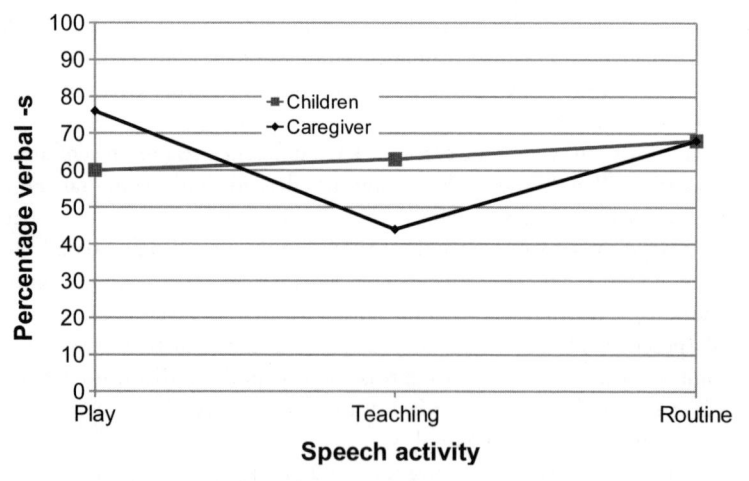

Figure 7.3 Percentage verbal (-s) by speaker and speech activity (adapted from Smith et al. 2007: 84)

social variation is related to the different prototypical roles played by parents and children. Notice that the roles in which power differences are highlighted are those in which the most 'standard' (ʌʊ) is used, while more equal, solidary situations have a higher 'vernacular' use. This pattern is a view into the dialectic between the pattern of the wider community and its use as a stance index, and shows how the indexical relationships in the community are recreated in new generations from early on. Note, however, that (-s) did not show such a pattern, as shown in Figure 7.3.

So in terms of both structural and social constraints, and age of acquisition, variables differ considerably. It is not clear at this point what is important in determining these differences. Some possibilities are the level of abstractness or complexity involved in the variable, the frequency with which tokens of the variable are present, the indexical order of the variable, the difference in rates of caregiver use (i.e., whether caregivers make big shifts as in the (ʌʊ) variable in Buckie, or small ones as for (-s)), and how that is related to the indexical order. Finally, note that one of the important general findings about language acquisition from these studies is that caregivers do not use one kind of speech to children, but can shift considerably depending on the situation.

OLDER CHILDREN AND ADOLESCENTS

Older children have been much less studied than both young children and adolescents. However, it is clear that this stage of life is important. While cultures differ in this respect, this tends to be the age range (about 6 to 12 years old) when children spend less time with caregivers and more with peer groups. In fact, in most studies it is not seen as a stage at all. Of course, life stages are social organisations of age, but in societies where there is a clear adolescent stage, the one before it is a mystery.

Kerswill and Williams (2005), however, do include 8-year-olds (along with 4- and 12-year-olds) in their sample in Milton Keynes. They find that for their (ou) variable (the fronting of the vowel in words like *goat*), the youngest group is correlated with caregivers, while this correlation disappears for the 8- and 12-year-olds. This result provides clear evidence that it is at this young stage that children begin to move to the variation norms of their peer group, and that this is probably where the incrementation of change begins to take place.

Eckert's study of two elementary schools in northern California is one of the only studies to investigate this stage. She shows that it is at this stage that children begin to enter what she calls the *heterosexual marketplace* as they build a 'peer-based social order'. This social order

> emerges in the course of fifth and sixth grades in the form of a heterosocial crowd, which is an alliance of smaller friendship groups of kids who have emerged as popular through early elementary school. The crowd brings boys' and girls' networks into a collaboration, combining social status and resources and yielding a sufficiently large social aggregate to dominate the local scene and to contrast with the other kids' small friendship groups. (2008b: 31)

This crowd is concerned especially with heterosexual pairs, and the girls are the organisers of the pairing (or 'trading'). Eckert shows how this heterosexual market becomes a linguistic one, and how linguistic variants become involved in the kinds of stances that girls and boys take in order to be successful on this market. It is clear from this work that at this point, the 'kids' are not so much reproducing the variation that they learned from their parents as using that variation as a resource for social work in this crowd. Eckert shows especially how differences in resources in the two schools – which differ in their dominant ethnicity and class background

– mean that different patterns of linguistic variation appear in each, and that different 'ethnolects' are maintained. Her work shows that this stage sees the beginning of the emergence of each generation's adolescent contribution to language change. It is clear from many studies that the adolescent stage is when most language change happens. Labov (2001a) shows that there is a peak of use for 'vernacular' variants in adolescence. Eckert's (2000) groundbreaking study of peer groups and variation, discussed in Chapter 4, showed how these changes are embedded into the social structure and practice of adolescents in high school. Central to that practice is the creation of what Eckert calls a persona, and most important for some kids is a persona that is distinctive. As one group moves to create the most distinctive stylistic practice (in Eckert's work, generally the burnouts, but that oversimplifies considerably), they increment changes further away from more 'conservative' speakers. These speakers don't experience themselves as incrementing a change, but as aligning themselves with certain stances and personae that are indexed by the most extreme variants, and in the process increment the change.

ADULTHOOD

Adulthood, as Eckert (2000) points out, is often not thought of as a developmental stage, but it is, and in fact one can identify different adulthood stages as well. However, linguists (variationists included) have often viewed adulthood as the endpoint of acquisition. While this may be the case for some variables (such as mergers), it is clear that changes do take place over the course of speakers' adult lives. For example, Guy and Boyd (1990) investigated whether CSD constraints changed over speakers' lifetimes. They found that most constraints remained constant, but that many speakers changed their analysis of the irregular past verb class that includes *told* and *slept*. These researchers argue that this shows that speakers continue to develop grammars across the lifespan.

There are also likely to be changes in adulthood as adults move into new speech situations and roles. Here again, there is very little work on how, for example, moving from being an unmarried 25-year-old to a 35-year-old parent changes the variable patterns a person uses, and what variables are sensitive to such a change.

TRANSMISSION AND INCREMENTATION OF CHANGES

What then is the role of children in the transmission and incrementation of changes? Transmission refers to the passing of the change from one generation to the next, while incrementation is the advancement of the change in the same direction by the next generation. Labov (2001a: 437) proposes that children learn the language of their caregivers, at least at first, and that they develop stylistic differences such that they associate a new or vernacular variant with 'nonconformity', which he argues is central in the incrementation or 'moving forward' of changes as well. From the research described above, this hypothesis seems sound at a very general level: some variables are differentiated by style (or speech activity, or stance) early on, and children match their caregiver's pattern. However, we don't see all variables being learned in this way; some are more complex, or they are not used by the caregivers to differentiate stance or speech activity. But it is clear that some variability is learned by children from caregivers.

Of course, it is what they do with that variability as they grow up and then grow old that is of central interest to a theory or model of change. For we have seen that children actively learn and sometimes create new ways of speaking in their peer groups. In most cases, this appears (at least once it is completed) to be a mechanical process in that many people move in the same direction – all the cities in the wide Northern Cities dialect area, for example, advance vowels in the same way. But observing this mechanical process does not provide us with an understanding of it. Rather, this incrementation seems to happen because the variability is a resource for social meaning locally and (it appears to each speaker at least) individually. The term 'acquisition of variation' is thus problematic, because at first children acquire only a general variation pattern; later on they actively create their own patterns of variation, thus moving a change forward, or reversing or recycling it.

Part III: Variation, change, and linguistic structure

Introduction to Part III

We can now move to a survey of how the field has begun to answer the main questions for the so-called *internal factors* affecting variation and change, which I will refer to more generally as *structural patterns* (referring to both the linguistic variable and the internal factors). As our discussion of the linguistic variable in Chapter 2 showed, variation in different domains of language – phonology, morphology, syntax, pragmatics and discourse, suprasegmentals, and lexicon – produces different sorts of linguistic variables and patterns of variation and change. So we will consider structural patterns in each of these domains separately. In this chapter we will consider phonology and morphology, which share some common problems. The division between phonology and morphology (and morphology and syntax) is not always clear; just to make the division manageable, I will consider phonological patterns to be those in which the sociolinguistic variable is defined on the basis of a phoneme or a shift in the phonetic realisation of a phoneme. Where a morpheme or morphology is involved in the variable, it will be considered a morphological variable. For example, the centralisation of diphthongs on Martha's Vineyard is clearly a phonological variable, while the alternation between [ɪn] and [ɪŋ] for the variable (ing) is a morphological variable; even though the latter is realised as a phonetic alternation (and is affected by phonological factors), the variable is identified by its status (mostly) as a morpheme. The criterion that moves a variable from morphology to syntax will be that the variable is involved in a phrase structure shift, such as word order. Thus an alternation between *was* and *were* with a plural subject in English is a morphological pattern, while an active–passive alternation is syntactic.

In addition, within each linguistic level, there are unique kinds of linguistic change that can be observed, such as mergers in phonology, paradigmatic levelling in morphology (in which parts of a paradigm lose differences), and word order in syntax. Therefore each kind of linguistic change will necessarily form another axis of organisation for these chapters. I will assume that readers have a basic familiarity with different kinds of changes from historical linguistics (for example, the definition of chain shifts, analogy, and grammaticalisation), and these concepts of historical linguistics will be addressed only through the lens of variationist research; introductory texts such as Trask (1996), Campbell (2004), McMahon (1994), or Hock (1991) are recommended to fill in the basic definitions and historical linguistics findings for the different kinds of changes. Note that we will concern ourselves largely with the changes in progress, not completed changes. In addition, we need to consider what counts as a change in progress and what does not, and the reverse side of the change questions: what leads to stability, and where does stable variability come from? Finally, although most changes we consider will be ones that appear to originate within one linguistic variety, we will also consider some changes that occur because of contact with other varieties.

In sum, we can approach the study of variation and change on a number of different axes:

1. structural (internal) factors or social factors influencing variation and change;
2. stable variation or variation indicating change;
3. phonology, morphology, syntax, or pragmatics;
4. types of change within:
   phonology: shifts and chain shifts, or mergers;
   morphology: analogy, levelling, reanalysis or morphologisation;
   syntax: grammaticalisation, reanalysis of surface structure, restructuring of grammars (e.g., in phrase structure);
   pragmatics: suprasegmentals (e.g., intonation), word order, and information structure.

Chapter 8

Structural patterns I: phonology and morphology

PHONOLOGICAL VARIATION: PATTERNS OF CHANGE, STRUCTURAL EFFECTS, AND EXPLANATION

We begin our survey of the structural factors in phonological variation by considering the four central questions surrounding phonological variation:

1. Does change operate gradually on a single phonetic feature of all instances of a phoneme (regular or Neogrammarian change), or does it operate on words, such that different words abruptly replace one phoneme with another (lexical diffusion)?
2. Are there universal constraints on the directionality of change?
3. If there are universal constraints on the directionality of change, is there some functional motivation for this direction? By 'functional', we mean whether the direction of change is created because language will function better in some way, either in the articulatory machinery of speaking or in the perception of different words (or in both).
4. Finally, are there any general principles of change in situations of dialect and language contact? For example, if phonemes differ phonetically in two varieties in contact, thus forming a variable, how is this difference resolved (e.g., by adopting one variant over the other, or by creating a third 'fudged' variant)?

CHANGE IN PROGRESS

As discussed in Chapter 3, we most often rely on age patterns in order to determine whether we are looking at changes in progress or stable variation. Labov's study on Martha's Vineyard was the earliest variationist study to use mechanical recording and show that a change in progress can be observed based on apparent-time patterns, and his 1966 study of New York City established that such a study can be performed in a large, complex urban community. Both of those studies relied on previous records of dialect surveys and other reports as real-time data to determine that the patterns they found were true generational change rather than age grading. In generational change, the individual is relatively stable, but the community is

132　Linguistic Variation and Change

Figure 8.1 /r/ use in New York City by department store at two different times (adapted from Labov 1994: 88)

changing. In age grading, the individual changes as they age, and the age patterns found actually reflect a relatively stable situation for the community. Most of the evidence so far from real-time studies suggests that, especially at the phonological level, speakers are fairly consistent in their productions of articulation once they reach adulthood. Labov (1994: ch. 4) presents several studies that make it evident that this is probably the case, although no one study is conclusive. The strongest evidence is simply the observations that adults who move to new dialect areas tend not to acquire that new dialect.

However, it also appears that results are different depending on aspects of the variable being studied. Two aspects seem to be particularly important. First is the so-called 'awareness' of the variation within the community, which we discussed as orders of indexicality in the previous chapter. Consider a variable such as (r) in New York City, which has become relatively noticeable to New Yorkers. In this case, there appears to have been some age grading (although dependent on class). Labov (2001a) discusses Fowler's (1986) replication of his department store study. At first, it appears that little has changed, as shown in Figure 8.1; there is a small rise, but considering that twenty-four years have intervened, the increases are small. However, in Figure 8.2, which takes into account the age of the respondent and shows the changes from 1962 to 1986, we see that the older group in Sack's (the highest-class store) has increased its [r] use much more than the same age group in Macy's (the middle-class store). Moreover, the difference between Sack's and Macy's is greater for the older group than for the younger. This points to the older group in the upper class having changed their (r) use throughout their lives, while the middle group has not changed as much. This pattern suggests that some speakers in New York (older middle- to upper-class speakers) have shifted their (r) pattern during their lifetimes, but not all. So it is possible for some shift to take place, but it is not necessarily the same for everyone.

On the other hand, systems of phonological category seem fairly resistant to

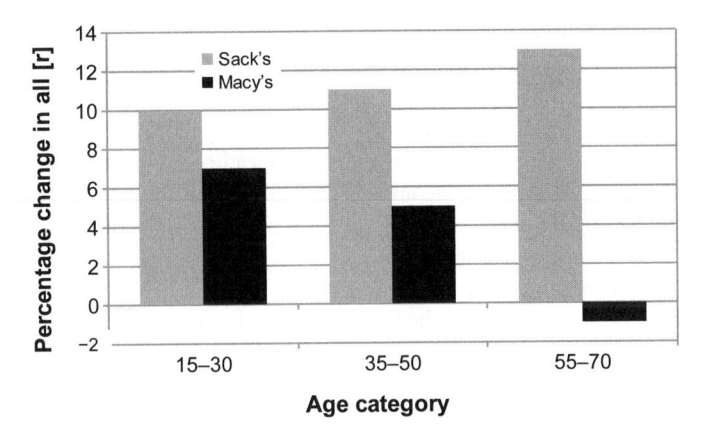

Figure 8.2 Change in /r/ use by department store and age (adapted from Labov 1994: 93)

change, such that distinctions learned or not learned in childhood will persist throughout adulthood. Labov (1994: 110–11) shows how a middle-aged New Yorker who has lived in Los Angeles for decades still shows much of the New York pattern that differentiates the low back vowels /ɑ/ and /ɔ/ (as in *cot* and *caught*).

The three main kinds of phonological change are shifts, mergers, and splits, although the latter two are sometimes discussed together. A shift is simply a phoneme which becomes realised differently phonetically, but for which the phonemic distribution stays the same. For example, in many English varieties, the back vowel /u/ as in *boot* is becoming fronted to a position that approaches [ɪ]. A similar shift is the glottalling of stops, especially /t/, across England. Once a shift occurs, the question becomes what happens to 'neighbouring' segments. That is, if a phoneme changes such that it becomes more and more like another phoneme, what happens to the second one? If it stays the same, then the two phonemes may become indistinct and *merge*. Once mergers take place, they tend not to reverse, but *splits* do occur, usually because of phonetic effects on segments.

So one outcome of a phonetic shift is merger. However, if the second phoneme also shifts and remains distinct from the first phoneme, then these phonemes are involved in a *chain shift*. The chain shift represented here is a *push chain*, because the first phoneme metaphorically pushes the second out of the way. For example, in the so-called Great Vowel Shift of English (Baugh and Cable 1993; Labov 1994), the low front vowel (as in words such as *mate*) moved up and forward from [a] to [e], and the mid front vowel (in words such as *meat*) then moved up as well, from[e] to [i]. *Drag chains* are also possible, such that the second phoneme occupies the old ground of the first phoneme. The Northern Cities Shift, discussed below, is an example of a drag chain.

We should briefly discuss how we know that a pattern is a chain shift, and how we can determine the order in which the changes have begun. The most direct manner is to use real-time data, records both from earlier surveys and from studies repeated at a later time. This is very direct evidence that the change found in the later study began after the changes apparent in the earlier one. A second method is to try to find when differences start to appear for different generations but only in apparent time. So if we find a difference earlier for one phoneme than another, we suspect that the one we find the change for first is leading a sound change.

Another way to determine the answer to the question of stage of change is to look at the magnitude of the effect of age on different vowels. In order to explain this, we must first take a short detour through some specific issues in analysing vowel variation, related to the discussion of Varbrul in Chapter 3. Labov (1994) argues that this can be accomplished on the basis of the regression coefficients for age that come out of multiple regression analyses. Labov's method, widely adopted by other researchers, uses formant measurements of vowels (see Labov et al. 2006). Each vowel is measured and coded as explained in Chapter 3. These measurements are then normalised so that researchers can compare men and women, although the topic of normalisation is somewhat controversial and would require too much discussion at this point (see Labov 2001a: 157–64; Johnson 2006). Because formant measurements are continuous variables (meaning that they are real numbers that have in theory infinite gradations and numbers of decimal places), rather than using logistic regression (the method in Varbrul) we can use a standard multiple regression, with each factor such as preceding and following environment, sex, and especially age as an independent variable. Rather than weights, the output of multiple regression yields coefficients that the factor is multiplied by. We generally use age *categories* rather than numerical age for this purpose, since we assume that linguistic change takes place more by generation than year by year. A multiple regression thus yields a model equation which predicts the value of a vowel's formant value from the values of the factors (for example, preceding and following environment, sex, and especially age). For instance, if we suspected that (aʊ) is fronting, as in Philadelphia, we would take measurements of the F2 of the nucleus of the vowel. Labov finds that the coefficient for age for this variable is −5.75 per decade, so that we can predict the likely F2 of a speaker from his or her age. All other things being equal, if a 20-year-old Philadelphian has an F2 for (aʊ) of 2,000 Hz, then a 40-year-old will have an F2 of 1,988.5 Hz (two decades multiplied by the coefficient is −11.5, which is taken from 2,000). Essentially, it is this coefficient which tells us the age and speed of a vowel shift. A larger coefficient means that the vowel is moving faster, whereas a small coefficient means very little movement (and if age turns out not to be significant, we may omit age in our final regression equation). If we have not performed a multiple regression, we can more simply (but less reliably) compare the differences from one generation to another for different vowels. Vowels that show bigger differences between generations are telling us that this vowel is shifting rather quickly. A regular pattern that is found in language change seems to be an S-curve, so we know that vowels moving more quickly than others are in the middle, steep slope of change, while those moving slowly are at the beginning or end of their shift (this curve is discussed in more depth in the next chapter).

These processes – mergers, splits and shifts – are the major general processes of sound change. Variationist studies have focused overwhelmingly on vowel shifts, with some work on consonantal changes. Nevertheless, we will review patterns in both areas, although the focus on vocalic variables will be clear.

SHIFTS AND CHAIN SHIFTS

Labov (1994: chs 5–6) provides an extensive catalogue of vowel chain shifts, both completed and in progress. Labov proposes several principles of vowel shifting in that work, exemplified by vowel shifts in progress, and identifies three patterns of vowel shifting. We should note that this catalogue heavily favours Germanic languages (especially English), and although there is some discussion of other Indo-European languages, the applicability of these processes universally is an open question. Part of the Germanic focus is Labov's claim that in Germanic languages and English specifically, the vowel space has a peripheral and non-peripheral space, as shown in Figure 8.3.

This conception of the vowel space is important in that it allows Labov to make claims about the directionality of vowels in these different spaces. These claims he calls 'principles', which are 'maximal projections of generalizations', and thus more abstract than generalisations, or 'a generalization that is unrestricted in its application in time or space' (1994: 13). From their presentation and discussion, these principles are formulated as an answer to the constraints question, and are meant to be the dominant tendencies for vowel shifts. They can thus also be distinguished from the 'sound laws' of the Neogrammarians in that they are not as strict as those laws. In order to understand Labov's principles, we will briefly discuss a number of vowel shifts that lead to these generalisations: the Philadelphia Shift, the Northern Cities Shift, the Southern Shift, and the Canadian Shift. The Great Vowel Shift is also discussed by Labov in his formulation of generalisations, but since it is a completed change we wil leave it aside for the most part.

The Philadelphia Shift

The vowel shifts in Philadelphia are characterised by a shift in the diphthongs /aʊ/ and /aɪ/, where the nucleus of /aʊ/ is moving up and forward and the nucleus of

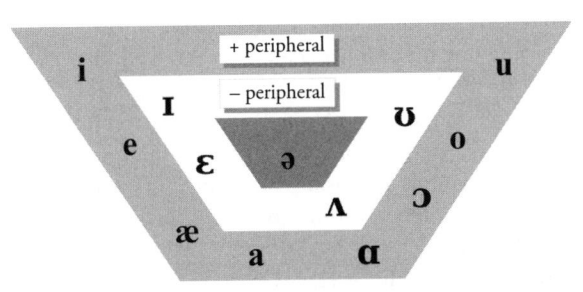

Figure 8.3 Vowel space core and periphery (adapted from Labov 1994: 177)

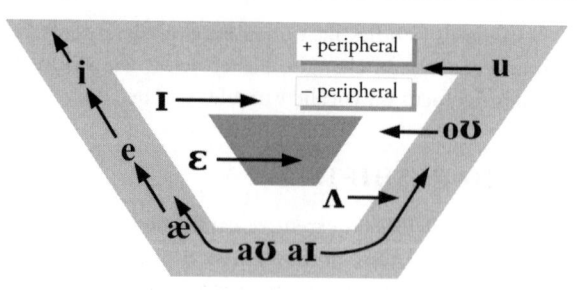

Figure 8.4 The Philadelphia Vowel Shift

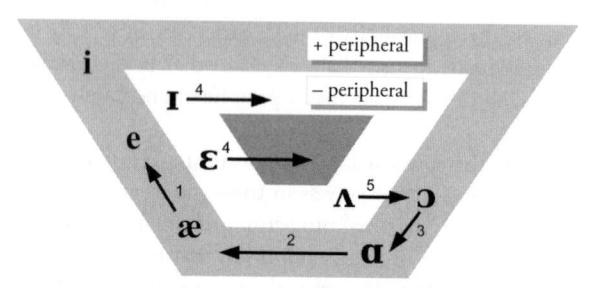

Figure 8.5 The Northern Cities Vowel Shift (adapted from Labov 1994, in press)

/aɪ/ is moving up and back (Labov 1994: 59). Philadelphia also shows the raising and fronting of /i, e, æ/ as in *seat, straight,* and *sat.* Moreover, the back vowels /u/ (*suit*) and /oʊ/ (*sowed*) are being fronted. Last, it seems that the short vowels /ɪ, ɛ, ʌ/ (*sit, set, but*) are all beginning to move down or back. So it appears that the diphthong changes happened first, and that there are two, not necessarily connected, chain shifts in progress, with the front and back vowels reorganising separately, as shown in Figure 8.4.

The Northern Cities Shift

The Northern Cities Shift (NCS) is studied by many more researchers than the Philadelphia Shift, but probably fewer speakers have actually been studied. This shift is occurring in a much wider geographic area as well, that is, the northern or Great Lakes cities in the USA, including Buffalo, Rochester, Cleveland, Detroit, and Chicago. This shift is the most comprehensive and connected of those we will consider, and the most agreed-upon pattern is shown in Figure 8.5.

The peripheral front vowels are raising, while the low vowels are fronting behind them. Finally, the non-peripheral front vowels are lowering or backing, both of which count as less open in Labov's final scheme. There is thus a wholesale rotation of the vowel system going on. However, as Gordon (2001) shows, there is fairly thin evidence for such a neat picture. He advocates a more complex picture, in which

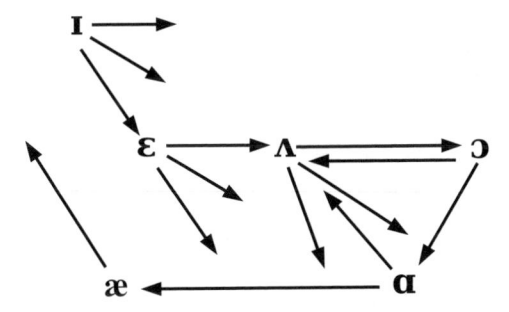

Figure 8.6 A more complex view of the Northern Cities Vowel Shift (adapted from Gordon 2001)

the tense vowels continue the rotation as claimed by Labov, but the non-peripheral vowels are characterised by variation in the direction of their movement as shown in Figure 8.6.

Gordon points out that vowel variation and shift, when viewed in terms of many tokens even in a single individual, are in fact much more complex and variable that those presented by the neat charts in Figures 8.5 and 8.6. So we must keep in mind that the changes we are discussing are abstract theoretical creations to a large extent.

Both of these shifts point to patterns that lead Labov to formulate the following vowel shift principles:

Principle I: In chain shifts, tense nuclei rise along a peripheral track. This pattern is present for both Philadelphia and the Northern Cities for the /i, e, and æ/ vowels, and in Philadelphia for the diphthong nuclei.

Principle II: In chain shifts, lax nuclei fall along a non-peripheral track. Both again show this pattern, for /ɪ, ɛ, ʌ/ (at least when they are falling).

Principle III: In chain shifts, tense vowels move to the front along peripheral paths, and lax vowels move to the back along non-peripheral paths. Here we find the peripheral /u/ and /oʊ/ moving forward in both shifts, and the non-peripheral /ɪ, ɛ, ʌ/ moving back.

The next two shifts also exemplify these principles, but in a less straightforward manner.

The Southern Shift

The Southern Shift is so called because it is characteristic of a number of 'souths', including the US south, the Southern Hemisphere countries of Australia, New Zealand, and South Africa, and the southern UK. In this shift, the front vowels have switched peripherality: /i/ (*seat*) and /e/ (*straight*) become non-peripheral and /ɪ/ (*sit*) and /ɛ/ (*set*) become peripheral. Following this shift, the (now peripheral) /ɪ/ and /ɛ/ raise and the (now non-peripheral) /i/ and /e/ fall. The reader will note, I

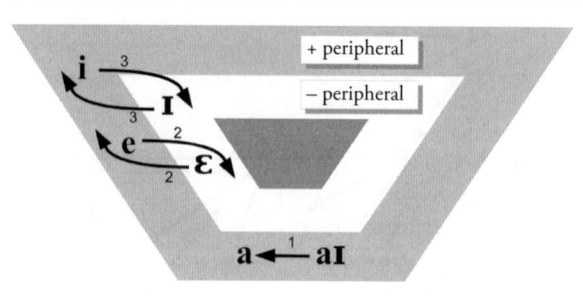

Figure 8.7 Southern Shift peripheral vowel raising (adapted from Labov 1994, in press)

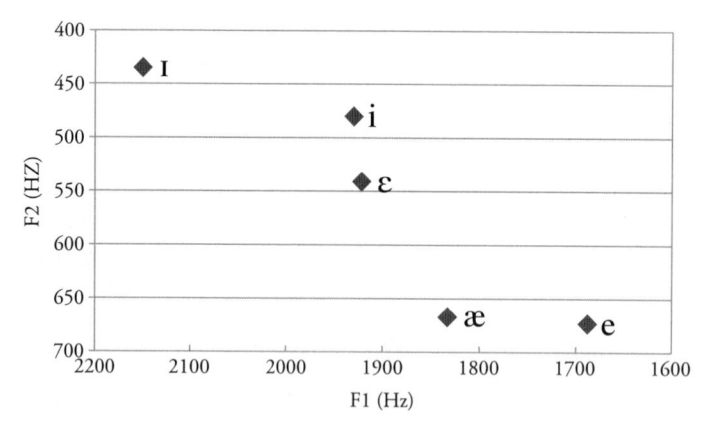

Figure 8.8 Southern Shift in Sydney, Australia

hope, that there is a danger of some serious *post hoc* reasoning in positing that these changes are taking place in this manner. We might worry that an apparent counter-example to Labov's principles is explained by 'magically' redefining which vowel track is being followed by particular vowels. However, this view can be checked by inspecting actual vowel plots by speakers from these areas. In all cases, we find that the (i) and (e) are to the back of /ɪ/ and /ɛ/, a pattern represented in Figure 8.7. Figure 8.8 shows this pattern in speakers from Sydney, Australia, based on data I collected in 1997–8 (see Kiesling 2005 for details). Note that /ɪ/ is to the front of /i/, and /ɛ/ is to the front of /e/.

The Canadian Shift

The Canadian Shift is a purported shift that again centres on the status of /æ/, except that rather than moving up and forward in vowel space as in the NCS, there is a lowering and backing towards [ɑ]. There is disagreement about the status of the other front lax vowels. Clarke et al. (1995) argued that /ɪ/ and /ɛ/ are falling in a chain shift, on the basis of data from Ontario. However, Boberg (2005) finds that in Montreal the higher two vowels are moving more towards the back rather than lowering. This difference is similar to the variation in short vowel trajectory that Gordon (2001) discusses for the NCS, suggesting that these vowels are likely to move either back or down, or both when they shift. It is possible that in the Canadian shift they are participating in a *parallel* shift rather than a chain shift.

Eventually, Labov boils the three principles down to one overarching principle, based on the idea that the articulation of vowels is actually not triangular, but rather more ovoid. He assigns the following degrees of openness to particular vowels (Labov 1994: 258):

5 4 3 2 1
a æ ɛ e I

8 7 6 5 4 3 2 1
a ɑ ɔ o u ʉ ü I

He then provides a single overarching principle: in chain shifts, peripheral vowels become less open and non-peripheral vowels become more open.

There are thus what appear to be some fairly robust patterns of vowel shift that address the constraints problem. However, these internal forces, while fairly strong, are not invariant and universal. Kerswill et al. (2008) and Torgersen and Kerswill (2004) both show that other forces – including language contact as well as social mechanisms and motivations such as network structure and identity – can override the principles. So it seems there are propensities for directions of vowel shift, but that they are far from universal 'laws'.

We do not have other patterns of phonological variation such as consonant shifting (or even shifting of, say, manner or sonorance). Other constraints on phonological variation have to do with well-known phonological processes: assimilation, dissimilation, resyllabification, etc. But there have been no proposals that, for example, stops tend to go to fricatives, or voiced to voiceless, or coronals to palatals. However, phoneticians have made some proposals in this regard, and many seem to be supported by variationist studies. Ohala (2003) argues that sound changes such as assimilation and dissimilation can be shown to be almost universal, and are based on the kinds of variation that appears because of the way sound segments are perceived. This claim is important for the variationist research programme because it predicts stable variation patterns and also asymmetric pressures that push changes one way or another. For example, Ohala argues that articulatory facts about /t/ productions before high vowels bias language in favour of the palatalisation of /t/, as in the pronunciation of *actual* as [æktʃuəl]. This could also be seen as part of the larger process often called *lenition or weakening*, although these terms are not used in linguistics in a consistent manner, and so whether variation studies show a trend towards lenition are not clear. Kallen (2005) compares /t/ lenition in several studies of Irish English, and finds that a general process of lenition is not likely. Ohala also argues that speech perception produces certain biases, such as the likelihood

Table 8.1 Factors in coronal stop deletion (CSD)

Features of Preceding Segment	Factor Weight
Sonority	
[-son]	0.58
[+son]	0.42
Continuancy	
[-cont]	0.65
[+cont]	0.35
Coronal Place	
[-cor]	0.65
[+cor]	0.35
Voice (preceding sonorants only)	
[α voice]	0.64
[-α voice]	0.36
Log likelihood = 535.033	

of a shift from /k/ to /t/ or /tʃ/ before high front vowels and glides. He cites work from Winitz et al. (1972) that shows that /pi/ is likely to be misheard as /ti/ in an experimental study, and that this is much more likely than other misperceptions. Unfortunately few variation studies of consonants take a wider view, and most focus on the internal factors of their particular data set. We might propose and test, for example, Ohala's prediction of directionality back in the mouth for labial and coronal segments before high front vowels, and pressure for /k/ to /p/ before high vowels. We might also propose that segments found more rarely in the world's languages are likely to shift to more common ones (such as /θ/ to /t/ in English).

We do find assimilatory patterns in variationist work, especially in cases of deletion. For example, in /l/-vocalisation in Pittsburgh, we find that there is more likely to be vocalisation with a following consonant, such as in *felt* rather than in *fell* when the /l/ is word-final. These are well-known historical and phonological processes, and we would be surprised if they didn't provide some of the stucture for 'orderly heterogeneity'. Similarly, Guy and Boberg (1997) argue that CSD is sensitive to the Obligatory Contour Principle or OCP (Leben 1973; Odden 1986). The OCP (very simplified) basically says that adjacent segments prefer to be different; the original formulation was for tone and thus the argument was that there should be a contour rather than level tone. Guy and Boberg find a constraint on deletion such that segments that have more in common with a coronal stop ([-sonorant], [-continuant], [+coronal], and the same voicing as the segment) are more likely to be deleted, as shown in Table 8.1. While this is a study of deletion, it could have implications for other studies of phonetic shift, such as those showing backing of consonants adjacent to high front vowels. Future work in this area could consider the relative strength, and contexts for, the OCP or assimilation in changes in progress.

Up until now we have considered consonantal sound changes to be based on a linear phonetic scale, but recent work has shown that close phonetic analyses reveal more complex variation. One example of such a situation is the realisation of /t/ word-finally in Newcastle-upon-Tyne, England. Milroy et al. (1994) identify five variants for this variable, and show that they are not organised on a single scale of lenition. The researchers found ten variants, and conflated these ten to five: [r], [t], voiced or flapped /t/ such as [ɾ], a glottalised variant [ʔt], a glottal stop [ʔ]. They are particularly interested in the latter two, because they have often been collapsed into a single variant in other studies. But Milroy et al. show that this assumption is suspect at best, especially since the [ʔt] and [ʔ] variants pattern different socially and linguistically. In addition, when all voiceless stops are considered, they find that [ʔ] is favoured with /t/, while glottalisation ([ʔp], [ʔt], [ʔk]) is favoured for /p/ and /k/. Work such as this suggests that for phonetic change, shifts may be other than binary, such that one variable has numerous variants and that many of them are involved in a change. While the main patterns of Labov may hold in further studies, it may also be true that more phonetically sensitive studies such as Milroy et al.'s will reveal that such generalisations have proved premature.

MERGERS

The second major phonological change that variationists have studied is the spread of mergers. This area has been one of the most contentious with respect to other areas of linguistic change, because it is where some of the more striking claims have been made. Before we get to those, however, let us consider how we might discover a vowel merger taking place (and most work in this area has been on vowel merger or on *conditioned* vowel mergers, such as the *pin–pen* merger in the US south or the *pool–pull* merger in Utah, discussed below). For chain shifts we looked for a relationship between two phonemes; in studying mergers we need to demonstrate a relationship between two vowels. However, in this case, rather than moving in the same direction in vowel space, we find that the two vowels are collapsing into a single area, either because one vowel is moving into the other vowel's space or because they are both moving into the same space. We can thus simply plot vowels and inspect whether they are occupying different areas, and do t-tests or other statistical tests to determine whether or not a speaker shows a significant difference in their formants.

For example, Eberhardt (2009a, 2009b) investigated whether the well-known low back merger (LBM), which is well established in the White population of Pittsburgh (Labov et al. 2006; Johnstone and Kiesling 2008), is also taking place in the African American population. This merger is the collapsing of the vowel category /ɑ/ as in *cot* and /ɔ/ as in *caught*, and is present throughout the Midland and Western dialect areas of the United States, and in Canada. Eberhardt performed measurements on the first two formants of the two vowels involved in the LBM, with a sample of thirty-four African American speakers in Pittsburgh. She first performed independent t-tests for each speaker, and found only sporadic statistical significance. She also employed a more rigorous multiple regression analysis for each speaker in which the word class (/ɑ/ or /ɔ/) was only one factor of many. Only one speaker showed any difference. From this pattern she argued that the African American speech community in Pittsburgh has adopted the merger. This result was, from a structural pattern standpoint, expected, because in general it has been found that mergers tend to expand (which Labov (1994: 313) calls *Herzog's Principle*: mergers expand at the expense of distinctions). We also might argue that a merger is in progress if we find generational changes such that older speakers show a statistical significance while younger speakers show no difference.

Another way to determine whether a merger has taken place or is in progress is to test the perceptions of the speech community; if two segments have merged, speakers should not be able to hear the difference. So if we ask speakers whether they hear a difference between two words that are different – but still within the range of the merged area – and they don't hear a difference, then we probably have a merger. There are a number of methods to assess this perception. One is simply to ask people whether two words sound the same or not. This method is the least reliable, of course, because speakers may not be accurate in their assessment, especially if they are looking at written pairs, which give them orthographic cues that they should sound different. A second way is to provide a list of pairs and ask whether the words are the same or different. This is more reliable, because it is in response to a standard set of stimuli and sound is the only cue. Finally, a procedure known as the commutation test has been used in some instances. Labov (1994) used this method in Philadelphia, where there is an apparent merger of /ʌr/ and /ɛr/, so that words pairs like *murray/merry* and *furry/ferry* are pronounced and heard the same. In the commutation test, speakers are asked to read a list containing the words involved in a random order, with some words repeating (for example, *murray, murray, merry, murray*). Once finished, the recording is set to a predetermined spot by the researcher (such as the third item) and then played while the speaker tries to identify the words. In a merger situation, in addition to the production in the list being statistically indistinguishable, the speaker should score randomly.

Finally, the most robust test is one in which speakers are not even aware that they are being tested about language, but have their attention on something else. In one of the most creative experiments in sociolinguistics, Labov developed the 'Coach test', so called because it involves speakers reacting to the actions of a coach in a story in which he is deciding whether or not to play a player named Murray (which speakers will hear as 'put Murray in there') or Merion ('put Merion there'). The story is read by a native Philadelphian who nevertheless adjusts his pronunciation so that one version of the test is *Murray* and the other is *Merion*. The story is played to the speakers and then they are asked whether the coach made the right decision. From the answer it is possible to determine how the speakers heard the story, but they focus on the actions of the coach and not on whether the name is *Murray* or *Merion*.

These perception tests have led to one of the most controversial linguistic findings of variationist literature: perception and production do not always match. In Philadelphia, there are a significant number of speakers who clearly produce a difference in the two vowels, but cannot hear the distinction. Almost everyone encountering these facts for the first time is incredulous: how can it possibly be that we can produce distinctions that we can't hear? However, we know that we are born with the ability to hear any distinction presented by our language, but that we eventually lose the ability to hear those distinctions (except with explicit language instruction and practice). It is entirely possible that we learn the subtle distinctions between two close phonemes and learn to reproduce the differences while we are young, and as we become older we adjust our perceptual system. Note that this story still assumes that we have relatively stable *production* throughout our lives while our grammar or perceptual system may be revised. (However, it seems unlikely that we could reorganise our production in such a way as to produce a split into the previous classes, unless they were based on something like orthography.)

I often fail to convince students of near mergers; unfortunately the data are real and robust, and I tell students, as I now caution readers, that one can continue to disbelieve in near mergers if one can find another explanation for the data, or provide a new data set that challenges the previous ones. This kind of reasoning is the hallmark of variationist linguistics (and science more generally): our empirical work may present us with inexplicable results that are nevertheless real. These results cannot be ignored, or else we are not doing science, but ideology. In fact, this is only the tip of the iceberg when it comes to 'strange things' that happen in language perception; as we saw in Chapter 6, perception can be influenced by many factors including how a speaker looks, without necessarily changing how speech is produced. In this wider context, near mergers are not all that strange.

REGULARITY VS. LEXICAL DIFFUSION

We now turn to whether patterns of change are regular or move through so-called lexical diffusion, an issue we have not addressed yet. The previous discussions, while they don't exactly state that changes are regular, nevertheless suggest that they are so. This impression of regularity comes from the discussion of changes in phonemes. In fact, most changes, once they are completed, are regular. Since variationists are looking at change in progress, they ask whether the actual progression of a change happens constantly for a single variety, or whether it happens first in one word and then in another. Here is a made-up example of the two. Imagine that in some language, /r/ is shifting to /l/. This shift will be regular, if it does it a little bit in every word. If there are internal phonological constraints (such that, for example, it happens more between vowels), this is still a regular change in our terminology. This is what we mean by regular change being phonetically gradual. If the change happens all at once in one word, and then all at once in another, then we are looking at lexical diffusion. So let's say there is a word /keres/ and another word /teres/. Now, if *teres* becomes pronounced [teles] 100 per cent of the time before *keres* changes at all, then we have an abrupt change, and evidence for lexical diffusion. Note that we have to be careful that what appears to be an effect from a particular word is not a phonetic effect. For example, we may find that another word – *terdes* – is less likely than *teres* to shift. Is this a lexical effect? We need to look at other words that have /d/ after /r/ in order to determine this. If we find that all /rd/ words are more likely to have the shift, then we are looking at a regular change. If we find, for example, that a word like /gerdes/ does not shift while /terdes/ almost always does, then we have evidence for lexical diffusion. While regularity is often presented as being opposed to lexical

Table 8.2 Types of sound change (Labov 1994: 543)

Regular Sound Change	Lexical Diffusion
Vowel shifts in place of articulation	Shortening and lengthening of segments
Diphthongisation of high vowels	Diphthongisation of mid and low vowels
Consonant changes in manner of articulation	Consonant changes in place of articulation
Vocalisation of liquids	Metathesis of liquids and stops
Deletion of glides and schwa	Deletion of obstruents

diffusion in sound change, there is really no reason to suppose that all changes work through the same mechanism. In fact, the 'debate' has raged for as long as it has because one can find data supporting lexical diffusion and regular sound change.

The best-known example of lexical diffusion in variationist linguistics is the tensing of /æ/ in Philadelphia (Labov 1994, 2001a). This tensing happens in words with following front nasals and fricatives (that is: /f, θ, s, m, n/); this pattern looks pretty regular so far. But /æ/also tenses before three words that have a following /d/: *mad, bad, glad*. These are the only three with a following /d/ that tense – all other words with /æd/ (*dad, sad*, etc.) are not tensed. (I have simplified somewhat for purposes of discussion; for the complete story see Labov 1994: 429–37.) Here we have a split into the tensed variable that Labov calls (aeh) and a lax one he calls (ae). (aeh) is raising in Philadelphia, and it appears that this raising is regular and gradual. Labov thus shows that in different kinds of change – with very similar segments and in the same location – we can find both lexical diffusion (phonetically abrupt tensing of /æ/ by word) and regular sound change (phonetically gradual with no lexical effects). He argues that these different kinds of change appear in different situations, as shown in Table 8.2.

Labov stresses that this division of types of sound change is not a final conclusion, but really a hypothesis that needs to be tested. Changes in progress that are found to deviate from this hypothesis will serve to update this work.

PHONOLOGICAL PATTERNS OF VARIETY CONTACT

Most of the discussion up until now has focused on so-called internal change, in which a variety or variable changes because of some, possibly only hypothetical, property of the language (such as the principles we have just discussed). However, varieties are rarely completely isolated from other varieties; even the most isolated language has a neighbour. So, when determining patterns of variation and change, we also need to take into account such patterns in situations of contact. These patterns are quite different in character from internal changes, because the direction of change depends on the differences in the two varieties. Thus, we characterise such patterns in terms of what kinds of influences different varieties will have on one another. Just as in our discussion above, we will discuss the structural internal patterns here only.

In varietal contact, the identification of a variable can be complex, because we have variability within each of the varieties in question and also between the varieties. In addition, there are a number of different demographic reasons for contact (such as migration, urbanisation, etc.), but since we are focused on language-internal patterns here, we will leave those to a different chapter. Trudgill's (1986) book is one of the central works in this area. In it and further revisions such as Trudgill (2004), he identifies a process of *new dialect formation* or *koineisation* (as indicated earlier, this term for new dialect formation derives from the Greek *koine*, the lingua franca form of Greek from around 300 BCE to 300 AD). After the mixing of the varieties, he argues, there are processes of levelling, simplification or unmarking, interdialect development, reallocation, and focusing.

Levelling and simplification are two processes that work at the beginning of varietal contact. Levelling is the process by which some of the initial variation of the mixing of variants is removed. Trudgill argues that levelling basically removes variation that is used by a minority of speakers in the new speech community. As such it is not an internal linguistic process. Unmarking or simplification, however, is an internal process. A straightforward example might be the survival of a merger in a case where two varieties are in contact and one variety has merged two phonemes that the other variety keeps distinct. The merged phonological system is simpler, and thus is more likely to be the one adopted by the new variety. (Note that this pattern would also follow Labov's 1994 'Herzog's Principle', discussed above.) An example of simplification is given in Kerswill's (2002: 676) discussion of koineisation in the Norwegian towns of Odda and Tyssedal, two towns which developed in the early twentieth century. These both have mixes of the Eastern and Western Norwegian varieties, but in different proportions. The Western dialect has a complex pattern of palatalisation in which nouns that have stems ending in velar stops are realised as palatals in definite forms (which also have a schwa following), but do not change in the indefinite. Thus we have /tɑ:çə/ for 'the roof' and /tɑ:k/ for 'roof'. However, the new variety has removed this complication so that the velars are not changed: 'the roof' is simply /tɑ:kə/.

MORPHOLOGICAL VARIATION

Morphological studies of variation and change present somewhat different questions from phonological ones, although the core concerns are shared. Of course, these variables are all discrete, providing speakers with clear choices in whether and how to mark morphological information. Regularity is less of an issue, although we can still ask whether a morpheme changes in the same way in all conditions and with all words, or whether there are some words for which the change is more or less likely to occur. Functional explanations for patterns of variation are more prominent in morphological variation: many morphological variables involve the deletion of a morpheme, and thus the loss of whatever that morpheme encodes in the language. For example, one variable we will explore is the deletion of plural {s} in Spanish and Portuguese. We might propose, then, that {s} is less likely to delete in situations where a hearer wouldn't be able to recover the plural information through other means. Finally, we are still concerned with whether there might be some universal directions of variation and change, although this concern has not been widely discussed in the literature. We could propose, for example, that the tendency of languages is for morphemes to be lost if they are part of the grammatical system (so we might suggest that the deletion of {s} just discussed is part of a universal pattern). The study of morphosyntactic change known as *grammaticalisation* in fact makes explicit proposals about the development of new morphemes from so-called content words, and we will be considering some patterns of variation in grammaticalisation in the next chapter on syntactic patterns.

There are two kinds of morphological variables, if we take these variables to be those for which the variable set is a single morpheme of the language. The first kind are really morpho*phonemic* variables in which a single morpheme has different phonetic realisations as variants, including deletions, which we should more neutrally refer to as *zero-marking* unless there is clear evidence that there is a process of deletion. The second type of morphological variable is a morphological *alternation*, such as the alternation in some varieties of English between *was* and *were* in the same grammatical person/number (e.g., *you was* alternating with the standard *you were*).

The best-known of this kind of variable is the alternation of (ing) in English. This is a stable variable, in that it has been present in the English language for several centuries. Houston (1985) found that the grammatical effect reflects 'an historical process, a partially completed merger between two originally distinct morphemes in English' (1985: 360). She establishes this fact through differences in (ing) use in south England dialect areas and correlated differences in the history of the morphology in these areas. Houston shows that the difference in variable rates between noun and verbal categories can be better explained through the history of English, rather than appealing to morphology or the functional characteristics of nouns and verbs. However, the reflexes of this change are still evident in the variable in present-day Englishes, and it is an exemplary variable in terms of the internal constraints that affect it.

Recall that the variants of (ing) are [ɪn] and [ɪŋ]. In some cases, [in] and [ɪŋk] are also present. Houston (1985) and Labov (1989) show that, because of the way the {-ende} verbal morpheme collapsed with the original a {-inge} nominal morpheme (among many others), we find a grammatical category effect for this variable. In short, more verbal categories are more likely to show [ɪn]. Houston also found that this sensitivity is a gradual, rather than categorical, scale: more 'noun-like' words had a higher rate of [ɪŋ] than 'verb-like' words. Thus, in her multiple regression analysis of speech from interviews in England, she found that the more noun-like a word, the more likely that it will have the [ɪŋ] variant. However, the statistical groupings fit not into the categories identified by describing words as +/−Noun and +/−Verb, but into less discrete categories on a continuum. Table 8.3 shows an example of the grammatical category effect from my data in the USA, which agrees more or less with Houston's findings (see Houston 1985 for detailed definitions of these categories). These are logistic regression (Varbrul) results, where a weight of over 0.5 indicates that factor favours the [ɪn] variant. Examples are either my own or from Houston (1985: 60–2).

Table 8.3 Grammatical category effect on (ing) variation

Grammatical status	weight	%	N
Progressive: *I'm lookin' for a plug.*	.61	69	313/453
Verb complement: *I don't mind watchin' rugby.*	.59	72	43/60
Preposition: *I fell asleep during class.*	.54	60	9/15
Participle: *and it was a dead end, twenty hefford bulls comin'.*	.48	54	47/87
something, nothing	.41	45	29/64
Mono-morphemic Noun: *morning*	.38	47	9/19
Proper name: *Hethering*	.38	67	2/3
Appositive: *We've been to Jersey, drivin' all over.*	.38	60	9/15
Adjunct modifier (participial): *the plain workin' man today in England, either he has roast beef . . . .*	.27	38	8/21
ACC ING: *cause it's either you gettin' battered or him gettin' battered.*	.27	36	4/11
Sentential complement: *you just gotta be so quick chucking answers back at them.*	.26	25	¼
WHIZ deletion: *That dude walking behind me is scary.*	.23	33	2/6
Derived nominal: *It's gone up into the netting.*	.16	14	2/14
Gerund: *I was shocked by the handling of the disaster.*	.16	24	49/201
Adjunct Modifier (gerundive): *Am I on the waiting list?*	.16	30	8/27
Adjective: *tempting*	.11	18	2/11
Input/total	**.62**	**57**	**623/1100**

We see that the most favouring factor is the progressive morpheme, and almost all favouring factors are verbal (with the exception of preposition). However, all verbal categories do not act the same; there are different weights for the progressive and participle factors. This shows that the variable is sensitive to small distinctions in grammatical category, and that these are due to the history of this variable. We might argue on these data that in fact we are looking at different morphemes, and that the variable context should be defined differently. Although this is not an argument that has been pursued, it would be a valid hypothesis since we have clear evidence that speakers are treating the different grammatical morphemes in different ways. If we were to follow this path, we would simply define the variable context as only progressive marking, and proceed from there. I did something of a similar analysis using the above data, and I found that by using only progressive, we arrive at results similar to the Varbrul ones for the social factors (e.g., speaker). In other words, we control the grammatical category effect by using only progressive tokens, but don't find much different in the way of other patterns. This result suggests that it is good practice to include all grammatical categories in the variable context, as long as we code for that factor and use a technique such as logistic regression which will take many factors into account. The results for (ing) – which are repeated in many different studies – show us that morphological variation especially reflects the history of the language. This is perhaps the only universal we can extract from (ing).

There is also an effect of the following phonological segment for (ing). This is essentially an assimilation effect based on whether the following segment is more front or back. Table 8.4 shows the results from the same analysis as above.

Table 8.4 (ing) assimilation

Following environment	Weight	%	N
Liquid	.65	74	31/42
Labial	.57	67	89/132
Alveolar	.56	60	166/278
Vowel	.51	57	197/345
Palatal	.50	38	5/13
Semivowel	.49	60	29/48
Pause	.36	41	75/184
Velar	.34	53	31/58
Input/total	.62	57	623/1100

Thus we see that basically front segments promote the [ɪn] variant, whereas a pause and velar segments promote the velar variant. While this is an unsurprising effect in the light of our discussion of phonological variation above, it points to the importance of coding for many different possible factors on many domains for morphological variables. These kinds of variables can be sensitive to many different constraints, including syntactic and phonological.

Deletion of morphological markers is another widespread morphophonological variable type. Morphological plural {-s} deletion in Spanish – which I will refer to as (sSpan) – is one of the most extensively studied. Just as (ing) is a variable in all varieties of English, (sSpan) is a variable in almost all varieties of Spanish, although unlike (ing) there are different processes and different variants across varieties. This process is morphological in that it applies to the plural marking in Spanish, which marks the plural with an /s/ on the determiner, adjective, and noun in any plural noun phrase, as in (1):

(1) Tienen muchos juegos de esos pintados en el suelo diferentes.
    'They have many different games like that painted on the ground.'
    (Poplack 1980: 372)

In essence there is always some sort of lenition process, such that /s/ is realised with less closure, either as [h] or being deleted altogether. The variants of (sSpan) are therefore [s], [h], or [Ø].

Poplack (1980) investigated patterns of (sSpan) for Puerto Ricans living in Philadelphia, and she collapsed the variable so it was binary, meaning that the variants were [Ø] or [s] and [h] combined. Poplack found both grammatical category and phonological effects, similar to the findings for (ing). As shown in Table 8.5, she found that deletion was favoured most on adjectives and nouns, and disfavoured on determiners. The following phonological segment was also significant, as was the stress that followed the (s).

Poplack also hypothesised, however, that there was an effect based on whether or not there was a preceding (s) environment, and whether or not there was deletion in that environment. So for each (s), she coded whether it was the first, second, or third in a series, and if it wasn't the fist (s), what the variants were for the preceding tokens. The results are shown in Table 8.6.

Structural patterns | 149

Table 8.5 (sSpan)-deletion in Philadelphia by grammatical category, following segment, and stress

Grammatical Category	Weight	Following Segment	Weight	Following Stress	Weight
Adjective	0.63	Pause	0.61	Heavy	0.55
Noun	0.61	Consonant	0.51	Weak	0.45
Determiner	0.28	Vowel	0.38		

Table 8.6 Weights for s-deletion by preceding environment

	Position of token in string		
	3	2	1
Marker(s) preceding token			
ØØ	0.76		
SØ	0.56		
Ø		0.55	
S		0.39	
ØS, SS	0.39		
Initial			0.33

In the table, the left-hand column shows the pattern of deletion preceding the segment of interest. So 'SØ' indicates that before the segments being coded, there was an -s that was articulated, followed by one that was deleted; 'initial' means that nothing precedes the segment. Blank cells are those combinations that are not possible (we have two -s segments preceding only if the one of interest is third). Deletion is again the application value, so these results show that the initial position shows the least likelihood for deletion, while the most likely position for deletion is an (s) that is last in a string of three (e.g., the (s) at the end of *bonitas* in *unas nenas bonitas* 'some pretty girls'). Most importantly, if an (s) is preceded by one or more deleted segments, it is more likely to be deleted. This 'birds of a feather' effect (after the colloquial phrase 'birds of a feather flock together'; see Chapter 9 below) has been found in other cases of variation, for example by Scherre and Naro (1991).

In these examples of morphophonological variation, we have seen a number of important patterns. For the phonological factors, it's clear that effects are not always of assimilation or dissimilation: segments exhibit both tendencies. (s) showed a dissimilation, with more s-retention with a following vowel than a consonant, while (ing) showed assimilation based on place of articulation. It must be noted, however, that these are really different kinds of effects. (s) is showing an effect of phonotactics in Spanish to avoid final consonant clusters, while (ing) is exhibiting a place-of-articulation constraint. In terms of grammatical patterns, we find that the history of a language can cause complex, unpredictable patterns to arise, as shown by the grammatical constraint on (ing). Finally, we find a persistence constraint that suggests that variants occurring immediately preceding a variable will affect the variant realisation of that variable.

Harasowska (1999) found an even more complex and intriguing pattern in her study of morphophonemic variation in the Slavic language Rusyn, spoken in western Ukraine. She investigated factors influencing the palatalisation of /k/ before word-final plural /i/. Thus, the word *Rusnak* 'a Rusyn man' is pluralised as *Rusnaci*, with the 'c' indicating a palatalised segment /rusnatsi/. Harasowska used a clustering statistical procedure to determine that there were three groups of speakers in her data, and each group had a slightly different pattern of palatalisation. She found that it is not grammatical but semantic features of the word in question that are important in predicting whether or not the velar is palatalised. Simplifying quite a bit, the general picture is that animate nouns are more likely to be palatalised, and the highest probability of palatalisation occurs in terms that refer to ethnic groups, such as *rusnak*.

We have thus seen that morphophonemic variables are sensitive not only to phonological factors, but to a wide range of types of other factors: grammatical category, semantics, frequency, and preceding realisations. These are some of the most complex variables studied because of these differing factors, and great care should be taken when they are analysed. However, they also show us how highly sensitive variation can be – the order in orderly heterogeneity is much richer than was probably initially imagined by WLH.

Now, however, let's look briefly at the analysis of the alternation of morphemes – or morphosyntactic variables. In these kinds of variables, two morphemes alternate in one slot, rather than a single morpheme being phonologically altered. Our example is the alternation of *was* and *were* in past tense sentences of English, such as *You were/was a crazy kid*. This alternation occurs in many English varieties to varying degrees, and in all person/number configurations. Of course, the 'standard' English verbal paradigm provides a somewhat complex pattern here, with second person singular and first, second, and third person plural requiring *were* (*you were, we/you/they were*) and first and third singular taking *was* (*I was, she/he/it was*). This means that *were/was* does not uniquely mark person or number. As with (ing), this pattern is a leftover of the regular Old English pattern which has been lost in all other verbs except *be*, and there is thus a tendency to 'regularise' this pattern, or make it more like the regularity of other verb forms. Like (ing), this variable has been studied in many varieties. As an example, Tagliamonte (1998) shows that (pastBE) is also sensitive to historical patterns and echoes those patterns. The overall analysis is quite complex, so here we will focus on her analysis of 'non-standard *was*', or those cases when *were* is used where standard English would require *was*. Tagliamonte's study of this variable in York, England, is notable in that she found what looks to be a change in progress in this community. She found strong internal effect for the polarity of the clause and the nature of the subject noun phrase, as shown in Table 8.7.

Tagliamonte also found that younger speakers were the most likely to use *were* in standard *was* contexts. It turns out that the change is focused in existentials and full noun phrases; in other words, it seems that the non-standard use of *were* occurs only in very specific grammatical constructions. In fact, it is likely that the negative tag *weren't it* is spreading as a discourse feature, which suggests that Tagliamonte should investigate the distribution of this tag question in her corpus as a discourse

Table 8.7 were probability by polarity and grammatical subject (Tagliamonte 2008: 176)

	Weight	%	N
Polarity			
Affirmative	0.53	97	4808
Negative	0.15	85	217
Negative tag question	0.01	43	74
Grammatical person			
He/She	0.54	97	2681
I	0.53	97	955
There	0.43	94	477
It	0.42	72	127
NP	0.39	95	863

variable rather than a morphological one. Here again, we find a complex array of features tied to a correspondingly involved history, reflected and reshaped in the grammar of a language.

One of the main questions regarding morphological variation is whether the patterns of variation and change can be said to be motivated by the functional reasons of the speaker. Most simply, the question is: do speakers organise their linguistic choices in order to make it easier for their hearers to extract relevant denotational information? The uncomfortable answer is: sometimes, but often not. In the case of (ing), there is clearly no functional reason for the variability in grammatical category; Houston (1985) convincingly shows that this is the reflex of the historical collapse of several morphemes. In the case of (sSpan), there is some indication of some functional effect, since we could argue that determiners are the carriers of the grammatical information for the phrase (DP or NP). But the pattern in which some deletion produces more deletion is clearly counter-functional: if I deleted the first (s), I would be more likely to mark subsequent tokens if I wanted to mark the plural clearly. Tagliamonte's data (and other data on the same alternation in other varieties) show that we might argue that *was* or *were* function to indicate polarity. But a verb paradigm motivated by functional concerns would certainly not end up looking like the *was/were* alternations that Tagliamonte and others have found.

What appears from the morphological studies is a picture of variation that is extremely sensitive to many different factors, regardless of information. Labov (1989, 1994) argues that these patterns reflect the fact that variation is learned by matching probabilities of particular contexts. This points neither to a completely functionalist nor to a structuralist view of variation, but to one that is more cognitivist. One might even argue that this is a neo-behaviourist view, such that speakers respond to the stimuli in the input. However, the fact that humans know what probabilities to pay attention to and match is not behaviourist at all. Theories of linguistics that incorporate probabilities are called *stochastic* theories, and there are a number of proposals for how to incorporate statistical information into grammars (a good summary for morphophonemic theory is Anttila 2004).

The most radical linguistic theories that incorporate statistical information are those that are simply statistical models. One of the most promising is exemplar theory (Pierrehumbert 2001, 2006). In broad outlines, this 'cognitivist' theory argues that language is stored in memory in a rich form, such that the details of each utterance of every word are stored, and connections made between these memories create clouds of exemplars. As memories fade, these exemplars are stored in more abstract distributions (enrichment). A single exemplar, say when we choose how to say a word, is picked randomly from the cloud (which of course has a stochastic structure based on our experience). So all the information that might go into the creation of constraints is stored at the same time, and choices about how to speak are made on the basis of these statistical distributions. The most important aspect of exemplar theory is that memories are stored not (at least initially) in a representational form, but with all of their phonetic detail (and possibly other, social details as well). Exemplar theory as a model for variation (and for linguistics in general) seems promising, but it is still controversial, even among variationists. A good introduction is Bod et al. (2003).

Chapter 9
Structural patterns II: syntax, lexical variables, and suprasegmentals

DESCRIPTION: THE PROBLEM OF 'SAYING THE SAME THING'

Variability in language is not limited to the morphophonological domain, but extends to all levels, including syntax and pragmatics. However, the way variables are studied at these levels requires a slightly different approach, because the idea of 'saying the same thing' becomes less reliable; that is, choices at these levels are often made by speakers precisely because there is some meaning difference. It is also more difficult to determine the closed set of variants. Lavendera (1978) was the first and most forceful proponent of the idea that syntactic variation was different from phonological variation. She had several arguments, but her main one boiled down to her contention that 'the quantitative studies of variation which deal with morphological, syntactic, and lexical alternation suffer from the lack of an articulated theory of meanings' (1978: 171). For Lavendera this has several consequences. First, the idea that a variable refers to 'the same thing' cannot be tested reliably. Thus, in a syntactic study one might have to 'ignore' many contexts of use in order to maintain the semantic equivalence condition (Lavendera 1978: 175) cites Sankoff and Thibault's 1977 study of the use of *être* and *avoir* in Montreal French). She argues instead that we should assume that different syntactic constructions have different meanings (although these may be social meanings), but that we should use variationist methods in order to discover what those meaning differences are. This view is a precursor of the definition of variable I suggested in Chapter 2, in which a variable merely represents any choice that can be made by the speaker about how to say something. This question has not been resolved, and is in general not a matter of deep discussion for sociolinguists at this point, although it should be a concern (good recent discussions are Cheshire 2006, 2009). However, as the 'variable rule' has been relaxed, so has the 'same thing' rule in sociolinguistic studies, as long as a reliable variable context can be defined. This issue of the variable context is one that is common to all non-morphophonological variables, as we see first in the next section.

SYNTACTIC VARIABLES

What do we mean when we identify something as a syntactic variable? The shortest answer is that we have two sentences with differing word order, or that use different words, to convey the same meaning. The example given in Chapter 2 – Weiner and Labov's (1983) study of the use of the passive and active – comes close to meeting these criteria, but as Lavandera (1978) notes, if one sentence specifies a subject and another doesn't, there is a meaning difference.

There is no clear boundary between morphosyntactic variables and completely syntactic variables. For instance, we could consider the discussion of *was/were* in the previous chapter to be a morphosyntactic variable rather than a morphological one. For our purposes, we will consider syntactic variables to be those that are involved in what in generative linguistics is considered phrase structure, and features associated with phrase structure. This will include the field known as grammaticalisation.

One possible drawback of syntactic studies has to do with obtaining enough tokens of a variable in order to find the pattern. That is, in a single sociolinguistic interview, or in conversation, there are not as many opportunities to utter a syntactic variable as there are for phonological ones. However, this concern has not proven to be as limiting as first thought. First, the kinds of variables chosen sometimes occur quite frequently; even though they are not as frequent as phonological variables, they tend to be frequent enough. Moreover, syntactic variables have one advantage over phonological ones: they can be represented in writing. This means that real-time historical studies are possible, as long as aspects of historical documents such as genre (letter, novel, etc.) are controlled for. And as the internet develops and produces more and more easily searchable text, resources for the investigation of syntactic variables are increasing almost exponentially.

In practice, researchers have used several strategies to analyse syntactic variables. One is indeed to focus on word order such that every clause or phrase can be abstractly categorised. A second also focuses on word order, but creates a variable based on the abstract phrase structure syntax of the language. Finally, and probably most productively (judging from the number of studies performed), one can analyse how a variety variably encodes grammatical information, such as negation, complementation, tense, number, and gender. These categories provide a way of delimiting the variable in an abstract way. This last kind of analysis is possible even if there is a shift in meaning for something that, for example, originally encoded tense but has undergone a change such that it becomes an aspect marker, as is the case for *been* in AAVE. An analysis of the variable encoding of these so-called functional categories can also be approached by analysing the variability of agreement, for example person and number agreement in verbs, or number and gender agreement for determiners, noun, and adjectives. Agreement patterns have already been discussed under morphological factors (Poplack's 1980 study on number agreement in Spanish, and Tagliamonte's 1998 and other studies on *was/were* alternations in English).

Syntactic variation has no work like Labov's (1994, 2001a) studies, although we will try to identify some principles by investigating some of the literature on syntactic variation. One set of likely principles can be found in the literature on grammaticalisation. Hopper and Traugott (2003), in their work on the subject, identify a number of possibilities for the directionality of syntactic change, and thus address the constraints-and-transition problems of WLH (although not necessarily using this term). Indeed, Hopper and Traugott's work is as much about syntactic change in language as it is about the specific process of grammaticalisation. They argue for a number of tendencies or directionalities for grammaticalisation, most prominently that there is a general tendency for grammaticalisation to take place beginning with changes in semantic and pragmatic functions of words, which then become more and more grammaticalised, or used to signal purely syntactic information.

A good example comes from negation in French. Negation is a topic that has been studied extensively in a number of language varieties. In French, the standard *ne* VERB *pas* construction leaves lots of room for variability. The study of this variable also shows us how syntactic variables can be studied both in real-time historical studies and in apparent time. In 'Standard' Continental French, negation is expressed through two elements: *ne*, which appears preverbally, and another postverbal negative element (most commonly *pas* but also *rien* 'nothing', *point* 'not', *jamais* 'never', and *personne* 'nobody'). Martineau and Mougeon (2003) provide an example of a real-time study, and the difficulties inherent therein. They find evidence that *ne*-deletion began fairly recently in both Quebec and Continental French, but that the rise was much steeper in Quebec French. Both increases began around the end of the eighteenth century. These researchers also find that the deletion is most pronounced in sentences with subject clitics rather than with full pronouns or NPs, a process that Martineau and Mougeon link to phonological sources. Their historical analysis supports the findings of Ashby (1981), who studied the process in Tours, France. Ashby found a strong effect for age, in which the younger speakers were using much less *ne* than older speakers. He found too that *ne*-deletion was stronger in more informal situations and was used more by the lowest-class speakers in his sample. He also found that the change was led by a few common and salient phrases, such as *je ne sais pas* 'I don't know', which is often reduced to [ʃepa], along with a number of other syntactic effects, including one for clause type and mood (e.g., dependent subjunctive, independent declarative, etc.), for which he found most deletion in the independent declarative types. This finding suggests some constraints that might be found on syntactic variables. In this case, we might suspect that changes such as that in *ne* in French will begin in certain types of clauses, which perhaps has to do with the frequency or markedness of this clause type (since independent declaratives are likely to be the most frequent and unmarked). However, this kind of generalisation has not yet been proposed.

Another perspective on syntactic variation and the constraints problem comes from the study of pidgins and creoles, in that this field is concerned with how languages in contact form a new language: What is the relative influence of each language, and what is the relative influence of so-called universals? Meyerhoff (2002) addresses this question in her analysis of the variable realisation of object

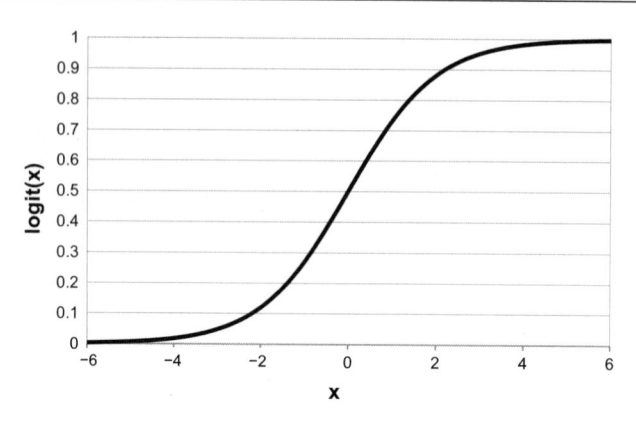

Figure 9.1 S-curve as defined by the logit function

pronouns in the Pacific creole Bislama. Her analysis is complex, but the important points for this discussion have to do with what she calls the *alienability constraint*. She finds that inalienable possessions (such as body parts) are more likely to be realised as objects than are alienable possessions (such as one's clothes). The alienable/inalienable distinction is marked in one of the languages that contribute to the creole (the Melanesian substrate), but the realisation differs from that in Bislama (being a syntactic marker rather than a tendency to delete a sentence argument). Meyerhoff's finding suggests that syntactic variables can be 'repurposed' for a number of different kinds of syntactic functions. In this case the additional function is related to cultural views of personhood (in which possessions help establish the self). In other words, the constraint on this syntactic variable, *even in its internal constraints*, is specific to its linguistic and cultural context, suggesting that principles of the kind Labov formulates for phonological variation will not be likely for syntactic variables beyond some of the general clines discussed by Hopper and Traugott (2003; see above).

We can also find some principles in studies of the rate in which new forms enter a speech community (the transition problem for WLH). First, it has been found that new forms replace older forms at a particular mathematical rate which generally follows an s-shaped curve, as shown in Figure 9.1.

Kroch (1989) argues that this curve can be hypothesised to be the logit function, a well-known pattern in changes in which one form replaces another; Kroch cites work in evolutionary biology that shows that one organism replaces another along this function (Spiess 1987). This s-shape is uncontroversial, but in the same article Kroch makes another claim which has attracted controversy, yet which also seems to have some support. Let me introduce the idea with an example.

A simple example is the use of the definite article before possessives in Continental Portuguese as reported by Oliveira e Silva (1982). This change is the increase in using a definite article in the same phrase as a possessive, as in (1), where (o) shows the variable placement of the definite article.

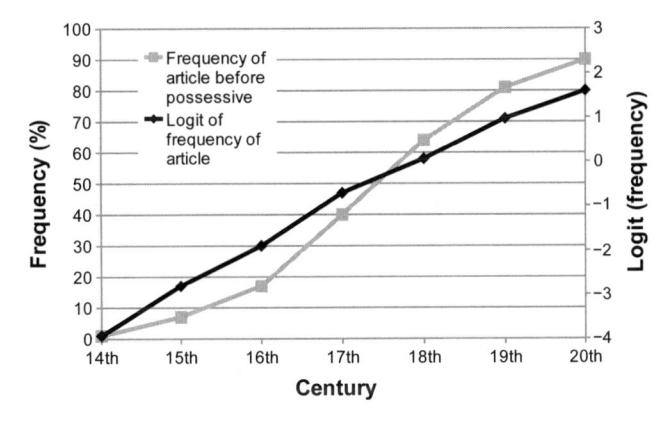

Figure 9.2 Definite article use before possessive in Portuguese (adapted from Kroch 1989: 209)

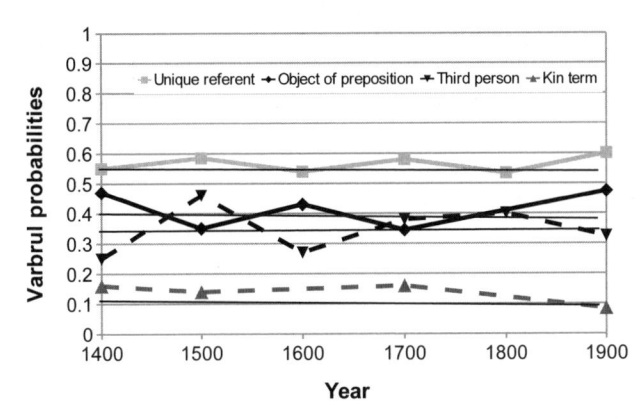

Figure 9.3 Probability of definite article before possessive in Portuguese by constraint type and century (adapted from Kroch 1989: 210)

(1) Maria conhece (o) meu irmão.
Maria knows (the) my brother.

Figure 9.2 shows the increase over the centuries in the use of the possessive, which Kroch shows is basically the logit function.

What is interesting is that the effect of various constraints across the centuries remain consistent, even as the rate goes up, as shown in Figure 9.3. In each time period, each constraint has almost exactly the same weight. The rate of change for each environment is thus the same, and the frequency of use for each is different, but their relationship to each other is stable.

So we have a single change in linguistic structure that affects a number of different contexts. The change is whether or not a definite article is used before possessives, and the different contexts are the kinds of nouns that might be possessed. There are

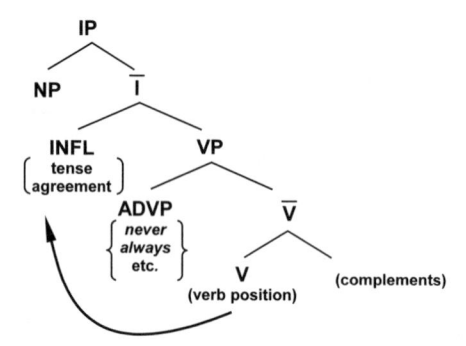

Figure 9.4   *Do*-support in Modern English (adapted from Kroch 1989: 219)

two ways this change could spread through the language. First, it could change in one context completely, and then move on to another. If this were the case for the Portuguese example, then the change would act only on the 'unique referent' nouns, and only after it was used 100 per cent of the time in this context (that is, when it was categorical) would it start to change in the next. Thus, there are different rates for different contexts. The second possibility appears to be the actual case, where the change happens for all kinds of nouns at the same *rate*, but at different *frequencies*. So in this example, 'unique referent' always shows more definite article use than 'kin term', but if the rate of one goes up, so does the other. That's what the parallel lines in Figure 9.3 show us: the rates of change are the same. Because the change happens at a constant rate, this is called the *constant rate hypothesis*.

A slightly more complex example involves Kroch's analysis of the rise of '*do*-support' in the history of English. *Do*-support refers to the use of *do* to take inflection in negative declaratives and interrogatives as well as a number of other sentence types. So, for example, *does he eat?* in modern English would have been *Eateth he?* in Middle English, and *He doesn't eat* would have been *He eateth not. Do* appeared only as a main verb in English until the fifteenth century, and its use in all contexts rose dramatically in the sixteenth. Kroch argues that this change is the result of an underlying change (which he argues also affected modal auxiliaries) in English phrase structure: Middle English had 'V-to-I raising' in which the verb raised to a category in the sentential phrase structure known as Infl (for Inflection), where features such as tense, number, aspect, and agreement are taken, while in Modern English the verb essentially stays put, as shown in the tree in Figure 9.4.

So the constant rate hypothesis applies here because, if the rise of *do* in these different environments (negatives, questions, etc.) are all related to V-to-I raising, then we would assume that *do* would increase at the same rate in all of the environments. It is important to remember that *do* will not appear at the same *frequency* in each of these environments, because each has other, different constraints that affect the appearance of *do* (semantic factors, prosodic factors, etc.). After all this explanation it should not be a surprise that Kroch does find them changing at the same rate. First, notice in Figure 9.5 that the curves, if smoothed out, would have roughly the

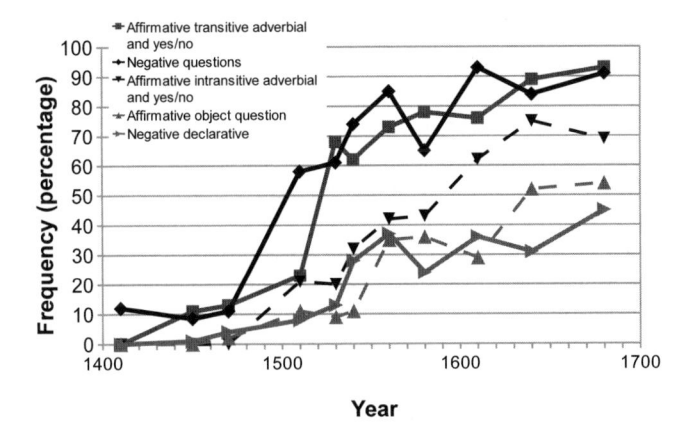

Figure 9.5 *Do*-support in English by constraint type and century (adapted from Kroch 1989: 223)

same shape, but at different frequencies. That is, the shape of the different curves in terms of more or less *do* is the same for each century.

Kroch finds that when the change is modelled mathematically using a logistic regression algorithm, the slopes (which represent the rate of change) for each of the different environments are not significantly different, although the intercepts (representing the frequency of use) are different. This analysis lends strong support to the idea that the general shape of the curve for each environment is not significantly different.

Kroch models the *do*-support change theoretically by positing that there are two different categorical grammars in competition in the speech community. However, Henry (2004) argues that variation is actually modelled better by a grammar that incorporates variation. That is, rather than positing two grammars (one that is learned first and the other later, as Kroch supposes), Henry argues that the frequencies of use for each form are part of the grammar, not epiphenomenal to it; i.e., the rates aren't just a 'by-product' of how two grammars interact, but there is some part of the grammar that specifies the rate of variation. This debate is an important one that stretches beyond variationist theory to the most basic assumptions of linguistic theory, at all levels of language.

Another question in syntactic variation and change is whether any generalisations can be made about the path taken in going from one 'state' to another. Grammaticalisation theory posits, for example, that purely lexical forms move through a stage in which pragmatic information is indicated, and then they complete the change to a purely syntactic function. The synchronic variation that results is called 'layering' in grammaticalisation theory (Hopper and Traugott 2003: 124–6). Hopper and Traugott point out that new forms do not necessarily fill a functional need, and often forms simply compete with one another. We do find, however, that forms begin to specialise if viewed from a statistical perspective. An example of this intermediate stage comes from the study of quotatives, especially the study of *like* when used as a quotative in English. This variable is the word or phrase used to introduce speech or thought in discourse, such as *He said* or *She thought*. The system of quotatives has been undergoing rapid change over the past fifty years in every variety of English studied, with new terms being used and often taking over from *say*. The two most common are *go* and *be like*. Both of these forms have taken over some of the contexts of *say*, but have not replaced it. Buchstaller and D'Arcy (2009) show that *be like* is more likely to be used in relating thought, when the subject is first person (obviously related to the thought), and when used for 'mimetic re-enactment', which describes speech that is not just reported but 'produced with a different "voice" (Bakhtin 1981) from that which encodes the surrounding material in terms of prosody, pitch, accent, etc. (Klewitz and Couper-Kuhlen 1999). Mimesis also often encodes sound or gestural effects' (Buchstaller and D'Arcy 2009: 297). The forms are thus 'layered' in the syntax. It is also possible that such a change could end with a phonological reduction and become a clitic-like morpheme such as [aik] or [ãik], which I have heard produced by young Pittsburghers. The transition is also likely to be affected by register, in which one term is used more often in a colloquial register (*be like* in this case). These kinds of register specialisations have also been found by Shi (1989) for the development of the aspectual particle *le* in Mandarin, and in Montreal French for non-clitic plural pronouns, which alternate simple forms such as *nous* 'us' and *nous autres* 'us others' (Blondeau 2001).

As Henry (2004) notes, 'within variationist studies . . . there has been little discussion of what type of factors can affect choice of variants, or of how the particular factors are chosen for analysis in any given case'. Even so, there are some linguistic factors that seem to recur, depending somewhat on the variable in question. The following is a list of such factors for cases in which the noun and verb categories are involved in some way, including subject–verb agreement and number agreement.

1. **The syntax and semantics of the noun**: Is the noun a pronoun, full noun, animate, etc.? We saw that this was central to Meyerhoff's analysis, and other variables are also sensitive to it, especially patterns of subject–verb agreement. However, as shown by Meyerhoff's analysis, this kind of constraint does not seem to have a universal application; it depends both on other aspects of the system and on cultural and linguistic values about what should be indicated by the grammar. Syntactically, the role and case are likely to be important: subject/object, agent/patient, etc., as well as the nature of the entire noun phrase (e.g., is it simple or complex, does it include a relative?).
2. **Syntax and semantics of the verb/clause**: This kind of constraint appears most commonly and unsurprisingly in such changes as subject–verb concord, negation, transitivity, tense, mood, and aspect. For example, Alamillo (2009) shows that the rate of deletion of object pronouns in Spanish is sensitive to whether the clause is interrogative or declarative, and whether it has a positive and negative polarity. Similarly, Schwenter and Cacoullos (2008) show that the choice of the present perfect and the preterite forms in two varieties

of Spanish is sensitive to the type of temporal reference, the type of clause, and the aktionsart (durative or punctual). It is probably not possible to make sweeping generalisations about these factors beyond the possibility that they might be present – the actual important factors are likely to depend on the variable being investigated.

3. **Co-occurrence factors**: This group of factors could also be thought of as indications of the way that a new syntactic construction is being used. For example, in the case of the Spanish preterite–present perfect alternation, the present perfect is more likely to be used when a proximate or frequency adverb is present (e.g., *ahora* 'now' and *cada año* 'each year', respectively). These co-occurrences are often adjectival or adverbial, and give clues about how the constructions are functionally distributed. In the Spanish present perfect case, the adverbs that favour the perfect show that this construction is a 'continuative perfect' that carries past time actions into the present.

4. **Serialisation factors**: Also known generally as *priming* or 'birds of a feather', this kind of constraint is the tendency (also observable in phonological and morphological studies) for the preceding variant to be likely to affect the appearance of the next one. This effect was shown by Scherre and Naro (1991) to have an effect on noun phrase plural marking in Brazilian Portuguese: If previous plurals were marked, then the next plural tended to be marked as well. Rickford et al. (2007) show that this constraint also affects the appearance of quotative *all* in their analysis of the use of the form in a diverse corpus dominated by American English. However, the direction of factors changes from one corpus to another over time, and these researchers argue that this change reflects a difference in the way quotative *all* is used in discourse.

PRAGMATIC AND DISCOURSE VARIABLES

As we saw in the previous section, many syntactic changes can be shown to be related to how languages use syntactic constructions for different pragmatic functions in a language, and thus provide us with an interface with syntactic and pragmatic variables. In this section we will briefly review three ways in which pragmatics are involved in language change. *Pragmatics* is defined in many different ways, from 'the use of linguistic structure' to language above the level of the sentence (see Levinson 1983: 5–35 for a discussion). *Discourse* is a similarly difficult concept to define, as discussed by Schiffrin (1994). Here we will take a very wide and general view of both these areas of research. We will explore three ways of approaching such variables.

First, we will review some of the ways that syntactic constructions that seem to be alternative word orders are sensitive to the *information status* of the entities they discuss. Second, we will expand our view to tag questions and general completers (the equivalent of *et cetera*). Finally, we consider the patterning of speech act forms through the quantification of politeness strategies. In general, we find that these variables are correlated with other syntactic constructions or pragmatic functions in order to uncover the general pragmatic function they serve for speakers.

One research tradition, pioneered by Ellen Prince, seeks to understand the functional motivations for the realisation of alternative syntactic constructions, such as preposing in English, as shown in (2) (from Birner and Ward 2009: 1173), in which 'the rosary' in the final sentence is preposed.

(2) Tico Feo was eighteen years old and for two years had worked on a freighter in the Caribbean. As a child he'd gone to school with nuns, and he wore a gold crucifix around his neck. He had a rosary too. The rosary he kept wrapped in a green silk scarf that also held three other treasures: a bottle of Evening in Paris cologne, a pocket mirror and a Rand McNally map of the world. ('A Diamond Guitar', in Truman Capote, *Breakfast at Tiffany's and Three Stories*, Vintage Books 1993, p. 144)

So non-canonical word order for English is non-SVO order. The method for this kind of work is usually to count clause types, so that the variable context is all clauses that could possibly contain the alternative constructions. This approach to pragmatic variation has provided renewed theoretical understanding of the Prague School insight (Seuren 1998: 157–60), repeated in many research traditions, that languages tend to put old information earlier in a clause and new information later, and has updated and operationalised the notions of old and new information in important ways (for details, see Birner and Ward 2009; also Ward and Birner 2004).

Other kinds of discourse features have been studied using variationist methods as well. Note, however, that discourse and conversation are overwhelmingly studied in a qualitative manner, because discourse functions are so much more open-ended than even syntactic variables. Thus, the focus is inclined to be on particular particles and lexical items and the pragmatic functions they tend to serve. However, quantitative pragmatic work often focuses on the frequency of use by speaker (and their social characteristics).

For example, tag questions were claimed by Lakoff (1975) to be used more by women. This claim, she readily admitted, was based on her own intuition, and it set off a search to investigate whether her intuition was true. Among these studies, Holmes (1995) is one of the more rigorous. Holmes noted that tag questions had a number of different functions. Some had a function of expressing epistemic modality; that is, indicating that the speaker was uncertain of what she was saying. However, Holmes noted other functions for tag questions, among these the *facilitative* function, in which the tag invites 'the addressee to contribute to the discourse' (1995: 81). She found that men in her sample were more likely to use epistemic modal tags, while women were more likely to use facilitative tags.

Holmes widened her analysis to consider discourse *strategies* as opposed to single particles. Holmes (1995), reviewing a number of her own studies, concludes that women are more likely to be *positively polite* than men. *Positive* and *negative politeness* are politeness strategies identified in the politeness theory of Brown and Levinson (1987). These terms refer to politeness strategies which ameliorate or build up a

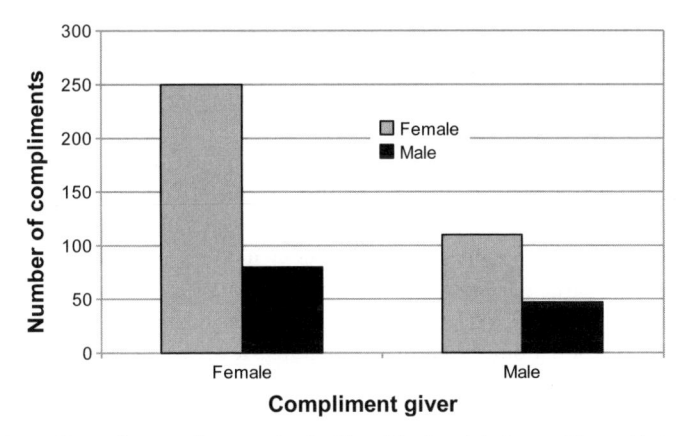

Figure 9.6 Compliments by gender in New Zealand (adapted from Holmes 1995: 123)

hearer's positive or negative *face*. *Positive face* is the need of people to be appreciated by others, so, for example, a compliment is a positive politeness strategy. *Negative face* is the need to act unimpeded and not be imposed upon, so an example of a negative politeness strategy is to give options when making a request. Circumscribing the variable context in this situation is nearly impossible; for instance, how can we say at any moment whether a speaker has the option to give a compliment or not? In essence, we are forced to assume that a compliment is possible at any time! Given this problem, Holmes simply collected compliments heard 'in the wild' by a group of speakers in New Zealand. This method is a fairly unreliable measure because we would want, for example, to control for the amount of speech and interaction a person hears over a given time period. However, speech forms like this may also be hard to find in corpora of recorded speech. In any case, the students who helped Holmes gather the data recorded information such as the sex of speaker and hearer and also the actual compliment. As shown in Figure 9.6, Holmes found that women used the most compliments with other women, while the fewest compliments were recorded between men. She finds a similar pattern for apologies.

Pragmatic and discourse variables thus form a much more heterogeneous class than any others we have considered so far, and present considerable challenges for an analysis from a quantitative perspective. As such, almost every discourse study that looks to find the structure of optionality in discourse in fact uses quantitative analyses as a supplement to arguments that are often more qualitative. As noted in Chapter 3, a quantitative analysis always begins with a qualitative understanding of the variable and its variants, and the definition of categories that can be coded reliably for quantitative analysis. Discourse and pragmatics are highly context-dependent, so exact coding can be challenging: new uses often provide contexts that can't be coded in the original coding scheme. However, the studies reviewed here provide some possibilities for how to go about such a project.

There are advantages to using quantification in discourse studies. The main advantage is that we might be able to discern a core abstract meaning for a form in discourse, which is made more precise in context. For example, the functioning of discourse markers can be uncovered through a quantitative view of their positioning and relationship to other elements of an utterance. Andersen (2001) provides a detailed account of *like* used as what he calls a pragmatic marker (which is essentially a notational variant of *discourse marker* or *pragmatic particle*), including the quotative use. He finds that in fact *like* is used relatively rarely as a quotative (about 7 per cent), and that it is often used (35 per cent) for purely discourse functions such as in false starts, self-repairs, etc. (Andersen 2001: 270). This is a pattern that only becomes clear once a quantitative approach forces the researcher to take into account every production of a particular discourse feature.

LEXICON

Lexical variables, in which speakers can use one word or the other, are also a possibility. As noted in Chapter 2, the use of *pop* or *soda* is variable in North America. In fact, lexical variation was one of the main ways that early dialect geography determined isoglosses for different dialects, especially in North America. When identifying referring terms for nouns, the variable context for lexical items is fairly straightforward: both *pop* and *soda* refer to a carbonated beverage, and *juice* is not an alternative since it does not refer to beverages which are carbonated. However, other types of lexical items can be considered as well; in fact, we can consider words that fulfil similar functions. We will consider two: intensifiers and address terms.

Intensifiers

Tagliamonte and Roberts (2005) study the rise of the use of *so* as an intensifier over all the seasons of the sitcom *Friends*, which was popular in many English-speaking countries in addition to the USA. Intensifiers are words 'that boost or maximize meaning' (Tagliamonte and Roberts 2005: 280), such as *pretty, really, very,* and *so* in the following (from Tagliamonte and Roberts 2005; names in square brackets are the characters whose utterance is reported):

(3) a. I think it is *pretty* exciting. [Chandler]
     b. Oh, Janine, the *really* hot dancer girl. [Monica]
     c. Oh, come on man. You can dance with my partner. She's *real* uh – mellow. [Joey]
     d. Trust me, it was actually – it was *very* funny. [Rachel]
     e. And this is *so* weird. [Joey]
     f. Well, Frank has to quit college because his *super* fertile sister is having three babies! [Phoebe]
     g. Oh, you're *totally* welcome! [Monica]
     h. Well, actually, she only did it the one time. But it was *pretty* weird. [Phoebe]
     i. Look, it is not my fault that your chairs are *incredibly* ugly! [Joey]

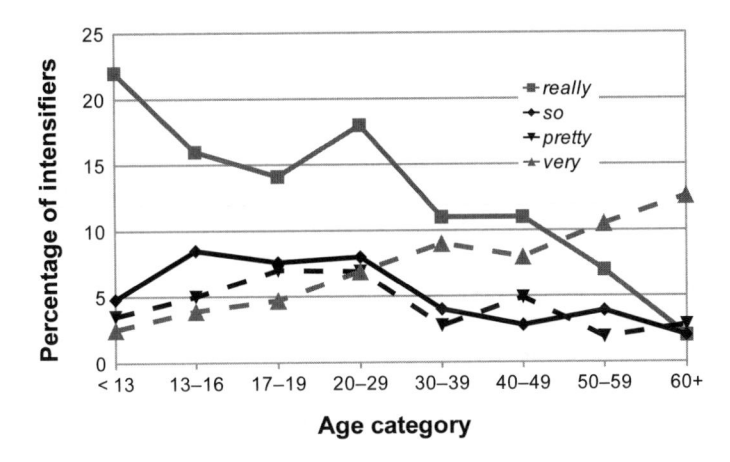

Figure 9.7 Intensifier use in Toronto by age (adapted from Tagliamonte 2008: 372)

As can be seen from these examples, intensifiers in English provide a variety of options for the speaker. While they are not all necessarily equal in the level of intensification (so that *pretty* marks a lower level of intensification than *really*, for example), the pre-adjectival intensifier slot in English is a clearly defined functional category that can be viewed as a variable. While it is a syntactic slot, I discuss it under lexical variation because essentially the choice is among a set of lexical items. Tagliamonte and Roberts (2005) show that *so* is the dominant intensifier used across all eight seasons of the show, and that it is more likely to be used by women than by men (in fact, the female characters were more likely to use intensifiers in general, but the gender difference was most pronounced with *so*). Tagliamonte (2008) investigates the change in intensifier use in a much bigger corpus for speakers in Toronto, Canada. Her Canadians were most likely to use *really*, with *very, so,* and *pretty* used much less often. However, she did find interesting patterns of change, including semantic change. As shown in Figure 9.7, she finds a rapid apparent-time increase for *really* and a corresponding decrease for *very*.

Tagliamonte also finds a number of interesting semantic and collocational changes that go along with the rise of *really*. For example, as *really* becomes more popular, it is more likely to be used with predicate adjectives (as in *The CN Tower is really tall*, as opposed to *I went to Toronto to see the really tall tower*.) Tagliamonte argues that these changes reflect a change in the semantics of *really* from an intensifier used in limited collocations to one used more generally.

Address terms

Semantic change almost always accompanies lexical change, and can be seen in the two address terms we will consider. The first is *dude* in US English, investigated in a study of my own (Kiesling 2004) and one by Hill (1994). An address term is a word that is used to address someone rather than refer to someone; the distinction usually needs to be made in use, because referring terms are usually used as address terms as well. For example, *Ms Holland* is a referring term in *Ms Holland was one of the best teachers I ever had* but an address term is *Here is my homework, Ms Holland*. *Dude*, as it is currently employed in American English, has both uses, but started out only as a referring term for rags, then clothes, and then a sharp-dressed man. As a referring term, it has since expanded to refer to a man in general, as in *I saw a dude you know in the airport*. The address term arose in the 1940s among gangs in the southwest and western USA who dressed flamboyantly, and expanded from there into the California counter-culture.

Address terms like *dude* are both simple and difficult to study from a variationist perspective, because it is not clear what the variable context should be. Most address terms are used as greetings, and we could simply take a very restrictive view and code only greetings. Of course, such an approach would also require a strategy for gathering data other than interviews, because greetings typically occur at the beginnings of interactions only, in fact before the interview proper starts. We would thus want to record greetings as they happen 'in the wild'. Another approach is simply to record all of the instances of the word we are interested in, which is a little less reliable but nevertheless can give indications on changes of use. In either strategy, a specific time frame or number of tokens should be identified in advance, so we don't only write down tokens that are particularly noticeable. I took the second strategy with a group of students in Pittsburgh. Each student chose a specific time to start listening for *dude* and then wrote down the next ten instances of the word, along with contextual information about the speakers and the utterance in which *dude* occurred. Since the researchers were college students, the vast majority of tokens were between speakers under the age of thirty, but there was a clear interaction for gender: overwhelmingly, men use *dude* with other men (and the class was composed of women more than men, which increases the possibilities for it to be used with women), as shown in Figure 9.8.

Note that *dude* follows a pattern that is similar to that of intensifiers in a very abstract sense: specific referring terms, when they change their meaning and use, tend to expand their meaning to be more generalised and more focused on 'subjective' types of meanings: from a word simply referring to rags to an address term whose meaning is entirely non-referential. Traugott (1989) argues that such changes move following a cline from propositional (i.e., referring terms) to textual (such as discourse markers) to expressive (such as address terms). In both of these cases of lexical variation we have seen such a movement, although this hypothesis would benefit from more testing from variationist studies.

SUPRASEGMENTALS: INTONATION AND RHYTHM

Popular stereotypes about how kinds of speakers talk are often discussed in terms of features that linguists find difficult to quantify, yet given such stereotypes, it is important to discuss these kinds of features in language as well. The sound of a language is not merely the way an inventory of phonemes is pronounced, or the order

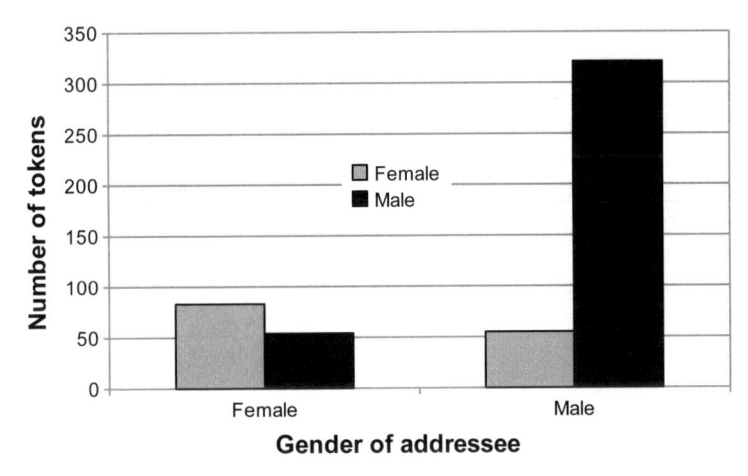

Figure 9.8 Use of *dude* by gender of speaker and addressee (adapted from Kiesling 2004: 285)

of its nouns and verbs. It is also the rhythm and intonation in which these other variables find themselves embedded. Moreover, such *suprasegmental* features may impact, for example, on the way a vowel is pronounced, since a vowel that is longer in a strictly durational sense has more time to do things like diphthongise. But there is no reason to think that these parts of language do not also change over time.

Such characteristics can, however, be difficult to quantify. In the realm of rhythm, there has been relatively little work on how to quantify things such as stress in the variationist literature, although such a study in certainly possible. The measurement of *stress-timed* versus *syllable-timed* languages has been an issue for some time (and current thinking seems to indicate that a simple dichotomy is too strict; see Roach 1982; Cummins and Port 1998; Deterding 2001). The strategy in such a study would be to determine how 'equal' adjacent syllables are in terms of duration (known as a variability index, or VI; also called the Pairwise Variability Index, or PVI; see Grabe and Low 2002), since in a syllable-timed language, there is a regular relationship among syllable length and stress. This kind of measurement is not as straightforward as it might seem, because there are all sorts of issues involving, for example, where to mark syllables and speech rate. Deterding (2001) provides a good example of how such a measurement might work, using 10 minutes of interview speech for British English and Singapore English speakers. He finds, as predicted, that the British English speakers have more variability in their syllable length, which he argues is an indication that their variety is more stress-timed. Szakay (2006) finds a similar difference between Maori New Zealand English and Pakeha (i.e., Anglo) New Zealand English, and also finds that younger speakers in general show a lower VI, indicating a movement towards syllable timing.

Speech rate has recently been investigated in a sophisticated study over a large number of American English utterances by Kendall (2009). He found that pause length was significantly different especially according to the region of the United States the speaker came from (although his sample included only three main regions: Ohio, Washington, DC, and North Carolina), with Ohioans having a shorter pause length. He also found that pause length differed significantly depending on ethnicity and gender. In addition, he measured speech rate and found parallel differences, although in this case there were interactions among the social variables. There was an important effect of utterance length, such that longer utterances had a higher speech rate than shorter ones, meaning that speakers tended to speed up when they had longer utterances. Finally, Kendall found that pause and speech rate were related, such that longer pauses were correlated with slower speech rate. Interestingly, however, he found that this effect too differed depending on the region and ethnic group. His findings are suggestive, and these variables should be investigated further by sociolinguists, though the explanations need to be supplemented by more qualitative analyses of the interviews he used as data.

Pitch and intonation have also been investigated as sociolinguistic variables. One of the most prominent variables is so-called 'high rising tone', or HRT, investigated especially for New Zealand and Australian English. HRT is the sharp intonational rise at the end of a declarative utterance, sometimes also called *question intonation*. One of the earliest studies was that of Guy et al. (1986) for Sydney English. They found strong evidence that there was an increasing use of HRT in the speech community, with teenagers in their sample using significantly more of the intonational contour than adults did. The contour is also used more by women, although gender interacts with class such that the gender difference is the most for lower working- and middle-class speakers. Like other linguistic variables, HRT is used more in descriptions and narratives (as opposed to statements of fact and opinion) and in multi-clause turns.

Intonation, much like other suprasegmental variables, shows that defining the variable is difficult. Paul Warren (2005) demonstrates some of the complexities involved in such variables which appear at first to be fairly straightforward. He investigates HRT in New Zealand English. Like Guy et al., Warren finds that younger speakers and women use significantly more HRT with statements. However, he also finds that the location that the rise begins in the *intonational phrase* (Ladd 1996) is different for different speaker groups, with younger speakers showing an earlier rise than older speakers. This finding raises questions about whether all rises should be compared together, or whether another method should be entertained (such as categorising every intonation phrase for a speaker, thus expanding the variable context). Warren also speculates that not only the direction of a rise but also the shape (concave or convex) should be considered in a rigorous investigation of intonation. It should be clear at this point that one reason why variationists have avoided suprasegmental variables has been the usual suspects of needing a lot of data and difficulty in defining the variable context. However, as our methods become more sophisticated, especially in terms of corpus management and labelling, it is likely that these types of variables will be studied more frequently and inform our understanding of the patterns of variation in language.

Part IV: Conclusions

Chapter 10

The life and times of linguistic changes

Throughout this book, we have examined variation and change either retrospectively once a change has occurred, or from the perspective of what is happening at one time point during a change. In this final chapter, I'd like to summarise the issues by considering the 'life course' of linguistic changes. But rather than proposing a short definitive list of such stages, in this chapter I bring together the previous discussions in order to consider the *possibilities* of how a change might (or might not) occur. I return to the question of how and when which factors (structural, cognitive, or social) affect different kinds of linguistic change. The general approach is not one of determinism, but of possibility. In a sense, this is a reorganisation of the questions posed by WLH. The issues we will explore are: the source and actuation of change; the early development and spread of change (problems of embedding and transition); and how change is further propagated in the speech community and goes 'to completion'.

SOURCES AND ACTUATION OF CHANGE

Where do linguistic changes come from? Are some changes more likely than others? These are the main questions to address about the beginnings of change, and both relate to what seems like a paradox: if language is for communication, why does it keep changing, since we might assume that such changes would make communication more difficult? This is a paradox only in so far as the assumption is correct. But remember that we have seen that language variation, particularly during changes in progress, is actually very efficient at communicating *social* information. Given the creativity and variation that are built into language, it should not be surprising that we develop new ways of talking.

In general, the 'natural' variability of pronunciation provides us with a possible source of change. This variability (perhaps having to do with the mechanics of articulation) may put pressure on language to move in certain directions. At the same time, there is the cognitive factor that there may also be perceptual asymmetries that lead to changes. That is, not all sounds may be heard the same, and these differences may lead to 'mishearings' that then provide the source of sound change.

In morphology and syntax, there is less 'natural' variability than in phonetics.

Although grammaticalisation studies show us that there are some general directions that changes are more likely to take, it is clear that speakers do not begin such a change with any kind of teleological purpose. For example, when a verb begins its course from lexical verb to tense/aspect marker (for example, *going to* began to develop into the future-marking auxiliary verb *gonna*), no speaker abruptly begins to use the verb in its new sense. Rather, these changes move in small steps, gradually. So incipient grammaticalisation and syntactic changes do resemble the minor, random variation of phonetics; in our example, a lexical verb simply begins to be used more when certain tense/aspect situations are expressed. This is a process that must happen quite often without developing into a fully fledged change, just as phonetic variation is common but rarely becomes a linguistic change.

Another source of change occurs when there is contact. That is, the new variant is heard by a speaker when interacting with someone who uses it natively. While this contact is a source of change, such 'borrowing' only really becomes a linguistic change when it begins to spread throughout a community, which is brought about when large groups migrate from one place to another, or when local communities take up regional or national 'standards'.

Finally, we must remember that humans use language expressively and creatively, and that changes can come about when someone is newly expressive with a variation that is already occurring. However, such expressiveness – for the interactional or identity motivations discussed in Part II –cannot push the boundaries of intelligibility, so speakers must recruit some kind of already-occurring variability. For example, there was already (ing) variability in English before it began to alternate and take on social significance. In another example, the word *like* in English could already describe an action (*I looked at him like this*), so we can see it would not be hard to use it for thought (and then direct quotation) without misunderstanding (*I was like 'He's not too bright'* and *I was like 'Hi Killah'*). The point is that there has to be a source of variability that someone in a speech community begins to use in a regular manner to make some expressive point. So actuation must be some combination of available variation and a need for social expressiveness of some sort.

EARLY DEVELOPMENT AND SPREAD OF CHANGE

Once someone uses a new form, though, it must 'get a foothold'; it has to be taken up by others to become a linguistic change that affects the entire speech community. We haven't actually seen changes at the very earliest stages, but we do know that other speakers must take them up. The three kinds of factors – structural, cognitive, and social – again can affect the spread of a change, and in fact can be instrumental in determining whether it spreads or not.

How a change fits into structure has important consequences. On the phonological level, changes are likely to be affected by whether or not there are already similar phonemes in the language. For example, glottal stops can spread in English because there is no glottal phoneme. Note, however, that this factor is not determinative:

mergers show us that phonemes can collapse even if the new category does end up containing some new homophones. Cognitive factors may also favour certain sound changes over others, as there are asymmetries in the perceptions and misperceptions of sounds. In this line of thinking, a new way of saying something is more likely to be taken up by other speakers if they simply misperceive it. Labov (1994) argues that extreme outliers ('mispronunciations') of a vowel in most cases are not heard as the vowel intended by the speaker in variation that is not involved in change. But during a vowel shift, a mispronounced vowel will be heard as the intended vowel and thus will be added to the set of vowels hearers use to decide how to pronounce these vowels themselves.

In syntax, we suspect that changes will be more likely to spread if they provide some functional usefulness, but the layering observed in grammaticalisation studies shows us that languages often develop new ways of expressing something they already encode, so it is not clear how determinative structural factors in syntax are. The cognitive factors in morphosyntactic change have been less studied, but again they must relate to how speakers understand the uses and meanings of syntactic constructions.

In all of these cases, we see the crucial role that speakers play both as producers of language and as perceivers of language. There is thus an important interaction in the systems of perception and production that move linguistic changes forward. Hearers must perceive the new way of speaking as such, and decide on some level to adopt it; for example, I may hear someone speak r-lessly, but perceive that they are not part of my native speech community, and thus not adopt r-lessness because it is 'foreign'.

This point leads us to consider the social factors in the early spread of change. The primary pressure for the way change is embedded in society is for the variants involved in a change to develop *meanings* – to become indexed to some non-linguistic and non-symbolic meaning. These meanings can be at three levels of social understanding which are interrelated: interactional indexes (for example, stances), speech activity indexes (for example, an index of a change in speech activity from chatting before a class to the class proper), and social group indexes (for example, masculinity or 'burnouts'). We suspect that at the very earliest stages of a change, variants are indexed with stances (see Chapter 5), or with particular people rather than large groups. As a change spreads and is used by more people for more varied stances, the meaning of the variants will change (as noted in Chapter 6), but it is impossible for a 'brand new' variant to be associated with a large social group if only a few of that group have used it. The very earliest meanings of variants must therefore be very 'local' – restricted to particular kinds of moves in interaction or to very specific people. Dorian (2010) in fact shows that in small communities without the group identity distinctions of modern urban society, variation remains highly individualised. Once a variant has some small bit of this kind of meaning, or it has been adopted by a critical mass of speakers, or both, it becomes possible for the change to propagate further through the speech community.

PROPAGATION, DIFFUSION, TRANSMISSION, AND COMPLETION

Once a change 'catches on' in some subgroup of the community, the next step is its propagation throughout the entire community. Because most research has been done on changes at this stage (notwithstanding older, completed changes), most of what has been discussed over the previous chapters is about propagation, which the embedding and constraints problems (as explained in Chapter 1) mostly address.

We have seen a number of structural factors in the propagation of a change. Within sound change, the issue of regularity has been central; there seems to be no complete consensus, but a majority of phonological changes seem to be regular, affecting all instances of a particular phoneme, with phonetic effects depending on things like a preceding and following environment. Note that this way of defining the change determines what is considered to be the sociolinguistic variable, such that in our studies we compare only instances of a phoneme in the same phonetic environment rather than all tokens of a phoneme. Some recent approaches to change, called *exemplar* approaches (see Chapter 8), challenge the notion that individual variables should be compared in this way, though, so the regularity question is still not resolved within the field. For example, Bybee (2000) and Pierrehumbert (2001) have found that at least sometimes word frequency has an effect on some variables. Labov (1994) proposes that change is regular in some situations and proceeds by lexical diffusion in others. Within syntax we discussed the constant rate hypothesis, which says that a new phrase structure change propagates through a linguistic system at the same rate even if the frequencies of particular constructions vary. We also saw that propagation does not seem to be very sensitive to so-called functional concerns, such as whether or not the loss of morphology causes information about person or number to be lost.

Much of Part II was concerned with how a change propagates socially. We saw some principles proposed that state that changes are 'led by' certain groups, which means those groups use more of the new variant than other groups. Specifically, women and the 'interior' (neither lowest nor highest) social classes are argued to be leaders. Labov also argues that traits such as 'nonconformity' play a role. The network structure of a community seems to be important too, such that weak ties promote change across networks, and strong ties within networks tend to reinforce a norm and could slow a change.

These class, gender, and network factors are social *structure* factors, but other groups of speakers, as well as the dominant ideologies of a community, play a large role as well. We saw that variants develop social meanings, which also change over time, and that these social meanings are most often the reason people adopt or do not adopt different variants. It is these meanings that people deploy when they talk to each other, and they must form the explanation for the social structure patterns that have been found. There seems to be a recurrent pattern to how these meanings work. At first, the community uses them, but they are relatively unnoticed and unremarked upon. As more people use a new variant, or especially if one group uses a new variant more (such as jocks in Eckert's 2000 study, or women, or the working class), or a variant is used more often for particular stances, the indexing of a variant with a group or stance becomes stronger in the community. A variable might stay this way, and after a time its indexicalities might change or possibly be weakened and fall away. But a variable and index might become so tightly connected that they (and probably other variables that go with them) become *enregistered*. If the variant becomes very strongly enregistered, the change may cease, but it could just as well expand further, depending on the community's ideology towards language (for example, if the new variant challenges their idea of 'linguistic purity') or towards the group who uses the variant.

A variant could also quite easily not become so strongly enregistered, and keep changing. Eventually the indexicalities of such a variant might change and it might become the new norm (at which point we could say it is 'complete'). These processes, while we have a general idea of their working, are still some of the more mysterious in variation and change. One question that lingers is which kinds of linguistic items are more likely to become enregistered and change (for example, what kinds of sounds or words are more likely to be enregistered, or whether words have more of a propensity for enregisterment than sounds). Silverstein (1981) provides suggestions for which linguistic forms get this *metapragmatic awareness*, and Trudgill (1986) suggests that a related notion – *salience* – is an explanation for why some features of dialects in contact are adopted (propagated) and some are not. Kerswill and Williams (2002), however, show that the notion of salience is a slippery one, and (like many things in variation and change) is not predictive, but tends to be a *post hoc* explanation.

There is still much that is mysterious in how change works. One open question is the relative strength of social and structural factors in change. It seems that some changes can go on without any enregistration (such as the low back merger (LBM) in the speech of African Americans in Pittsburgh), but that others are strongly influenced by ideologies (such as the monophthongisation of /aʊ/ among White and African American Pittsburghers). Another open question is how a change actually propagates in a community, both how it is *transmitted* to younger generations and also how and why those younger generations *increment* the change: what is their motivation for speaking differently from the older generation, in the same direction that that older generation spoke differently from the one before them?

In the case of socially influenced changes, one possibility is that the social meanings and enregistrations that develop in one generation are re-indexed in different (and often unrelated) ways by the next generation, for its own peer-related purposes, and these new indexations propel the change forward. The reason for the directionality of the change is likely to be structural or perceptual, but the motivation for the change (especially as experienced by the speakers) is likely to be social. Thus the re-indexings need not change the directionality of the change; rather, they may simply change the way the change is incremented. Moreover, those meanings may change as the generation ages and passes through the life stages that are relevant in the community. In this sense change is not a set of fixed rails moving a language from one state to another, but a wending path with switchbacks and forks that its speakers may or may not stay on (and which allows speakers to make their own new paths), but inevitably leads down the mountain unless some unusual obstacle is encountered. In most cases once a change begins it tends to keep going unless arrested by an unusually strong social influence or very large-scale demographic reasons. To expand the metaphor even further, the path does not end; varieties only pause at different points. Although changes are sometimes considered 'completed', this notion is really an analytical fiction that linguists have imposed on language so it may be studied. In reality, language is ever-changing, just as it is ever-variable.

References

Agha, A. (2003) The social life of a cultural value. *Language and Communication, 23*, 231–73.
Agha, A. (2007) *Language and Social Relations*. Cambridge: Cambridge University Press.
Alamillo, A. R. (2009) Cross-dialectal variation in propositional anaphora: null objects and propositional *lo* in Mexican and Peninsular Spanish. *Language Variation and Change, 21*(3), 297–317. doi: 10.1017/S0954394509990111.
Andersen, G. (2001) *Pragmatic Markers and Sociolinguistic Variation: A Relevance-Theoretic Approach to the Language of Adolescents*. Amsterdam: John Benjamins.
Anderson, B. (2006) *Imagined Communities: Reflections on the Origin and Spread of Nationalism* (rev. edn). London: Verso.
Anttila, A. (2004) Variation and phonological theory. In J. Chambers, P. Trudgill, and N. Schilling-Estes (eds), *The Handbook of Language Variation and Change* (pp. 206–43). Oxford: Blackwell.
Ashby, W. J. (1981) The loss of the negative particle *ne* in French: a syntactic change in progress. *Language, 57*(3), 674–87.
Baayen, R. H. (2008) *Analyzing Linguistic Data: A Practical Introduction to Statistics using R*. Cambridge: Cambridge University Press.
Bailey, G., Wile, T., Tillery, J., and Sand, L. (1993) Some patterns of linguistic diffusion. *Language Variation and Change, 5*, 359–90.
Baker, A. (2008) Addressing the actuation problem with quantitative models of sound change. *University of Pennsylvania Working Papers in Linguistics 14*: 1–13.
Bakhtin, M. (1981) *The Dialogic Imagination: Four Essays*. Austin: University of Texas Press.
Baugh, A. and Cable, T. (2003) *A History of the English Language*. Saddle River, NJ: Prentice Hall.
Becker, K. (2009) /r/ and the construction of place identity on New York City's Lower East Side. *Journal of Sociolinguistics, 13*(5), 634–58.
Bell, A. (1984) Language style as audience design. *Language in Society, 13*(2), 145–204.
Bell, A. (2001) Back in style: reworking audience design. In P. Eckert and J. R. Rickford (eds), *Style and Sociolinguistic Variation* (pp. 139–69). Cambridge: Cambridge University Press.
Benor, S. (2001) The learned /t/: phonological variation in Orthodox Jewish English. *University of Pennsylvania Working Papers in Linguistics 7*(3): 1–16.
Benor, S. (2004) Second style acquisition: the linguistic socialization of newly orthodox Jews. Unpublished doctoral dissertation, Stanford University, Palo Alto, CA.
Bernard, H. R. (2006) *Research Methods in Anthropology: Qualitative and Quantitative Approaches*. Lanham, MD: Altamira.
Bickerton, D. (1971) Inherent variability and variable rules. *Foundations of Language 7*, 457–92.
Birner, B., and Ward, G. (2009) Information structure and syntactic structure. *Language and Linguistics Compass, 3*(4), 1167–87. doi: 10.1111/j.1749-818X.2009.00146.x.

Blake, R., and Josey, M. (2003) The /ay/ diphthong in a Martha's Vineyard community: what can we say 40 years after Labov? *Language in Society, 32*(4), 451–85.
Blondeau, H. (2001) Real-time changes in the paradigm of personal pronouns in Montreal French. *Journal of Sociolinguistics, 5*(4), 453–74.
Boas, F. (1911) *Handbook of American Indian Languages*. Washington, DC: Government Printing Office.
Boberg, C. (2005) The Canadian shift in Montreal. *Language Variation and Change, 17*(2), 133–54. doi: 10.1017/S0954394505050064.
Bod, R., Hay, J., and Jannedy, S. (eds) (2003) *Probabilistic Linguistics*. Cambridge, MA: MIT Press.
Boersma, P., and Weenick, D. (2009) Praat: doing phonetics by computer. [Software.] www.fon.hum.uva.nl/praat.
Bortoni-Ricardo, S. M. (1985) *The Urbanization of Rural Dialect Speakers: A Sociolinguistic Study in Brazil*. Cambridge: Cambridge University Press.
Bourdieu, P. (1991) *Language and Symbolic Power* (trans. G. Raymond and M. Adamson). Cambridge, MA: Harvard University Press.
Britain, D. (1991) Dialect and space: a geolinguistic study of speech variables in the Fens. Unpublished doctoral dissertation, Essex University, Colchester.
Britain, D. (2004) Space and spatial diffusion. In J. K. Chambers, P. Trudgill, and N. Schilling-Estes (eds), *The Handbook of Language Variation and Change* (pp. 603–37). Oxford: Blackwell.
Brown, P., and Levinson, S. C. (1987) *Politeness: Some Universals in Language Usage*. Cambridge: Cambridge University Press.
Bucholtz, M., and Hall, K. (2004) Theorizing identity in language and sexuality research. *Language in Society, 33*(4), 469–515. doi: 10.1017/S0047404504334020.
Buchstaller, I., and D'Arcy, A. (2009) Localized globalization: a multi-local, multivariate investigation of quotative *be like*. *Journal of Sociolinguistics, 13*(3), 291–331. doi: 10.1111/j.1467-9841.2009.00412.x.
Bybee, J. (2000) Lexicalization of sound change and alternating environments. In M. Broe and J. Pierrehumbert (eds), *Papers in Laboratory Phonology, Vol. 5: Acquisition and the Lexicon* (pp. 250–68). Cambridge: Cambridge University Press.
Cameron, R. (1992) Pronominal and null subject variation in Spanish: constraints, dialects, and functional compensation. Unpublished doctoral dissertation, University of Pennsylvania, Philadelphia.
Campbell, L. (2004) *Historical Linguistics: An Introduction*. Cambridge, MA: MIT Press.
Campbell-Kibler, K. (2007) Accent, (ing), and the social logic of listener perceptions. *American Speech, 82*(1), 32–64. doi: 10.1215/00031283-2007-002.
Campbell-Kibler, K. (2008) I'll be the judge of that: diversity in social perceptions of (ING). *Language in Society, 37*(05), 637. doi: 10.1017/S0047404508080974.
Campbell-Kibler, K. (2009) The nature of sociolinguistic perception. *Language Variation and Change, 21*(1), 135–56. doi: 10.1017/S0954394509000052.
Cedergren, H. (1973) The interplay of social and linguistic factors in Panama. Unpublished doctoral dissertation, Cornell University, Ithaca, NY.
Cedergren, H., and Sankoff, D. (1974) Variable rules: performance as a statistical reflection of competence. *Language, 50*, 333–55.
Chambers, J. (1995) *Sociolinguistic Theory: Linguistic Variation and its Social Significance*. Oxford: Blackwell.
Cheshire, J. (1982) *Variation in an English Dialect: A Sociolinguistic Study*. Cambridge: Cambridge University Press.
Cheshire, J. (2006) Discourse variation, grammaticalisation and stuff like that. *Journal of Sociolinguistics, 11*(2), 155–93.

Cheshire, J. (2009) Syntactic variation and beyond. In N. Coupland and A. Jaworski (eds), *The New Sociolinguistics Reader* (pp. 119–35). Basingstoke: Palgrave Macmillan.

Clarke, S., Elms, F., and Youssef, A. (1995) The third dialect of English: some Canadian evidence. *Language Variation and Change, 7*, 209–28.

Clyne, M., Eisikovits, E., and Tollfree, L. (2001) Ethnic varieties of Australian English. In D. Blair and P. Collins (eds), *English in Australia* (pp. 223–38). Amsterdam: John Benjamins.

Cochran, M., Larner, M., Riley, D., Gunnarsson, L., and Henderson, C. R. (eds) (1990) *Ex-Tending Families: The Social Networks of Parents and Their Children*. Cambridge: Cambridge University Press.

Collins, R. (1975) *Conflict Sociology: Toward an Explanatory Science*. New York: Academic Press.

Coupland, N. (1980) Style-shifting in a Cardiff work-setting. *Language in Society, 9*, 1–12.

Coupland, N. (1984) Accommodation at work: some phonological data and their implications. *International Journal of the Sociology of Language, 46*, 49–70.

Coupland, N. (2007) *Style: Language Variation and Identity*. Cambridge: Cambridge University Press.

Cummins, F. and Port, R. (1998) Rhythmic constraints on stress timing in English. *Journal of Phonetics*, 24, 145–171.

Deterding, D. (2001) The measurement of rhythm: a comparison of Singapore and British English. *Journal of Phonetics, 29*(2), 217–30.

Dinkin, A. (2008) The real effect of word frequency on phonetic variation. *University of Pennsylvania Working Papers in Linguistics 14*(1): 97–106.

Dorian, N. C. (2010) *Investigating Variation: The Effects of Social Organization and Social Setting*. Oxford: Oxford University Press.

Doxsey, J. (2005) /ai/ monophthongization on the Alabama coast. Presentation at the 35th Annual Meeting of New Ways of Analyzing Variation, Columbus, OH, 9–12 November.

Dubois, S., and Horvath, B. (1999) When the music changes, you change too: gender and language change in Cajun English. *Language Variation and Change, 11*(3), 287–313. doi: 10.1017/S0954394599113036.

Durkheim, E. (1933) *The Division of Labor in Society* (trans. G. Simpson). New York: Free Press. (Original work published 1893.)

Eberhardt, M. (2006) Leadership and style-shifting: women's use of (ING). PhD comprehensive paper, University of Pittsburgh, PA.

Eberhardt, M. (2009a) Identities and local speech in Pittsburgh: a study of regional African American English. Retrieved from ProQuest Digital Dissertations (AAT 3375240).

Eberhardt, M. (2009b) The sociolinguistics of ethnicity in Pittsburgh. *Language and Linguistics Compass, 3*(6), 1443–54.

Eckert, P. (1989) *Jocks and Burnouts: Social Categories and Identity in the High School*. New York: Teachers College Press.

Eckert, P. (2000) *Linguistic Variation as Social Practice*. Oxford: Blackwell.

Eckert, P. (2008a) Variation and the indexical field. *Journal of Sociolinguistics, 12*(4), 453–76. doi: 10.1111/j.1467-9841.2008.00374.x.

Eckert, P. (2008b) Where do ethnolects stop? *International Journal of Bilingualism, 12*(1–2), 25–42. doi: 10.1177/13670069080120010301.

Eckert, P., and McConnell-Ginet, S. (1992) Think practically and look locally: language and gender as community-based practice. *Annual Review of Anthropology, 21*, 461–90.

Eckert, P., and McConnell-Ginet, S. (2003) *Language and Gender*. Cambridge: Cambridge University Press.

Eckert, P., and Rickford, J. (2001) *Style and Sociolinguistic Variation*. Cambridge: Cambridge University Press.

Elliott, N. (2000) A sociolinguistic study of rhoticity in American film speech from the 1930s to the 1970s. In R. Dal Vera (ed.), *Standard Speech and Other Contemporary Issues*

in Professional Voice and Speech Training Presented by the Voice and Speech Review (pp. 103–30). Cincinnati, OH: VASTA.
Fasold, R. W. (1991) The quiet demise of variable rules. *American Speech, 66*(1), 3–21.
Fischer, C. S. (1982) *To Dwell Among Friends: Personal Networks in Town and City*. Chicago: University of Chicago Press.
Fischer, J. (1958) Social influences on the choice of a linguistic variant. *Word, 14,* 47–56.
Fought, C. (1999) A majority sound change in a minority community: /u/-fronting in Chicano English. *Journal of Sociolinguistics, 3*(1), 5–23.
Fought, C. (2003) *Chicano English in Context*. Basingstoke: Palgrave Macmillan.
Fought, C. (2006) *Language and Ethnicity*. Cambridge: Cambridge University Press.
Foulkes, P., Docherty, G., and Watt, D. (1999) Tracking the emergence of structured variation: realisations of (t) by Newcastle children. *Leeds Working Papers in Linguistics, 7,* 1–23.
Fowler, J. (1986) The social stratification of /r/ in New York City department stores twenty-four years after Labov. Unpublished manuscript, New York University, NY.
Gerritsen, M., and Jansen, F. (1980) The interplay of dialectology and historical linguistics: some refinements of Trudgill's formula. In P. Maher (ed.), *Proceedings of the 3rd International Congress of Historical Linguistics* (pp. 11–37). Amsterdam: John Benjamins.
Ghosh Johnson, S. E. (2005) Mexiqueño? Issues of identity and ideology in a case study of dialect contact. Retrieved from ProQuest Digital Dissertations (AAT 3206779).
Giles, H. (1973) Accent mobility: a model and some data. *Anthropological Linguistics, 15,* 87–105.
Giles, H., and Powesland, P. (1975) *Speech Style and Social Evaluation*. London: Academic Press.
Giles, H., Taylor, D., and Bourhis, R. (1973) Toward a theory of interpersonal accommodation through speech: some Canadian data. *Language in Society, 2,* 177–92.
Giles, H., Coupland, J., and Coupland, N. (1991) *Contexts of Accommodation: Developments in Applied Sociolinguistics*. Cambridge: Cambridge University Press.
Goffman, E. (1974) *Frame Analysis: An Essay on the Organization of Experience*. London: Harper and Row.
Goffman, E. (1981) *Forms of Talk*. Philadelphia: University of Pennsylvania Press.
Gordon, E., Campbell, L., Hay, J., Maclagan, M., Sudbury, A., and Trudgill, P. (2004) *New Zealand English: Its Origin and Evolution*. Cambridge: Cambridge University Press.
Gordon, M. J. (2001) *Small-Town Values and Big-City Vowels: A Study of the Northern Cities Shift in Michigan*. Durham, NC: Duke University Press.
Grabe, E., and Low, E. (2002) Durational variability in speech and the rhythm class hypothesis. *Papers in Laboratory Phonology 7*. Berlin: Mouton de Gruyter.
Gramsci, A. (1971) *Selections from the Prison Notebooks of Antonio Gramsci* (trans. Q. Hoare and G. Nowell-Smith). New York: International Publishers.
Granovetter, M. (1973) The strength of weak ties. *American Journal of Sociology, 78*(6), 1360–80.
Green, L. J. (2002) *African American English: A Linguistic Introduction*. Cambridge: Cambridge University Press.
Guy, G. (1980) Variation in the group and the individual: the case of final stop deletion. In W. Labov (ed.), *Locating Language in Time and Space* (pp. 1–36). New York: Academic Press.
Guy, G. R. (1990) The sociolinguistic types of language change. *Diachronica, 7*(1), 47–67.
Guy, G. R. (1991) Explanation in variable phonology: an exponential model of morphological constraints. *Language Variation and Change, 3,* 1–22. doi: 10.1017/S0954394500000429.
Guy, G. R., and Boberg, C. (1997) Inherent variability and the obligatory contour principle. *Language Variation and Change, 9*(2), 149–64.
Guy, G., and Boyd, S. (1990) The development of a morphological class. *Language Variation and Change, 7*(1), 101–12.

Guy, G., Horvath, B., Vonwiller, J., Daisley, E., and Rogers, I. (1986) An intonational change in progress in Australian English. *Language in Society, 15*(1), 23–52.
Haas, M. (1944) Men's and women's speech in Koasati. *Language, 20*, 142–9.
Haeri, N. (1997) *The Sociolinguistic Market of Cairo: Gender, Class, and Education*. London: Kegan Paul International.
Halliday, M. A. K., and Matthiessen, C. M. (2004) *An Introduction to Functional Grammar*. London: Arnold.
Hanneman, R., and Riddle, R. (2005) *Introduction to Social Network Methods*. Riverside, CA: University of California, Riverside. (Published in digital form at http: //faculty.ucr.edu/~hanneman.)
Harasowska, M. (1999) *Morphophonemic Variability, Productivity, and Change: The Case of Rusyn*. Berlin: Mouton de Gruyter.
Hay, J., Nolan, A., and Drager, K. (2006) From fush to feesh: exemplar priming in speech perception. *Linguistic Review, 23*, 351–79.
Henry, A. (2004) Variation and syntactic theory. In J. Chambers, P. Trudgill, and N. Schilling-Estes (eds), *The Handbook of Language Variation and Change* (pp. 267–82). Oxford: Blackwell.
Hill, R. (1994) You've come a long way, dude: a history. *American Speech, 69*(3), 321–7.
Hindle, D. (1980) The social and structural conditioning of phonetic variation. Unpublished doctoral dissertation, University of Pennsylvania, Philadelphia.
Hock, H. H. (1991) *Principles of Historical Linguistics*. Berlin and New York: Mouton de Gruyter.
Holmes, J. (1995) *Women, Men, and Politeness*. London: Longman.
Hopper, P., and Traugott, E. (2003) *Grammaticalization*. Cambridge: Cambridge University Press.
Horne, J., and Östberg, O. (1976) A self-assessment questionnaire to determine morningness-eveningness in human circadian rhythms. *International Journal of Chronobiology, 4*(2), 97–110.
Horvath, B. M. (1985) *Variation in Australian English: The Sociolects of Sydney*. Cambridge: Cambridge University Press.
Horvath, B. M, and Horvath, R. (2001) Short /a/ in Australian English: a geolinguistic study. In D. B. Blair and P. Collins (eds), *Varieties of English Around the World: English in Australia* (pp.341–54). Amsterdam: John Benjamins.
Horvath, B. M., and Horvath, R. J. (2002) The geolinguistics of /l/ vocalization in Australia and New Zealand. *Journal of Sociolinguistics, 6*(3), 319–46. doi: 10.1111/1467-9481.00191.
Houston, A. (1985) Continuity and change in English morphology: the variable (ING). Unpublished doctoral dissertation, University of Pennsylvania, Philadelphia.
Hutcheson, N. (producer) (2001) *Indian by Birth: The Lumbee Dialect*. [Television documentary.] Raleigh, NC: North Carolina Language and Life Project.
Hutcheson, N. (producer) (2004) *Mountain Talk*. [Television documentary.] Raleigh, NC: North Carolina Language and Life Project.
Hutcheson, N. (producer) (2005) *Voices of North Carolina*. [Television documentary.] Raleigh, NC: North Carolina Language and Life Project.
Hymes, D. (1972) Models of the interaction of language and social life. In J. Gumperz and D. Hymes (eds), *Directions in Sociolinguistics: The Ethnography of Communication* (pp. 35–71). New York: Holt, Rhinehart and Winston.
Hymes, D. (1986) Discourse: scope without depth. *International Journal of Sociology of Language, 57*, 49–89.
Jaffe, A. M. (2009) *Stance: Sociolinguistic Perspectives*. Oxford: Oxford University Press.
Johnson, D. E. (2009) Getting off the GoldVarb Standard: introducing Rbrul for mixed-effects variable rule analysis. *Language and Linguistics Compass, 3*(1), 359–83. doi: 10.1111/j.1749-818X.2008.00108.x.

Johnson, K. (2003) *Acoustic and Auditory Phonetics*. Oxford: Wiley-Blackwell.
Johnson, K. (2006) Resonance in an exemplar-based lexicon: the emergence of social identity and phonology. *Journal of Phonetics, 34*(4), 485–99. doi: 10.1016/j.wocn.2005.08.004.
Johnson, K. (2008) *Quantitative Methods in Linguistics*. Oxford: Blackwell.
Johnstone, B., and Kiesling, S. F. (2008) Indexicality and experience: exploring the meanings of /aw/-monophthongization. *Journal of Sociolinguistics, 12*(1), 5–33.
Johnstone, B., Andrus, J., and Danielson, A. E. (2006) Mobility, indexicality, and the enregisterment of 'Pittsburghese'. *Journal of English Linguistics, 34*(2), 77–104.
Kallen, J. (2005) Internal and external factors in phonological convergence: the case of English /t/ lenition. In P. Auer, F. Hinskens, and P. Kerswill (eds), *Dialect Change: Convergence and Divergence in European Languages* (pp. 51–80). Cambridge: Cambridge University Press.
Kendall, T. (2009) Speech rate, pause, and linguistic variation: an examination through the Sociolinguistic Archive and Analysis Project. Unpublished doctoral dissertation, Duke University, Durham, NC.
Kerswill, P. (1996) Children, adolescents, and language change. *Language Variation and Change, 8*, 177–202.
Kerswill, P. (2002) A dialect with 'great inner strength'? The perception of nativeness in the Bergen speech community. In D. Long and D. Preston (eds), *A Handbook of Perceptual Dialectology. Vol. 2* (pp. 155–75). Amsterdam: John Benjamins.
Kerswill, P., and Williams, A. (2000) Creating a new town koine: children and language change in Milton Keynes. *Language in Society, 29*(1), 65–115. doi: 10.1017/S0047404500001020.
Kerswill, P., and Williams, A. (2002) 'Salience' as an explanatory factor in language change: evidence from dialect levelling in urban England. In M. C. Jones and E. Esch (eds), *Language Change: The Interplay of Internal, External and Extra-Linguistic Factors* (pp. 81–110). Berlin: Mouton de Gruyter.
Kerswill, P., and Williams, A. (2005) New towns and koineization: linguistic and social correlates. *Linguistics, 43*(5), 1023–48. doi: 10.1515/ling.2005.43.5.1023.
Kerswill, P., Torgersen, E. N., and Fox, S. (2008) Reversing 'drift': innovation and diffusion in the London diphthong system. *Language Variation and Change, 20*(3), 451–91.
Kiesling, S. F. (1998) Men's identities and sociolinguistic variation: the case of fraternity men. *Journal of Sociolinguistics, 2*(1), 69–99.
Kiesling, S. F. (2004) Dude. *American Speech, 79*(3), 281–305.
Kiesling, S. F. (2005) Variation, stance and style: word-final -er, high rising tone, and ethnicity in Australian English. *English World-Wide, 26*(1), 1–42.
Kiesling, S. F. (2009) Style as stance: stance as the explanation for patterns of sociolinguistic variation. In A. Jaffe (ed.), *Stance: Sociolinguistic Perspectives* (pp. 171–94). New York: Oxford University Press.
Kiesling, S. F. (forthcoming) Ethnography of speaking. In C. Bratt Paulston, S. F. Kiesling, and E. Rangel (eds), *Handbook of Intercultural Discourse and Communication*. Malden, MA: Wiley-Blackwell.
Kiesling, S. F., and Wisnosky, M. (2003) Competing norms, heritage prestige, and /aw/-monophthongization in Pittsburgh. Poster presented at New Ways of Analyzing Variation 32, Philadelphia, 9–12 October.
Klewitz, G., and Couper-Kuhlen, E. (1999) Quote-unquote? The role of prosody in the contextualization of reported speech sequences. *Pragmatics, 9*(4), 459–85.
Kroch, A. (1989) Reflexes of grammar in patterns of language change. *Language Variation and Change, 1*, 199–244.
Labov, W. (1963) The social motivation of a sound change. *Word, 19*, 273–309.
Labov, W. (1966) *The Social Stratification of English in New York City*. Washington, DC: Center for Applied Linguistics.

Labov, W. (1969) Contraction, deletion, and inherent variability of the English copula. *Language*, 45(4), 715–62.
Labov, W. (1972a) *Language in the Inner City: Studies in the Black English Vernacular*. Philadelphia: University of Pennsylvania Press.
Labov, W. (1972b) *Sociolinguistic Patterns*. Philadelphia: University of Pennsylvania Press.
Labov, W. (1982) Objectivity and commitment in linguistic science: the case of the Black English trial in Ann Arbor. *Language in Society*, 11(2), 165–201.
Labov, W. (1989) The child as linguistic historian. *Language Variation and Change*, 1(1), 85–97.
Labov, W. (1990) The intersection of sex and social class in the course of linguistic change. *Language Variation and Change*, 2, 205–54.
Labov, W. (1994) *Principles of Linguistic Change. Vol. 1: Internal Factors*. Oxford: Blackwell.
Labov, W. (2001a) *Principles of Linguistic Change. Vol. 2: Social Factors*. Oxford: Blackwell.
Labov, W. (2001b) The anatomy of style. In P. Eckert and J. Rickford (eds), *Style and Sociolinguistic Variation* (pp. 85–108). Cambridge: Cambridge University Press.
Labov, W. (2007) Transmission and diffusion. *Language*, 83, 344–87.
Labov, W. (in press) *Principles of Linguistic Change. Vol. 3: Cognitive and Cultural Factors*. Oxford: Blackwell.
Labov, W., Ash, S., and Boberg, C. (2006) *The Atlas of North American English: Phonetics, phonology, and Sound Change: A Multimedia Reference Tool*. Berlin: Mouton de Gruyter.
Ladd, R. (1996) *Intonational Phonology*. Cambridge: Cambridge University Press.
Lakoff, R. T. (1975) *Language and Woman's Place*. New York: Harper and Row.
Lambert, W. (1967) A social psychology of bilingualism. *Journal of Social Issues*, 23, 91–109.
Lavandera, B. (1978) Where does the sociolinguistic variable stop? *Language in Society*, 7(2), 171–82.
Lawson, R. G. (2009) Sociolinguistic constructions of identity among adolescent males in Glasgow. Unpublished doctoral dissertation, University of Glasgow.
Le Page, R., and Tabouret-Keller, A. (1985) *Acts of Identity: Creole-Based Approaches to Language and Ethnicity*. Cambridge: Cambridge University Press.
Leben, W. (1973) Suprasegmental phonology. Doctoral dissertation, MIT, Cambridge, MA. [Distributed by Indiana University Linguistics Club, Bloomington.]
Levinson, S. C. (1983) *Pragmatics*. Cambridge: Cambridge University Press.
Lippi-Green, R. (1997) *English with an Accent: Language, Ideology, and Discrimination in the United States*. London: Routledge.
Maegaard, M. (2007) Social categories, social practice and linguistic variation in an urban school: combining variationism, ethnography and language attitudes research. Presentation at the 36th Annual Meeting of New Ways of Analyzing Variation, Philadelphia, PA, 11–14 October.
Martineau, F., and Mougeon, R. (2003) A sociolinguistic study of the origins of *ne* deletion in European and Quebec French. *Language*, 79(1), 118–52.
Marx, K., and Engels, F. (1867) *Das Kapital*. Hamburg: O. Meissner.
McMahon, A. (1994) *Understanding Language Change*. Cambridge: Cambridge University Press.
Mendoza-Denton, N. (2008) *Homegirls: Language and Cultural Practice among Latina Youth Gangs*. Oxford: Blackwell.
Mesthrie, R. (1996) Language contact, transmission, shift: South African Indian English. In V. de Klerk (ed.), *Focus on South Africa* (pp. 79–98). Amsterdam: John Benjamins.
Mesthrie, R. (2002) *Language in South Africa*. Cambridge: Cambridge University Press.
Mewett, P. (1982) Exiles, nicknames, social identities and the production of local consciousness in a Lewis crofting community. In A. P. Cohen (ed.), *Belonging: Identity and Social Organisation in British Rural Cultures* (pp. 222–47). Manchester: Manchester University Press.

Meyerhoff, M. (1994) Sounds pretty ethnic, eh? A pragmatic particle in New Zealand English. *Language in Society, 23*(3), 367–88.

Meyerhoff, M. (2001) Dynamics of differentiation: on social psychology and cases of language variation. In N. Coupland, C. Candlin, and S. Sarangi (eds), *Sociolinguistics and Social Theory* (pp. 61–87). London: Longman.

Meyerhoff, M. (2002) All the same? The emergence of complementisers in Bislama. In T. Güldemann and M. von Roncador (eds), *Reported Discourse: A Meeting Ground for Different Linguistic Domains* (pp. 341–59). Amsterdam: John Benjamins.

Milroy, L. (1980) *Language and Social Networks*. Oxford: Blackwell.

Milroy, L., and Gordon, M. (2003) *Sociolinguistics: Method and Interpretation*. Oxford: Blackwell.

Milroy, L., and Milroy, J. (1992) Social network and social class: toward an integrated sociolinguistic model. *Language in Society, 21*(1), 1–26.

Milroy, J., Milroy L., Hartley, S., and Walshaw, D. (1994) Glottal stops and Tynside glottalization: competing patterns of variation and change in British English. *Language Variation and Change, 6*, 327–57.

Moore, E. (2003) Learning style and identity: a sociolinguistic analysis of a Bolton high school. Unpublished doctoral dissertation, University of Manchester.

Mugglestone, L. (2003) *Talking Proper: The Rise of Accent as Social Symbol*. Oxford: Oxford University Press.

Naslund, D. (1993) The /s/ phoneme: A gender issue. Unpublished manuscript, University of Minnesota, Minneapolis.

Niedzielski, N. (1999) The effect of social information on the perception of sociolinguistic variables. *Journal of Language and Social Psychology, 18*, 62–85. doi: 10.1177/0261927X99018001005.

Niedzielski, N., and Preston, D. (2003) *Folk Linguistics*. Berlin: Mouton de Gruyter.

Nycz, J., and De Decker, P. (2006) A new way of analyzing vowels: comparing formant contours using smoothing spline ANOVA. Poster presented at the 35th Annual Meeting of New Ways of Analyzing Variation, Columbus, OH, 9–12 November.

Ochs, E. (1992) Indexing gender. In A. Duranti and C. Goodwin (eds), *Rethinking Context: Language as an Interactive Phenomenon* (pp. 335–58). Cambridge: Cambridge University Press.

Odden, D. (1986) On the role of the Obligatory Contour Principle in phonological theory. *Language, 62*, 353–83.

Ohala, J. (2003) Phonetics and historical phonology. In D. Joseph and R. Janda (eds), *The Handbook of Historical Linguistics* (pp. 669–86). Oxford: Blackwell.

Oliveira e Silva, G. (1982) Estudo da regularidade na variação dos possessivos no Português do Rio de Janeiro. Unpublished doctoral dissertation, Universidade Federal do Rio de Janeiro.

Otheguy, R., Zentella, A. C., and Livert, D. (2007) Language and dialect contact in Spanish in New York: toward the formation of a speech community. *Language, 83*(4), 770–802.

Parsons, T. (1964) *Essays in Sociological Theory*. New York: Free Press.

Patrick, P. (2002) The speech community: some definitions. http://courses.essex.ac.uk/lg/lg232/SpeechComDefs.html.

Patrick, P. (2004) The speech community. In J. Chambers, P. Trudgill, and N. Schilling-Estes (eds), *The Handbook of Language Variation and Change* (pp. 573–97). Oxford: Blackwell.

Peterson, G. E., and Barney, H. L. (1952) Control methods used in a study of the vowels. *Journal of the Acoustical Society of America, 24*, 175–84.

Paul, H. (1970) *Principles of the History of Language* (trans. H. A. Strong). College Park, MD: McGrath.

Payne, A. (1980) Factors controlling the acquisition of the Philadelphia dialect by out-of-state children. In W. Labov (ed.), *Locating Language in Time and Space* (pp. 143–78). New York: Academic Press.

Pierrehumbert, J. B. (2001) Exemplar dynamics: word frequency, lenition and contrast. In J. Bybee and P. J. Hopper (eds), *Frequency and the Emergence of Linguistic Structure* (pp. 137–57). Amsterdam: John Benjamins.

Pierrehumbert, J. B. (2006) The next toolkit. *Journal of Phonetics, 34*(4), 516–30. doi: 10.1016/j.wocn.2006.06.003.

Podesva, R. J., Roberts, S. J., and Campbell-Kibler, K. (2001) Sharing resources and indexing meanings in the production of gay styles. In K. Campbell-Kibler, R. J. Podesva, S. J. Roberts, and A. Wong (eds), *Language and Sexuality: Contesting Meaning in Theory and Practice* (pp. 175–89). Stanford, CA: CSLI.

Poplack, S. (1980) 'Sometimes I'll start a sentence in Spanish y termino en español': toward a typology of code-switching. *Linguistics, 18*(7/8), 581–618.

Preston, D. R. (1989) *Perceptual Dialectology: Nonlinguists' Views of Areal Linguistics*. Dordrecht: Foris.

Prince, E. (1981) Toward a taxonomy of given-new information. In P. Cole (ed.), *Radical Pragmatics. Vol 3* (pp. 223–56). New York: Academic Press.

Prince, E. (1992) The ZPG letter: subjects, definiteness, and information-status. In S. Thompson and W. Mann (eds), *Discourse Description: Diverse Analyses of a Fund Raising Text* (pp. 295–325). Amsterdam: John Benjamins.

R Development Core Team (2009) *R: A Language and Environment for Statistical Computing*. R Foundation for Statistical Computing, Vienna, Austria. www.R-project.org. ISBN 3-900051-07-0.

Rickford, J. R. (1986) The need for new approaches to social class analysis in sociolinguistics. *Language and Communication, 6,* 215–21.

Rickford, J. R., and McNair-Knox, F. (1994) Addressee- and topic-influenced style shift: a quantitative sociolinguistic study. In D. Biber and E. Finegan (eds), *Sociolinguistic Perspectives on Register* (pp. 235–76). Oxford: Oxford University Press.

Rickford, J. R., Wasow, T., Zwicky, A., and Buchstaller, I (2007) Intensive and quotative *all*: something old, something new. *American Speech, 82*(1), 3–31. doi: 10.1215/00031283-2007-001.

Rissel, D. A. (1989) Sex, attitudes, and the assibilation of /r/ among young people in San Luis Potosí, Mexico. *Language Variation and Change, 1*(3), 269–83. doi: 10.1017/S0954394500000181.

Roach, P. (1982) On the distinction between 'stress-timed' and 'syllable-timed' languages. In D. Crystal (ed.), *Linguistic Controversies: Essays in Linguistic Theory and Practice in Honour of F. R. Palmer* (pp. 73–9). London: Arnold.

Roberts, J. (1997) Acquisition of variable rules: a study of (-t, d) deletion in preschool children. *Journal of Child Language, 24*(2), 351–72.

Salami, L. O. (1991) Diffusion and focusing: phonological variation and social networks in Ile-Ife, Nigeria. *Language in Society, 20*(2), 217–45.

Sankoff, D., and Cedergren, H. J. (1974) Performance as a statistical reflection of competence. *Language, 50*(2), 333–55.

Sankoff, D., and Laberge, S. (1978) The linguistic market and the statistical explanation of variability. In D. Sankoff (ed.), *Linguistic Variation: Models and Methods* (pp. 239–50). New York: Academic Press.

Sankoff, G. (2006) Age: apparent time and real time. In K. Brown (ed.), *Encyclopedia of Language and Linguistics* (2nd edn). Amsterdam: Elsevier.

Sankoff, G., and Blondeau, H. (2007) Language change across the lifespan: /r/ in Montreal French. *Language, 83*(3), 560–88.

Sankoff, G., and Thibault, P. (1977) L'alternance entre les auxiliaires *avoir* et *être* en français parlé à Montréal. *Langue Française, 34,* 84–108.

Santa Ana, O. (1991) Phonetic simplification processes in the English of the barrio: a cross-generational sociolinguistic study of the Chicanos of Los Angeles. Retrieved from ProQuest Digital Dissertations. (AAT 9200383).

Santa Ana, O. (1996) Sonority and syllable structure in Chicano English. *Language Variation and Change, 8*(1), 63–89.

Sapir, E. (1921) *Language: An Introduction to the Study of Speech.* New York: Harcourt, Brace.

Saussure, F. (1983) *Course in General Linguistics* (trans. R. Harris). La Salle, IL: Open Court. (Original work published 1916.)

Saville-Troike, M. (2003) *The Ethnography of Communication: An Introduction* (3rd edn). Oxford: Blackwell.

Scherre, M., and Naro, A. (1991) Marking in discourse: birds of a feather. *Language Variation and Change, 3,* 23–32.

Schiffrin, D. (1994) *Approaches to Discourse.* Oxford: Blackwell.

Schilling-Estes, N. (1998) Investigating 'self-conscious' speech: the performance register in Ocracoke English. *Language in Society, 27*(1), 53–83. doi: 10.1017/S0047404598001031.

Schilling-Estes, N. (2004) Constructing ethnicity in interaction. *Journal of Sociolinguistics, 8*(2), 163–95.

Schwenter, S. A., and Cacoullos, R. T. (2008) Defaults and indeterminacy in temporal grammaticalization: the 'perfect' road to perfective. *Language Variation and Change, 20*(1), 1–39. doi: 10.1017/S0954394508000057.

Scott, J. (2000) *Social Network Analysis: A Handbook.* London: Sage.

Seuren, P. A. (1998) *Western Linguistics: An Historical Introduction.* Oxford: Blackwell.

Shi, Z. (1989) The grammaticalization of the particle 'le' in Mandarin Chinese. *Language Variation and Change, 1*(1), 99–114.

Shuy, R. (1990) A brief history of American sociolinguistics. *Historiographia Linguistica, 17*(1–2), 183–209.

Sidnell, J. (1999) Gender and pronominal variation in an Indo-Guyanese creole-speaking community. *Language in Society, 28*(3), 367–99.

Silverstein, M. (1981) The limits of awareness. In R. Bauman and J. Sherzer (eds), *Working papers in Sociolinguistics. Vol. 84* (pp. 1–30). Austin, TX: Southwest Educational Development Laboratory.

Silverstein, M. (2003) Indexical order and the dialectics of sociolinguistic life. *Language and Communication, 23,* 193–229. doi: 10.1016/S0271-5309(03)00013-2.

Smith, J., Durham, M., and Fortune, L. (2007) 'Mam, my trousers is fa'in doon!' Community, caregiver, and child in the acquisition of variation in a Scottish dialect. *Language Variation and Change, 19*(1), 63–99. doi: 10.1017/S0954394507070044.

Spiess, E. B. (1987) *Genes in the populations.* New York: John Wiley.

Strand, E. A. (1999) Uncovering the role of gender stereotypes in speech perception. *Journal of Language and Social Psychology, 18*(1), 86–100. doi: 10.1177/0261927X99018001006.

Strand, E. A. (2000) Gender stereotype effects in speech processing. Unpublished doctoral dissertation, University of California, Berkeley.

Strand, E. A., and Johnson, K. (1996) Gradient and visual speaker normalization in the perception of fricatives. In D. Gibbon (ed.), *Natural Language Processing and Speech Technology: Results of the 3rd KOVENS Conference, Bielefeld, October, 1996* (pp. 14–26). Berlin: Mouton de Gruyter.

Sweet, H. (1911) *A Primer of Spoken English.* Oxford: Clarendon Press.

Szakay, A. (2006) Rhythm and pitch as markers of ethnicity in New Zealand English. In P. Warren and C. I. Watson (eds), *Proceedings of the 11th Australian International Conference on Speech Science and Technology* (pp. 421–6). Canberra: Australian Speech Science and Technology Association.

Tagliamonte, S. (1998) *Was/were* variation across the generations: view from the city of York. *Language Variation and Change, 10*(2), 153. doi: 10.1017/S0954394500001277.

Tagliamonte, S. (2006) *Analysing Sociolinguistic Variation*. Cambridge: Cambridge University Press.

Tagliamonte, S. (2008) So different and pretty cool! Recycling intensifiers in Toronto, Canada. *English Language and Linguistics, 12*(2), 361–94. doi: 10.1017/S1360674308002669.

Tagliamonte, S., and Roberts, C. (2005) So weird; so cool; so innovative: the use of intensifiers in the television series *Friends*. *American Speech, 80*(3), 280–300.

Tannen, D., and Wallat, C. (1987) Interactive frames and knowledge schemas in interaction: examples from a medical examination/interview. *Social Psychology Quarterly, 50*, 205–16.

Torgersen, E., and Kerswill, P. (2004) Internal and external motivation in phonetic change: dialect levelling outcomes for an English vowel shift. *Journal of Sociolinguistics, 8*, 24–53

Trask, R. L. (1996) *Historical Linguistics*. London: Arnold.

Traugott, E. C. (1989) On the rise of epistemic meanings in English: an example of subjectification in semantic change. *Language, 65*(1), 31–55.

Trudgill, P. (1974) *The Social Differentiation of English in Norwich*. Cambridge: Cambridge University Press.

Trudgill, P. (1981) Linguistic accommodation: sociolinguistic observations on a sociopsychological theory. In D. S. Masek, R. A. Hendric, and M. F. Miller (eds), *Papers from the Parasession on Language and Behavior* (pp. 218–37). Englewood Cliffs, NJ: Prentice Hall.

Trudgill, P. (1983) *On Dialect: Social and Geographical Perspectives*. New York: New York University Press.

Trudgill, P. (1986) *Dialects in Contact*. Oxford: Blackwell.

Trudgill, P. (2004) *New-Dialect Formation: The Inevitability of Colonial Englishes*. Edinburgh: Edinburgh University Press.

Tufte, E. R. (1986) *The Visual Display of Quantitative Information.*. Cheshire, CT: Graphics Press.

Tufte, E. R. (2003) *The Cognitive Style of PowerPoint*. Cheshire, CT: Graphics Press.

Ward, G., and Birner, B. (1995) Definiteness and the English existential. *Language, 71*(4), 722–42.

Ward, G., and Birner, B. (1996) On the discourse function of rightward movement in English. In A. Goldberg (ed.), *Conceptual Structure, Discourse and Language* (pp. 463–79). Stanford, CA: CSLI.

Ward, G., and Birner, B. (2004) Information structure. In L. Horn and G. Ward (eds), *Handbook of Pragmatics* (pp. 153–74). Oxford: Blackwell.

Warren, P. (2005) Patterns of late rising in New Zealand English: intonational variation or intonational change? *Language Variation and Change, 17*(2), 209–30. doi: 10.1017/S095439450505009X.

Weber, M. (1947) *The Theory of Social and Economic Organization* (trans. A. M. Henderson and T. Parsons). New York: Free Press. (Original work published 1922.)

Weiner, E. J., and Labov, W. (1983) Constraints on the agentless passive. *Journal of Linguistics, 19*(1), 29–58.

Weinreich, U., Labov, W., and Herzog, M. (1968) Empirical foundations for a theory of language change. In W. Lehman and Y. Malkiel (eds), *Directions for Historical Linguistics* (pp. 95–188). Austin: University of Texas Press.

Wells, J. C. (1982) *Accents of English*. Cambridge: Cambridge University Press.

Williams, G. (1992) *Sociolinguistics: A Sociological Critique*. London: Routledge.

Winitz, H., Scheib, M., and Reeds, J. (1972) Identification of stops and vowels for the burst portion of /p, t, k/ isolated from conversational speech. *Journal of the Acoustical Society of America, 51*, 1309–17.

Wolfram, W. (1969) *A Sociolinguistic Description of Detroit Negro Speech*. Washington, DC: Center for Applied Linguistics.

Wolfram, W. (1974) The relationship of Southern White speech to Vernacular Black English. *Language, 50*, 498–527.

Wolfram, W. (1993) Ethical considerations in language awareness programs. *Issues in Applied Linguistics,* 4, 225–55.

Wolfram, W. (1998) Scrutinizing linguistic gratuity: a view from the field. *Journal of Sociolinguistics,* 2, 271–9.

Wolfram, W. (2000) Reconstructing the history of AAVE: new data on an old theme. *Berkeley Linguistics Society,* 26, 333–48.

Wolfram, W., and Schilling-Estes, N. (1998) *American English: Dialects and Variation.* Oxford: Blackwell.

Zelinsky, W. (1980) North America's vernacular regions. *Annals of the Association of American Geographers,* 70(1), 1–16.

Zhang, Q. (2005) A Chinese yuppie in Beijing: phonological variation and the construction of a new professional identity. *Language in Society,* 34(3), 431–66.

Zhang, Q. (2008) Rhotacization and the 'Beijing Smooth Operator': the social meaning of a linguistic variable. *Journal of Sociolinguistics,* 12(2), 201–22. doi: 10.1111/j.1467-9841.2008.00362.x.

Zilles, A. (2005) The development of a new pronoun: the linguistic and social embedding of *a gente* in Brazilian Portuguese. *Language Variation and Change,* 17, 19–53.

Index

Note: page numbers in italics denote figures or tables where separated from the textual reference

AAVE (African American Vernacular English), *73*
  been, 154
  copula deletion, 17–19
  differentiation, 72–3
  low back merger, 81
  monophthongisation, 81
  speech communities, 33
  systematicity, 31
  see also African American speakers
accommodation
  to addressee, 93
  audience design, 100, 104
  canonical patterns, 64–70
  identity, 52
  indexicality, 114
  solidarity, 98, 101, 103
  style, 92–3
  urban life, 62
active/passive constructions, 15–17, 129, 154
acts of identity model, 93, 95, 98, 117
actuation riddle, 10, 27–8, 171–2
address terms, 165–7
adolescent vernacular variants, 123–4
adoption of change
  Cajun example, 88
  eh, 102
  gender, 29–30, 33, 35, 36, 42, *43, 44,* 45–6

adulthood changes, 124
(ae) variation, 56, 57, *66,* 144
/æ/-tensing, 120, 144
(ae)-raising, *84,* 144
African American speakers
  low-back merger, 81, 82, 114, 141–2, 175
  monophthongisation, 81, 114
  negative concord, 60
  Pittsburgh, 81–2
  social networks, 67
  see also AAVE
age factors
  Cajun English, *86*
  canonical patterns, *78*
  describing patterns, 41–2, 44–5, 46
  as identity category, 53
  monophthongisation, 76, *77*
  negation, 155
  r-fulness, 57, *58*
  vowels, 134
age grading, 29, 131–2
Agha, A., 8, 95, 115
Alamillo, A. R., 160
alienability constraint, 156
all as quotative, 161
American Indian languages, 5–6
Andersen, G., 164
Anderson, B., 8
ANOVA, 47
Anttila, A., 151

apparent-time studies, 28–9
Arabic languages, 85
Ashby, W. J., 155
aspect markers, 62, 154
assimilation, 139, 140, 147–8
atomisation of category, 24–5
audience design (AD), 92–3, 98, 100, 104
auditory analysis, 16

Baayen, R. H., 3, 26, 46, 48
Bailey, G., 62
Bakhtin, M., 96, 160
Barney, H. L., 111
Baugh, A., 133
Becker, K., 28
been (AAVE), 154
Beijing, 118
Belfast, 65, *66*
Bell, A., 92–3, 100
Benor, S., 118
Bernard, H. R., 36
bias, 35, 111, 139–40
Bickerton, D., 22
Birner, B., 15, 162
Blake, R., 28
Blondeau, H., 15, 29, 160
Bloomberg, M., 106
Boas, F., 5–6
Boberg, C., 138–9, 140
Bod, R., 152
Boersma, P., 39
borrowing/imposition, 88
Bortoni-Ricardo, S. M., 60, 68
Bourdieu, P., 62
Boyd, S., 124
Brasilia, 60, 68
Brazilian Portuguese, 15, 60, 68, 161
Britain, D., 70–1
Brown, P., 102, 162–3
Bucholtz, M., 118
Buchstaller, I., 160
Buckie, 121, 123
burnouts, 75, *76,* 82–3, 85, 89, 117–18
Bybee, J., 28, 174

Cable, T., 133
Cacoullos, R. T., 160–1
Caipira language, 68

Cajun English, 86–9, 114
Californian school study, 123–4
Campbell, L., 129
Campbell-Kibler, K., 112–14, 115, 116
Canadian raising, 111
Canadian Shift, 138–9
Cane Walk village, 79, 80–1
canonical patterns, 51, 54
  accommodation, 64–70
  age factors, *78*
  challenged, 79–89
  differentiation, 70–9
carefulness of speech, 56, *57, 58,* 90, *91,* 92, 94
caregivers
  intraspeaker shift, 119, 121–2
  language acquisition, 119, 121, 123
  transmission of change, 119, 124–5
Caribbean, 74, 93
casualness of speech, 56, *57, 58,* 90, *91,* 93, 94
categoricity, 8, 11, 22; *see also* atomisation of category
Cedergren, H., 19–20, 48, 60
centralisation in diphthongs, 13, 16, 28, 117, 129
chain shift, 133–4, 135–41
Chambers, J., 53
change
  from above/below, 88
  completion of, 176
  directionality, 131
  early development/spread, 172–3
  propagation, 174–6
  see also adoption of change; diffusion of change; transmission of change
Cheshire, J., 65–7, 85, 153
Chicago, 72, 74
Chicano English, 74, 75
child language acquisition, 119–22, 123–4
chi-square test, 46–7
Chomsky, N., 3
Clarke, S., 138
class
  adoption of changes, 29–30
  canonical patterns, *78*
  consensus, 79–80
  gender, 83, 115

generalisations, 61–2
high rising tone, 168
ideology, 115
measures, 59–60
monophthongisation, 83, 115
negation, 155
and networks, 69
perception, 113
prestige, 63
pronunciation, 9
r-fulness, 57, *58,* 105–6
stereotyping, 107
stratification, 54, 56, 59
vocalisation, 100, *101*
class conflict, 80
Cleveland, 72
Clyne, M., 73
coach test, 142
Cochran, M., 69
coding scheme, 39–41, *91,* 98
cognitivist theory, 152
Collins, R., 80
colonialism, 72, 73
Columbus, 72
communication competence, 95
community of practice, 32, 35, 36, 85, 118
commutation test, 142
comparative philology, 4–8
confidence interval, 46
conformity, 78, 82, 83
constant rate hypothesis, 158
constraints, 9, 18–19, 27–8, 124
continuative perfect, 161
co-occurrence factors, 161
copula deletion, 17–19
copula insertion, 74
coronal stop deletion *see* CSD
correctness of speech/intelligence, 117
correlation/embedding problem, 53–4
Coupland, N., 93, 96, 100, 114
creativity, 96
creole languages, 93, 155, 156
cross-product display, 18, *19*
CSD (coronal stop deletion), *120, 140*
  constraints, 18, 27–8, 124
  interactons, 19–20
  as past tense marker, 18, 21, 22
  Philadelphia, 120, 121

cultural capital, 62
culture/language, 6
Curvilinear Principle, 61–2

D'Arcy, A., 160
database program, 40
debt incurred principle, 30–1
decision tree coding scheme, *91*
definite article/possessives, 156–8, *157,* 158
deictic words, 105
deletion, *144*
  assimilation, 140
  copula, 17
  (dh) in Northern Ireland, 65
  morphological markers, 148
  ne (French), 155
  plural, 145–6
  pronouns, 15, 160
  Spanish /s/ word final, 17, 24, 145, 148–9, 151
  see also CSD
Deterding, D., 167
Detroit
  African American speakers, 60
  burnouts/jocks, 75, *76,* 82–3, 85, 89, 117–18, 175
  Canadian raising, 111
  negative concord, *61, 76, 83*
  sociolinguistic icons, 67
(dh) and (th) stopping, Cajun English, 86, *87*
dialect
  community, 7
  contact, 68–9, 120–1
  North America, 71–2
  systematicity, 31
differentiation, 54, 103
  AAVE, 72–3
  canonical patterns, 70–9
  gender, 70
  geography, 70–1
  identity, 71, 72–4, 75, 82
  ideological, 72–4, 75, 82
  indexicality, 114
  orderly, 7
  race and ethnicity, 70, 72–4
diffusion of change, 59, 62, 64, 88, 143–4, 174–6

digital recorders, 38
Dinkin, A., 28
diphthongs, centralised, 13, 16, 28, 117, 129
directionality, 11, 131, 135, 140, 155, 175
discourse, 162–4
discourse particle, 102
discrete variants, 16, 39
dissimilation, 139
distribution of data, 46–7
Dorian, N. C., 173
do-support, 158–9
Doxsey, J., 83
drag chains, 133
Dubois, S., 63, 67, *86,* 88, 89, 114
dude address term, 165–6, *167*
Durkheim, E., 79

East Anglia, 71
Eberhardt, M., 81, 82, 97, 98, 114, 141
Eckert, P.
   Californian school study, 123–4
   community of practice, 35, 85
   Detroit school study, 67, 75, *76,* 82–4, 117–18, 175
   heterosexual marketplace, 89, 123
   (ing) variable, *116*
   negative concord, 75, *76*
   peer groups, 124
   social practice, 66
   style, 92
educational ranking, 55, *84*
Egyptian linguistic variables, 85
eh, ethnicity/gender, *102*
Elliott, N., 63
embedding problem, 10, 27–8, 29–30, 51, 53–4
endonorms, 63–4
Engels, F., 80
English–Spanish contacts, 74
enregistration, 63, 106, 114, 115, 175
epistemic modal tags, 162
error correction principle, 30
ethical linguistics, 30–1
ethics panels, 30
ethnicity, 29–30, 37; *see also* race and ethnicity
ethnography, preliminary, 31

ethnography of communication, 95
ethnolects, 124
ethno-metapragmatics, *108,* 111, 114
evaluation problem, 10, 27–8, 30, 51
exemplar theory, 152, 174
exonorms, 63–4, 114
experimental evidence, 107, 109–14

facilitative function, 162
Fasold, R. W., 18–19
Fens, 70–1
fidelity of recording, 38
FileMaker Pro, 40
Fischer, C. S., 69
Fischer, J., 75
fixed effects, 48
folk theories of language, 115
formants, 39, 40, 134
Fought, C., 74, 75, 85
Foulkes, P., 120
Fowler, J., 28, 132
frames, 95–6
fraternity study, 97–8, 101–2
French/English speakers
   Montreal, 15, 29, 153, 160
   negation, 155
   Quebec, 107, 109–11, 155
frequencies, 46
friendship, 89, 123
fronting of vowels, *77, 97,* 123, 133, 134

Gauchat, L., 76
gender
   adoption of changes, 29–30, 33, 35, 36, 42, *43, 44,* 45–6
   Cajun English, 89
   canonical patterns, *78*
   class, 75–6, 83, 115
   conformity, 83
   differentiation, 70, 75, 78–9
   glottalisation, 88
   high rising tone, 168
   identity, 75
   ideology, 75
   Koasati, 21–2
   matched-guise technique, 111
   monophthongisation, 76, *77,* 83, 115
   patterns, 42, 44

prestige, 75, 85
vernacular language use, 54
gender paradox, 75, 77–8
generalisations, 59, 61–2, 88–9
generational changes, 28–9, 131–2, 175
generational time, 28
generative linguistics, 23
genre, 95
geographical boundaries, 32–3, 70–1, *78*
Gerritsen, M., 62
Ghosh-Johnson, S. E., 74
Giles, H., 92
glottal stops, 172–3
glottalisation, 23, 88, 100–1, 120, 133, 141
go as quotative, 160
Goffman, E., 92, 95–6
going to/gonna, 172
GoldVarb, 19–20, 48
Gordon, E., 28, 139
Gordon, M., 3, 26, 36
Gordon, M. J., 136–7
grammar, 4, 11
grammaticalisation, 146, 154, 155, 159–60, 172
Gramsci, A., 80–1
Granovetter, M., 69
Great Vowel Shift of English, 133
group identity, 92
Guatemalan Spanish, 74
Guy, G., 19, 22–3, 58–9, 88, 124, 140, 168
Guyana, 80, 85

Haas, M., 21
Haeri, N., 85
Hall, K., 118
Halliday, M. A. K., 21
Harasowska, M., 149–50
Harlem study, 64, 67
Hay, J., 111
hearer types, 92
hegemony model, 80
Henry, A., 159, 160
Herzog, M., 6; *see also* WLH
Herzog's principle, 142, 145
heterosexual marketplace, 89, 123–4
high rising tone, 15–16, 168
Hill, R., 165–6
Hindle, D., 96–7

historical linguistics, 129–30
Hock, H. H., 129
Holmes, J., 162–3
homogeneity ideology, 7–8, 11
homophones, 173
Hopper, P., 155, 156, 159–60
Horvath, B. M., 36, 59, 62–3, 67, *86,* 88, 89, 114
Horvath, R., 62–3
Houston, A., 146, 151
Hyde County, 72, 81
Hymes, D., 95
hypercorrection, 57

icon, 105
identity
accommodation, 52
acts of, 93, 95, 98, 117
Cajun, 87–8
categories, 53
differentiation, 70, 71, 72–4, 75, 82
gender, 75
group, 92
Martha's Vineyard, 117
non-White, 74
prestige, 62
social practices, 117–18
speech communities, 94
stance, 98–103
ideology
and class, 115
differentiation, 72–4, 75, 82
gender, 75
perceptions, 143
personae of speakers, 118
standard/vernacular language, 94–5
idiolect, 6
imposition/borrowing, 88
income ranking, 55
index, 105, 106–7, 116–17
indexical cycling, 114
indexical field, 116, *116*
indexical meaning, 21, 104–7, 111–12
indexical order, 106, *108*
indexical webs, 114–17
Indian migrants, South Africa, 73
Indian South African English (ISAE), 73–4
indicator/marker/stereotype, 106, *108*

Indo-European language family, 4
information status, word order, 161
informed consent, 30
(ing) variable
　alternation, 146
　grammatical categories, 147–8
　indexical field, *116*
　stratification, 58–9, 75
　structural constraints, 120
　variability, 172
innovation, 75, 76, 88
intelligence, *113,* 117
intensifiers, 164–5
interactional analysis, 96
interactions
　Eckert, 82
　greeting, 166
　Kendall, 168
　norms, 32
　sex/class/age, 60–1
　social meanings, 89, 114, 118
　social variables, 79
internal review boards, 30
International Phonetic Alphabet, xvi, 4
interviewer--interviewee relationship, 37, 101
interviewing, 37, 96, 99
intimate diversification pattern, 75
intonation, 15–16, 166–8
intraspeaker variation
　attention-paid-to-speech, 94–5
　caregivers, 121–2
　community patterns, 90–4
　controlling for, 56
　stance, 100
　stratification, 104
　style, 90–4
inversion, 15
Irish English, 139
ISAE (Indian South African English), 73–4
isoglosses, 164
iterability, 96

Jaffe, A. M., 99
Jansen, F., 62
Japanese, 116–17
job suitability/friendliness scale, 110–11

jocks, 75, *76,* 82–3, 85, 89, 117–18, 175
Johnson, D. E., 48
Johnson, K., 3, 26, 46, 48, 111–12
Johnstone, B., 24, 63, 107, 114
Jones, W., 4
Josey, M., 28
judgement sample, 35

Kallen, J., 139
Kendall, T., 167–8
Kerswill, P., 68–9, 120–1, 123, 139, 145, 175
Kiesling, S. F., 24, 37, 95, 97–8, 118, 146, 165–6
Koasati language, 21–2
koines, 64, 67–8, 74
koinetisation, 145
Kroch, A., 156, *157,* 158–9

/l/ vocalisation, 63, 140
Laberge, S., 62
Labov, W., 3, 6
　active/passive, 15, 154
　class measures, 59–60, 79, 83
　coach test, 142
　commutation test, 142
　conformity, 82
　CSD and (ing), 120, 121
　Curvilinear Principle, 61–2
　decision tree, *91*
　dialect regions, 71
　diffusion, 59, 88
　ethical linguistics principles, 30–1
　formant measurement, 134
　fronting of vowels, 133
　gender paradox, 75, 77–8
　Harlem study, 64, 67
　indicator/marker/stereotype, 106, *108*
　intimate diversification pattern, 75
　intraspeaker variation, 90
　linguistic norms, shared, 32
　linguistic variable, 13
　Martha's Vineyard, 13, 28, 89, 117, 129, 131
　matched-guise technique, 110–11
　MFY Survey, 55–6
　mispronunciation, 173

negative concord, 60, *61*
neo-behaviourist approach, 151
networks, 64, 67
New York City, 8–9, 11–12, 28, 53, 54–8, 115, 131
nonconformity, 174
Philadelphia vowel system, 26–7, 69, 76–7
plural markings, 24
/r/ pronunciation, *132, 133*
real-time studies, 29
recording, 36–7
regularity of change, 174
social constraints, 51
The Social Stratification of English in New York City, 54–5
transmission of change, 59, 88, 119, 124–5
types of sound change, 144, *144*
variable rules, 17–20
variables' state of change, 84
vernacular variants, 124
vowel chain shifts, 135
see also WLH
Ladd, R., 168
Lakoff, R. T., 162
Lambert, W., 107, 109–10
language, 5, 6, 8, 11–12, 115
language acquisition, 119, 121, 123
language analysis, 26
Latinos, 74
Lavendera, B., 153, 154
Lawson, R. G., 85, 118
Le Page, R., 74, 93
Leben, W., 140
lenition, 139–40, 141, 148
Levinson, S. C., 102, 161, 162–3
lexical variables, 14, 143–4, 164–6
like, 160, 164, 172
Linguistic Atlas of New England (LANE), 28
linguistic gratuity principle, 31
linguistic norms, shared, 32
linguistic variables, 13, 14, 15–16
  awareness of, 59
  coded, 31
  criticisms, 20–5

gender, 75–9
  measuring, 39
  speech communities, 16–17
  stance, 100
  variants distinguished, 40–1
Lippi-Green, R., 115
literacy rates, 30
logistic regression, 19–20
logit function, *156*, 157
Los Angeles, 75
Louisiana, 87–8
low-back merger (LBM), 81, 82, 114, 141–2, 175
Lumbee interview, 99

McConnell-Ginet, S., 35, 82, 83, 85
McMahon, A., 129
McNair-Knox, F., 37, 101
Maegaard, M., 118
Mandarin, 160
Maori/Pakeha English, 167
Martha's Vineyard, 13, 28, 89, 117, 129, 131
Martineau, F., 155
Marx, K., 80
matched-guise technique, 107, 109, *109*, 110–11, 112–14
Matthiessen, C. M., 21
mean, 46
meaning, 107, 109–14, 173
measurements, 28, 39–40
median, 46
Mendoza-Denton, N., 85
mergers, 133, 134–5, 141–3
Mesthrie, R., 73, 74
metapragmatics, 106, 114–15, 175;
  see also ethno-metapragmatics
methodology, 26
methods text books, 3, 26
Mewett, P., 69
Mexican Spanish, 74
Meyerhoff, M., 102, 155–6, 160
Meyers, C., 96–7
microphones, 38, 98
Microsoft Excel, 40
migration, 68–9, 72–3
Milroy, J., 64–5, *66*, 69

Milroy, L., 3, 23, 26, 36, 64–5, *66*, 69, 88, 140–1
Milton Keynes, 68–9, 123
mimesis, 160
mispronunciation, 173
mixed effects modelling, 48
Mobilization for Youth Survey, 55–6
modelling variation, 45–8
monophthongisation
  African American speakers, 81, 114
  age factors, 76, *77*
  class, 83, 115
  educational ranking, *84*
  expected/observed, *47*
  gender factors, 76, *77,* 83, 115
  Pittsburgh, 24, 39, 41–2, 44–5, *47,* 76, *77, 84,* 114
  race factors, 82
  resisted, 82
  speech activity, *122*
Montreal French, 15, 29, 153, 160
Moore, E., 85, 118
morphological alternation, 146, 171–2
morphological markers, 148
morphological variation, 14, 145–52
morphology, 129
morphophonemic variables, 146, 150
morphosyntactic variables, 23, 67, 146, 154
Mougeon, R., 155
Mugglestone, L., 4, 115
mutual contact criterion, 34

Naro, A., 149, 161
nasalisation, 86, *87*
Naslund, D., 111
nationhood/language, 8
natural philosophy, 5
negation, French, 155
negative concord, 60, *61,* 75, *76, 83*
neo-behaviourist approach, 151
Neogrammarians, 5, 10, 131, 135
network analysis, 64–5, 67, 70
network of practice, 32
network sampling, 34
New England, 33, 75
New York City
  Harlem, 64, 67
  Labov, 8–9, 11, 28, 53, 54–8, 131

/r/ pronunciation, 63, 115, *132, 133*
New Zealand English, 28, 102, 111, 167
Newcastle-upon-Tyne, 88, 120, 140, 141
Niedzielski, N., 111, 115
nonconformity, 124, 174
non-standard language varieties, 31, 32, 60, 75
Northern Cities dialect area, 125
Northern Cities Shift, 83, 84, 133, *136–7,* 139
Norwegian varieties, 145
Norwich study, 53, 58–9, 75, 110
number agreement, 154

Obligatory Contour Principle, 140
observations, 46, *47*
occupational ranking, 55, 59–60, *84*
Ochs, E., 116–17
Odden, D., 140
Ohala, J., 139–40
Oliveira e Silva, G., 156
OpenOffice.org Calc, 40
orderly heterogeneity, 6–8
  constraints, 8–12
  examples, 140
  richness, 150
  variable rules, 20
Orthodox Jews, 118
Otheguy, R., 74

Pairwise Variability Index, 167
palatalisation, 145, 150
Panama City, 60
panel studies, 29
Parsons, T., 79
partitive construction, 74
passive/active constructions *see* active/passive constructions
past tense marking, 18, 21, 22
Patrick, P., 32
Paul, H., 6–8
pause length, 168
Payne, A., 96, 120
peer groups, 65–6, 123, 124
perception, 111–13, 139–40, 142–3, 173
performance register, 97
personae of speakers, 118

personal pronouns, 74
Peterson, G. E., 111
Philadelphia
  /æ/-tensing, 120
  class measures, 59–60
  CSD, 120, 121
  fronting, 97, 134
  gender/occupation, *84*
  negative concord, *61*
  Orthodox Jews, 118
  perception/production, 142–3
  Puerto Rican Spanish, 148–9
  vowel system, 26–7, 69, *77*
Philadelphia Shift, 135–6
The Philadelphia Story, 63
phonemes, 5, 133
phonetic analysis programs, 39
phonetic notation, xv–xvii
phonological variables, 14, 131, 132–3, 144–5
phonology, 129
pidgin languages, 155
Pierrehumbert, J. B., 28, 174
pitch, 168
Pittsburgh, 72
  address terms, 166
  African American community, 81
  enregistration, 63
  indexical order, *108*
  language ideology, 115
  low-back merger, 114, 141–2, 175
  /l/-vocalisation, 140
  monophthongisation, 24, 39, 41–2, 44–5, *47*, 76, *77, 84,* 114
  segregation patterns, 81–2
plural (s) deletion, 145–6
plural markings, 24, 148
Podseva, R. J., 118
politeness, positive/negative, 162–3
politeness theory, 102, 161–2
Poplack, S., 148, 154
population, 35–6, 46
Portuguese, Continental, 156–8; *see also* Brazilian Portuguese
possessives/definite article, 156–8
power, 64, 89, 98, 102, 103
Praat program, 39
pragmatic marker, 164

pragmatic/discourse variables, 15, 153, 161–4
Prague School theories, 162
preposing, 162
prescriptive grammars, 4
prestige
  class, 63
  gender, 75, 85
  identity, 62
  power, 89
  resisted, 80
  r-fulness, 90–1
  social, 61, 62, 79
  stratification, 54, 60, 62, 64, 67
Preston, D., 115, 117
preterite–present perfect, 161
priming, 111
Prince, E., 162
probability weighting, 48
pro-drop languages, 15
production/perception, 173
pronoun use, 15, 74, 160
pronunciation, 9
(ptk), Cajun English, 86–7
Puerto Rican Spanish, 74, 148–9, *149*
push chain, 133

qualitative analysis, 162
quantification, 163–4
quantitative analysis, 162
Quebec French, 107, 109–11, 155
question intonation, 16, 168
quotatives, 160, 161

R Development Core Team, 48
/r/ pronunciation, 60, *132, 133*; *see also* r-fulness
R statistical package, 48
race and ethnicity, 53, 70, 72–4, *78*, 82, 101
race relations, 99, 100
random effects, 48
random sample, 35–6
Rbrul, 48
Reading study, 85
real-time studies, 28–9
Received Pronunciation, 115
recording, 28, 36–7, 38–9

referee design, 93
referent, 105
region factors, 53, 113
register, 94–5
regularity in lexical diffusion, 143–4
relationships/stance, 99
resyllabification, 139
r-fulness
  age factors, 57, *58*
  careful/casual, 90–1
  class, 57, *58,* 105–6
  gender, 75–6
  indexical experience, 105–6
  Montreal French, 29
  New York, 9, 11–12, 54–8, 115
  prestige, 90–1
  standard form, 63
  topic, 99
rhythm, 166–8
Rickford, J. R., 37, 79, 80–1, 85, 92, 101, 161
Rissel, D. A., 60
r-lessness, 9, 12, 63, 173
Roberts, C., 164–5
Roberts, J., 120
rules of use, 106
Rusyn language, 150

/s/ fronted/alveolar, 111–12
Salami, L. O., 67
Salvadoran Spanish, 74
sample size, 36
sampling, 32–6
San Luis Potosi, 60
Sankoff, D., 19–20, 29, 48, 62, 88, 153
Sapir, E., 6
Saussure, F. de, 5, 11
Saville-Troike, M., 95
schematisation problems, 18–19
Scherre, M., 149, 161
Schiffrin, D., 161
Schilling-Estes, N., 91, 92, 97, 99, 100, 101
Schwenter, S. A., 160–1
semantic differential, 107, 109
serialisation factors, 161
Seuren, P. A., 4, 5, 162
sex/gender, 53

Shi, Z., 160
shifters, 105
shifts, 133, 134–5, 139; *see also* chain shift
Sidnell, J., 85
significance, 45, 105
signifier, 105
Silverstein, M., 106, *108,* 114, 116, 175
simplification, 145
Smith, J., 121, *122*
snowball sampling, 34, 35, 36
social categories, 82–3
social factors, 11–12, 51, 173
social identity knowledge, 111–12
social information, 171–2
social meaning, 62, 104–7, 117–18
social networks, 34, 64, 67
social order, peer-based, 123–4
social practice, 66, 117–18
social structure factors, 53, 79, 174–5
sociolects, 59
sociolinguistic icons, 67
sociolinguistic variables, 96, 174
sociolinguists, 30–1, 32–3, 37, 51
solidarity, 64, 89, 98, 101, 103
sound changes, 5, *144*
South Africa, 73
Southern Shift, 137–8
Spanish
  Mexican, 74
  number agreement, 154
  plural markings, 24, 148
  preterite--present perfect, 161
  pronouns, 15
  Puerto Rican, 148–9
  /s/ word final, 17, 24, 145, 148–9, 151
  verbs, 161
speech activity, 95, 113, *122*
speech analysis, 146
speech communities
  AAVE, 33
  boundaries, 32–4
  change, 11, 173
  community of practice, 35
  dialect, 7
  identification of, 31
  identity, 94
  intraspeaker variation, 90–4
  language analysis, 26

linguistic variables, 16–17
patterns, 22
perception, 142
sampling, 32–6
social networks, 34
solidarity, 64
structural/cognitive/social factors, 172
Sydney, 33
variable rules, 22
speech data, 36–7
speech event, 95, 99
speech rate, 167–8
Spiess, E. B., 156
splits, 133, 134–5
stance, 97, 98–103, 113, 116–17, 118
stance accretion, 118
stance index, 122
standard language, 94–5
statistical information theories, 151–2
statistical significance, 45–8
statistics programs, 40
statistics text books, 3, 26
status, 89
stereotyping, 106, *108*
  class, 107
  intelligence, 117
  perception, 111–12
  types of speakers, 166–7
stochastic theories, 151
Strand, E. A., 111–12
stratification, 54–64, 67, 75, 103, 104, 114–15
stress-timed languages, 167
structural constraints, 120
structure/variability, 45
style
  accommodation, 92–3
  acts of identity model, 93, 95, 98, 117
  intraspeaker variation, 90–4
  sociolinguistic, 91–2
suprasegmental variables, 15–16, 166–8
Sweet, H., 4
Sydney, 33, 59, *138*, 168
syllable-timed languages, 167
symbolic capital, 62
symbolic meaning, 21, 105
syntactic change, 155, 171–2, 173

syntactic variables, 15, 153, 154–61
syntax, 28, 129, 160–1
Szakay, A., 167

Tabouret-Keller, A., 74, 93
tag questions, 162
Tagliamonte, S., 3, 26, 46, 150–1, 154, 164–5
Tannen, D., 96
tense/aspect markers, 172; *see also* past tense marking
Texas, 62
Thibault, P., 153
Torgersen, E., 139
Toronto, 164–5
transition problem, 9–10, 27–8, 156
transmission of change, 59, 64, 88, 124–5, 174–6
transmission problem, 119
Trask, R. L., 129
Traugott, E., 155, 156, 159–60, 166
trend studies, 29
Trudgill, P.
  glottalisation, 100–1
  intraspeaker variation, 90
  koinetisation, 145
  Norwich study, 53, 58–9, 75, *76*, 110
  salience, 175
  wave model of diffusion, 62
t-test, 46, 47
Tyneside, 23
tyranny of correlation, 24

universal grammar, 3
unmarking, 145
urbanisation, 62, 68

validity, 39–40
Varbrul statistical method, 3, 19–20, 23, 48, 98, 134, 146
variability
  coding, 39–41
  linguistic, 10, 13
  as a natural, 11
  phonetics, 171–2
  stable/changing, 26
  structure, 45
  see also specific types of variables

variability index, 167
variable rules, 17–20, 22, 23
variationist theories, 3, 4–8, 24
verbs, 160–1, 172; *see also* past tense marking; tense markers
vernacular culture, 66–7, 85
vernacular language, 37, 54, 60, 94–5, 123–4
vocalisation, 100, *101*
voiceless stops, 23
voicing, 96
vowel shift principles, 76–7, 137
vowels
  age factors, 134
  backing, 65
  centralisation, 16
  core and periphery, *135*
  directionality, 135
  fronting, *77, 97,* 123, 133, 134
  job suitability/friendliness scale, 110–11
  mergers, 141–3
  New Zealand English, 111
  Northern Cities Shift, 83
  notation, xv
  ovoid articulation, 139
  Philadelphia, 26–7, 69, *77*
  Sydney, 59

Wallat, C., 96
Ward, G., 15, 162
Warren, Paul, 168

was/were alternation, 150, *151,* 154
Weber, M., 80
Weenick, D., 39
Weiner, E. J., 15, 154
Weinreich, U., 4, 6–8
Wells, J. C., xv
Williams, A., 68–9, 121, 123, 175
Winitz, H., 140
WLH
  actuation riddle, 10
  constraints problem, 9, 155
  embedding problem, 10, 51
  evaluation problem, 10, 51
  language change, 11–12
  orderly heterogeneity, 6–8
  transition problem, 9–10, 155, 156
  transmission problem, 119
  variation problems, 26, 27–8
  see also Herzog, M.; Labov, W.; Weinreich, U.
Wolfram, W., 18, 20, 22, 30–1, 60, *61,* 72
word frequency, 174
word order, 15, 161, 162

yinz term, 107
Yoruba language, 67

Zelinsky, W., 33
zero-marking, 146
Zhang, Q., 118
Zilles, A., 15